C000104032

Doubts and Certainties
in the
Practice of Psychotherapy

Josephine Klein

Doubts and Certainties
in the
Practice of Psychotherapy

Josephine Klein

London
KARNAC BOOKS

First published in 1995 by
H. Karnac (Books) Ltd.
58 Gloucester Road
London SW7 4QY

British Library Cataloguing in Publication Data

Klein, Josephine
    Doubts and Certainties in the Practice
    of Psychotherapy
    I. Title
    616.8914

    ISBN 1 85575 104 6

Printed in Great Britain by BPC Wheatons Ltd, Exeter

ACKNOWLEDGEMENTS

I am grateful to Peter Baynes for permission to quote from *Re: Verse—A Retiring Collection* (unpublished); to Faber and Faber Ltd. for permission to quote Louis McNeice's poem "Entirely" (from *The Collected Poems of Louis McNeice*, 1986); to Hugh MacDiarmid and the Carcanet Press for permission to quote from the poem "Stones" (from *Selected Poems*, 1992); and to Kenneth Wright and his publishers, Free Association Books, London, and Jason Aronson, North Vale, NJ, for permission to quote from *Vision and Separation: Between Mother and Baby*.

CONTENTS

PREAMBLE

The tension between free-ranging thought and the institutions that contain us is the unifying theme of this book, which started as a collection of occasional papers, mainly on the practice of psychotherapy, some for pre-qualification students but most for more experienced professionals. Many I met on those occasions supported the values that generate this tension, and many wished there were more discussion of them. They would acknowledge in a subdued sort of way that their experience often corresponded with mine as regards what works and what does not work in the practice of psychotherapy, and as regards what seems right and what seems wrong. They would lament that they often felt isolated and silenced by their fear of more authoritative-sounding voices—or just ones that are more difficult to understand. To bring to our attention and confirm and celebrate these often unexpressed values, I have included the first two chapters, which are not directly on the practices of psychotherapists but on the values that I think should govern us in our work:

- *modesty of scope:*   a preference for what works;
- *pragmatism:*   the idea that what works is to be preferred to what follows logically from any theory;
- *pluralism:*   the idea that a collection of practices which works is to be preferred to any single theoretical structure to which all other notions must submit;
- *openness in society:*   a preference for practices that enable people to share the good things of life more equally; in the realm of ideas, this involves our readiness to listen and learn, and inevitably also to care about the language in which we communicate our ideas in teaching and in therapy.

These values affect imagination and empathy in a particular way, and this book begins, accordingly, with one chapter whose main focus is on the place of imagination and empathy in social institutions, and a second whose main focus is on how this applies across the barriers that divide the more fortunate from the rest of us. The six chapters that follow come from my experiences as a psychoanalytically oriented psychotherapist. How we view therapy, and how we do it, is deeply influenced by the values that govern how we relate to people, and these chapters consider what it is that psychotherapists do that makes people better, what may be meant by a patient being "held", whether and when to interpret unconscious processes, whether and when to focus on the transference, and the very idea of well-being. Finally, two chapters put the development of some psychoanalytic theories into their social and historical context, to serve as reminders that logic and evidence are but two of the ingredients that determined their being.

Doubts and Certainties
in the
Practice of Psychotherapy

PART ONE

CONCERNING VALUES

CHAPTER ONE

Imagination
and the institutional mind

For more than twenty years, before I became a full-time psychotherapist, I was an academic, a university teacher of theories of social life. The move from the one profession to the other was eased by four transitional years at the University of London's Goldsmiths College, nurturing an experimental unit for community and youth workers. The course was intended for an older age-group with some experience of the world, and it compelled me to think about the particular problems of teaching mature adults and about the problems that arise generally in interactions between people in the caring and helping professions and the to-be-cared-for-and-helped.

More than ten years later, the College invited me, by now an established full-time psychotherapist, to give a lecture in memory of Ian Gulland, who had been eminent among those instrumental in setting up the course. What the other tutors

---

A version of "Imagination in Adult Education", a lecture given *In Memoriam Ian Gulland* at Goldsmiths College in March 1984.

and I had learnt while teaching the students, and what I had suffered during my training as a psychotherapist, came together under the title *Imagination in Adult Education*. That lecture was addressed to people in the world of adult education but when, more than ten years later again, I rediscovered it among my papers, it became the basis and inspiration for the present collection. This chapter is a version of that lecture, somewhat adapted, where I could do so without falsifying the tone, to make the ideas more accessible to the world of psychotherapeutics. Then, when I was preparing it for the printer early in 1994, I came across a review of a poet by a poet, which brought home to me the extent to which my own felicitous defences, at the time I was training, had protected me from being crippled by encounters with the theories of psychodynamics and therapeutics as mediated by all too many teachers and colleagues—though not, I record with continued gratitude, by my training therapist.

> One night, as a student at Cambridge, Ted Hughes had a strange dream. For some time he had been finding his weekly essay a torment to write, and once again he had ended up sitting over a blank page till 2 am before giving up and going to bed. He dreamt that a fox—a very large fox, as big as a wolf—walked into the room on hind-legs. It looked as if it had just stepped out of a furnace, its body scarred, its eyes full of pain. It came up to his desk, laid a bleeding hand on the blank page, and said: "Stop this— you are destroying us".
>
> Ted Hughes recounts the dream early on in his new book of occasional prose writing, Winter Pollen. It is almost caricaturely Hughesian: the wild animal; the appeal from nature to man "to stop destroying us". Hughes prints it without comment. What does it mean? It seems to describe, or allegorise, his feelings about literary criticism. He had chosen to read English at Cambridge, he tells us, because he thought this would help his own writing; the dream, we infer, changed his mind, warned him that literary criticism is unnatural, intrusive, a danger to creativity. For his Finals, Hughes switched to anthropology and archaeology. [Blake Morrison in *The Independent on Sunday*, 6 March 1994]

Ted Hughes' dream warned him—and should warn us—that what passes for education, or care or help, may destroy what we value. This is hardly ever what educators or helpers or carers intend. Education, I said in my 1984 address, particularly the education of adults, should enable people to open themselves to the stimulus of new ideas—to take in more, make sense of more, make use of more, bring more to, the riches that human culture has made available. This idea of education, I said, has implications for teachers in general, and also for educational institutions, and those who make policy or administrative decisions on educational matters. Ten years later I can add that it has implications for sister-disciplines in the caring and helping professions, and in counselling and psychotherapy. At its core is Imagination. Those who make policy need it, and those whose profession it is to teach and to help and to care need it, and so do those who are subjected to those processes of education, help, and care.

Imagination: creative or escapist

According to the *Shorter Oxford English Dictionary*, imagination is

1.   The action of imagining, of forming a mental concept of what is not actually present to the senses; the result of this, a mental image or idea (frequently characterized as vain, false, etc.).

2.   The mental consideration of actions or events not yet in existence
    (a)   scheming or devising
    (b)   expectation, anticipation (1654)

3.   That faculty of the mind by which we conceive of the absent as if it were present (frequently including the memory): the "reproductive imagination".

4.   The power which the mind has of forming concepts beyond those derived from external objects: the "productive imagination".

You can see, I said in 1984, that imagination may be either productive or reproductive, defensive or creative. The same, I said, is true of education. Imagination can keep you in your world dreaming up things to keep you feeling fine—so can education. Or it can make you reach out to discover new things—and so can education.

Psychoanalytic literature tends to subsume imagination under the heading of phantasy, and it has a similar difficulty in deciding whether phantasy (imagination) is escapist or creative, defensive or adaptive. Thus, according to Rycroft's *Critical Dictionary of Psychoanalysis*, imagination "is the process, or faculty, of conceiving representations of objects, events, etc. not actually present. The process produces results which are either (a) imaginary, in the sense of being fictitious, unreal, or (b) imaginative, in the sense of providing solutions to problems which have never previously been solved, or, in the arts, creating artefacts which nonetheless reflect or enhance experience."

We cannot always be sure what imagination is at work. One of Giradoux's characters in *The Tiger at the Gates* is quoted as saying, "There's no better way of exercising the imagination than the study of law. No poet ever interpreted nature as freely as a lawyer interprets truth." Here imagination equals lies.

The compilers of Roget's *Thesaurus* are less ambivalent. They put "Imagination (515)" under Section 7: *Creative Thought*, together with "(514) Supposition" and "(516) Meaning". *Creative Thought*, incidentally, is itself a sub-heading of "Class 4: INTELLECTUAL POWERS", not of "Class 6: SENTIMENT AND MORAL POWERS".

Of particular interest for us is the empathic imagination, empathy being "the power of projecting one's personality into, and so fully understanding the object of, contemplation" (*Shorter Oxford English Dictionary*). Or, as Rycroft (1968) puts it:

> The capacity to put oneself into the other's shoes. The concept implies that one is both feeling oneself into the object, and remaining aware of one's own identity as a person. [p. 69]

The proviso that one retain the sense of one's own identity is important: empathy is not about being one of the lads or lasses.

You must remain your individual self *and* have something to offer and be willing to receive what the other offers: a fair exchange between different people who each have something to offer the other.

"The capacity to put oneself into the other's shoes"! Here, Rycroft's good plain English already points up one limitation to our imaginative empathy. What about those who have no shoes? Does all the human race have shoes? Yes, as far as our imagination normally goes. We had better call empathy the capacity to put ourselves into another's place. Once we have been in that place where the other lives, we are not ever the same again. We identify with the other, we rejoice with their joy, agonize in their distress.

Empathic imagination

Imaginative literature, novels and such, help us to be empathic and imaginative. However, we must not make too much of the power of our imaginative writers helping us see things we are not ready to see. When Howard Brenton published a play in 1982 to show the corrupting influences of conflict and conquest, with each succeeding wave of rescuers and liberators inevitably screwing the peasantry who remained oppressed, it did not broaden Mrs Whitehouse's imagination. She took the author to court! The play was *Romans in Britain.*

Perhaps the metaphor used by Brenton was too much for our unstretched imaginations—not only for Mrs Whitehouse's, but also for many others'. I would want to consider Brenton's point seriously. To that extent, Brenton was unimaginative—did he want to communicate with us or did he want to shock?

I do not know. I know I am often angry at you, when I think of you not as the people I know, but as "the public" or "people" or "educators". In that frame of mind I can easily think that communication with you is impossible unless I shock you. When I am angry I find it easy to believe that being shocked is good for you, and a good way of communicating with you. My anger has limited my empathic imagination. In my anger I have used my imagination to falsify you, to imagine what is not, to imagine what is good for you without consulting you, to imagine an untruth, as the dictionaries warned I might.

Imagination as empathy, as identification with the other, can be contrasted with imagination as phantasy, as a projection of one's wishes or fears onto the other person without checking the truth of one's ideas, not caring how the other person sees the world, not meeting the other person and not becoming vulnerable to correction where one was mistaken.

For the artist, communication with any particular set of people is optional. For the educator or carer or helper, however, communication is of the essence, is part of the definition of the work. We can fail to communicate, blinkered by anger and the wish to shock, or by lack of empathy in some other direction. Indeed, we can have very unrealistic and vapid, and very nasty and hating, phantasies about those we are meant to serve.

Aunt Dot's world

Other people's blinkered imagination has often been used with great comic effect. Take Rose Macauley's portrait of Aunt Dot in *The Towers of Trebizond* (1956), a novel that begins:

> "Take my camel, dear", said my Aunt Dot, as she climbed
> down from this animal on her return from High Mass.

I should say for those who have not come across this pearl among funny novels, that Aunt Dot was living in St John's Wood at the time. *The Towers of Trebizond* is also a serious novel, about the conflict of personal values that seemed so important to us in the 1930s, 1940s, and 1950s, and in particular about conflict where the individualist wishes of a person stand over against the systematic values of a religion or ideology. Being a comic novel, it is therefore very funny about religious adherence as well. Aunt Dot belongs to that small proportion of people whose allegiance is to Anglo-Catholicism. But it does not matter what the target is. It could be monetarism or Marxism or psychoanalysis.

One of the main characters traces some of the influences which have shaped her family and her Aunt Dot.

We have inherited a firm and tenacious adherence to the Church of our country. With it has come down to most of us a great enthusiasm for catching fish. Aunt Dot maintains that this propensity is peculiarly Church of England. She has perhaps made a slight confusion between the words Anglican and angling. To be sure the French fish even more, as I sometimes point out, and, to be sure, the pre-Reformation monks fished greatly. "Mostly in fishponds", said Aunt Dot. "Very unsporting, and only for food".

Aunt Dot had married a missionary who had, as was then the convention, shot himself when in danger of capture by a heathen tribe. He also tried to shoot Aunt Dot, but fortunately he had missed. She was taken into the harem of the tribe.

"How did you escape from the harem?" I would ask her, when she told me this story in my childhood.

"One of the wives, who didn't want me to wait until the chief came back, bribed one of the tribe to take me away into the jungle and kill me. But he was afraid to do this, as I was a goddess, so he showed me a path out of the forest that led to a Baptist missionary settlement. I had never cared much for Baptists, but they were really most kind. You must never forget, Laurie, that dissenters are often excellent Christian people. You must never be narrow-minded".

I promised that I never would.

Other people's worlds

For more immediately relevant implications I turn to Bob Hescott, in the 1970s an actor at the Nottingham Playhouse, who became involved first in the theatre's Saturday morning drama workshops for children, and from there developed a number of other very interesting projects. He wrote a small book about his experiences (*The Feast of Fools*, 1983), illustrated with his own sketches.

At Broad Oaks, a hostel for adults of sub-normal intelligence, we played drama games, devised shows and discovered the inmates' delightful talent for giving new lyrics to old tunes. To describe Broad Oaks as a hostel makes it sound like roughing it and making do, but it wasn't like that, it was a real, warm, comfortable home with private and communal facilities for people who would never have experienced a home life without it. It was quite new and some of the older inhabitants had spent years previously in hospital wards.

"How long were you in hospital?" I asked Eileen.

"Seventeen years four months three days", she said. [p. 39]

I am learning something here. And again,

The inmates of Broad Oaks would quite happily devise mini-operas of their day's experiences. One of the inmates, Cathy, had a boyfriend, Jimmy, a young Irish alcoholic from St Mary's hostel. She would talk to us after sessions about Jimmy's drinking problem. She had a grasp of relationships, in her supposedly sub-normal mind, that was sophisticated to the extreme. "He has to do it for himself. I can't make him give up drinking for me. If ever we broke up he'd just start again. I don't want to be in charge of him like people have always been in charge of me".

I think before we ever begin to get it right, we must become attuned to all the wisdom that is available at all the levels throughout society. There is a certain kind of ignorance which is an advantage in Great Britain. I know exactly how to help my son "get on". I should keep him in ignorance. I should take him out of the community and put him in a public school where he will see and experience little of his fellow men. Then, on the strength of this selected ignorance he can go off to university, the more select and cut off the better—Oxbridge would be ideal, and a course like Classics divine. Finally, thoroughly ignorant of the life style and the needs of the mass of his countrymen, he would be considered qualified to govern them, to practise medicine on them, to dispense law and judgement on them. . . . [p. 40]

He goes on to say,

It is hard to hurt a friend, and therefore much better to build a wall to govern behind. It is easy to close down the hostels for the sub-normal when you don't know Cathy or Eileen. [p. 41]

In the same vein, Richard Hoggart (1958):

No doubt these things are better arranged now, but when I was a boy our area was shocked by the clumsiness of a Board of Guardians visitor who suggested to an old woman that, since she was living on charity, she ought to sell a fine teapot she never used but had on show. "Just fancy", people went around saying, and no further analysis was needed. Everyone knew that the man had been guilty of an insensitive affront to human dignity. [from the chapter on "Them and Us", p. 59]

Since then our imagination has expanded a little. Many of us do now know that this old lady should not have been made to feel ashamed of living on charity, but was morally entitled to support when she had worked all her life at useful things— keeping a house going, keeping an industrial worker fed and clothed and comfortable, bearing and caring for children some of whom may have died for their country while others lived and worked to keep the economy going. But not everyone's imagination, then *or* now, has yet sufficiently expanded to know this. Even now, when one of these instances of breath-taking heartless lack of imagination comes to me, I hear the people of Hunslet say: "Just fancy!"

The point to note here is how what is commonly called education may diminish rather than bring out the talent for empathic imagination. There may even be an idea afoot that *in order to* make good decisions you must be educated in a way that makes you remote from the people you will make decisions about. The process of what is commonly called higher education can be very damaging in this respect. Perhaps it was with this in mind that Lionel Trilling, in *The Liberal Imagination*, wrote that there is no connection between the political ideas of our educated class and the deep places of the imagination.

'Did you pick up on the underlying subplot emphasising the institutionalised colonialism of capitalism's megalomania for multinational expansionism and profit accountability?'

From Hescott (1983)

Experiencing differences in status

These thoughts lead me to make a plea for more imagination among those who have power, who make the decisions that so deeply affect the lives of others, for more imagination among politicians national and local, among administrators, among academics, dispensers of welfare services, social workers, psychotherapists, educators.

There is a definition of professionalism that is probably still impressed on some students in the caring professions and in teaching, which insists that students must not use empathic imagination, must not identify with the client, for fear that it would weaken their ability to "deal with" the client. Those of us who rank ourselves in the caring profession have a peculiar position. We think of ourselves as caring when we stand in our own shoes. From the place where those stand whom we imagine ourselves to be caring for, we are also powerful professionals and experts. From where they stand, we are experienced as able to confer benefits or withhold them, as caring or uncaring, as able to confirm self-respect or destroy it with a careless word and without redress. What redress do people have who feel they have come for a favour, a benefit? Professionals are not just caring, they are powerful.

> The toad beneath the harrow knows
> Exactly where each tooth-point goes;
> The butterfly upon the road
> Preaches contentment to that toad.
>
> Rudyard Kipling, *Paget M.P.*

People who are often at the lower-status end of relationships tend to be more conscious about status. Higher-status people tend not to experience status-differences so acutely—it is not such a salient factor in their imagination. They may not even be aware of the differences. At first glance this may look purely like a good thing: not to be status-conscious. But other factors are involved.

To be unconscious of a status-difference when the other person is painfully aware of it may be experienced by the other person as a form of indifference to their feelings, a form of bullying. I may not set out to bully the other, but that is the effect just the same when my assumption of our equality and mutual free confidence is not shared by the other. I guess that many readers of these lines are sure of their own harmlessness and feel that no-one should be so silly or neurotic as to be intimidated by *them.* That is exactly the oppression I am here trying to communicate: that feeling of impatience or superiority towards those who are intimidated by our way of doing things— that feeling that the other should not be so stupid as to feel what they are feeling. Yet there are people who could use the facilities our colleges have to offer, our social services, our advice centres, our psychotherapy departments, who are inhibited by the very entrance to the building. And there are people working in these places who never ask themselves how this entrance, these corridors, this room, this formality, might feel to a stranger already oppressed by a history of low-status feeling.

If, for one reason or another, a person is already accustomed to put forth his strength against another, is already accustomed through an inner confidence to do others down with reason or with banter, or to argue them into the ground, or to insist, to thump the table, to threaten, then such a person has no incentive to develop his imagination. On the contrary, if he could feel how it is for the other, it would detract from his ability to push people around in a carefree spontaneous way, or in an orderly disciplined way, or whatever.

This happens a great deal between men and women in some circles. It is for that reason that, just for once, in the paragraph above, I used the masculine pronoun "he" rather than the more general pronouns "we" or "they". It also conveys a sense of how it feels to be suddenly singled out by gender, implicitly, just through the language that is being used.

There is a definite relationship between the use of some kinds of imagination and the willingness to use some kinds of power, a simple linear relationship: the more you have of the one, the less you have of the other.

The figure below says that, on the whole, people with more empathic imagination are less likely to be experienced as bullying; people with less empathic imagination are more likely to be experienced as bullying. It also says that people with less

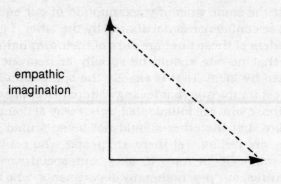

ability to imagine how the world feels to another person find it easier to impose their will on others. It implies that the more you have the ability to imagine accurately how the world feels to another person and how you come across to another person, the more you find it hard to impose your views and still think of yourself as a person of good will, fit to live in a democratic society.

I said that it is bullying to insist that others should not feel what they are feeling because it is inconvenient. I had in mind teachers and other professionals who believe themselves to be better than those they serve, better in other respects than their professional expertise. But I was also thinking of those who do not believe themselves to be better than other people, but who simply do not realize that there may be others who are going to feel a lowering of their self-respect, just from being in a role-relationship in which they are acutely conscious that the other has more resources and more power than they. People who get ahead have more of this capacity to remove from their consciousness any inconvenient feelings, and this is one factor in their ability to get ahead. And what this does is to obscure their consciousness of their own power, which is then consciously experienced only by the power*less* with whom they interact, the toads.

We have to accept that people differ in actual power—more money and more education mean more freedom of choice, more leisure, more time to think, less pressure, often more access to more powerful sources of help, networks of advice and "pull". And we have to accept that it is not to the obvious advantage of the more powerful to be imaginative about the less powerful. So there is likely to be some unconscious motivation not to be too imaginative, lest it hamper what we like to think.

The alienation is of course mutual, and mutually destructive. When there is no consultation or agreement between professional and client, or teacher and student, about the purpose of their meeting, then these people are strangers to one another, and when strangers are forced together for prolonged periods, past memories of humiliation in such unequal encounters may be so strong that cooperation is emotionally not possible, however determined our conscious disposition may be. Only by trying for mutual understanding in a relationship valued by each can we hope to undo the damage and reduce the mutual alienation. And in many cases it is up to the professionals to take the risky first steps, of learning how to meet people we fear, without use of force, and without those errors in tact that make such meetings painful—a difficult task, and not one in which we can hope to be inevitably successful, regardless of the social, institutional, or historical setting. Some kinds of organizations, in some contexts, make it almost impossible for people to meet in the sense I am thinking of here.

To sum up so far, to the extent that we are powerful, in the sense in which I am using the word, we can use power to oppress other people. This is easiest when we know least about them. It is less easy if we can empathize with them, if we can imagine how it is with them—their hopes, their fears, their views of the situation and of us. Knowing less about them makes it emotionally easier to impose our agenda on them. The temptation, therefore, is to see them as toads, ludicrous or dangerous. If we were to imagine their thoughts, we might be challenged, perhaps affronted; there might be danger to our image of ourselves as right and well-intentioned; it might undermine our feeling of confidence. That gives us quite an incentive not to be empathic about others, quite an incentive to avoid meeting those people skin-to-skin, getting our minds confused, quite an incentive to establish institutional and organizational patterns such that we do not have to meet those who do not want to take what we have to offer—patterns so that those with many resources are not faced by those with few, clients are not faced by professionals except on a clearly defined basis, managers do not meet the managed except in stereotyped role-relationships. The layout of our cities, the differential use of public transport, embody some of these segregations.

Status differences and repression

Meeting in role-relationships is hardly meeting at all. Still talking mainly about people of good will, my simple remedy against unwitting personal oppressiveness is obvious now. The prescription is: to meet others, not just in role-relationships but in a spirit of willingness to discover new things about oneself and the world round about. But this endangers the received opinions behind which we can shelter. Among the funny posters that people love to pin up in their offices is one that says, "Don't confuse me with facts, my mind's made up". We avoid people who might confuse us with new facts. Uncertainty seems hard to tolerate.

We have moved into an intellectual climate where there is pressure on us to have opinions on everything. Inevitably we then spawn our opinions faster and faster, without thought, there is no time—what do you think about Iran . . . about the Geneva talks . . . about capitalism . . . about disciplining your children? In such a climate, to have achieved an opinion becomes part of one's self-respect, and then one cannot welcome anyone who confuses that opinion with further considerations. Most certainly, one does not go out of one's way to discover confusing facts. This is yet another way in which confident-feeling people can be powerful over less confident-feeling ones. We have therefore quite a lot of incentive not to let our empathic imagination range and reach. It would increase the number of questions that have no single simple answer, and would increase our uncertainty and alienate us from those around us who appear to know. Dare I keep saying, "I'm not so sure?"

So what we do instead is to banish or alienate ourselves from facts that are not shared by the circle in which we move most comfortably. Or we banish or alienate ourselves from those whose selection of facts or opinions is different from ours; this increases our comfort and decreases the range of our imagination.

I can bring a similar line of thought to what goes on in our inner world. We are creatures with an almost infinitely rich inner potential for enjoyment and exploration and construction. We vaguely know this about ourselves, but we are also afraid. We are afraid of some of the things we might meet in an inner exploration. As Hamlet put it:

> I am myself indifferent honest; but yet I could accuse me of
> such things that it were better my mother had not borne
> me . . . with more offences at my beck than I have thoughts
> to put them in, imagination to give them shape, or time to

act them in. What should such fellows as I do, crawling between heaven and earth? [III, 1]

If throughout long stretches of our lives we have had to use energy to keep our inner lives in order, to keep under control our temper, our greed, our sense of being-hard-done-by, our malice, our depression, our interest in dirty things, or whatever has been the particular shaming aspect of our selves, how does that affect our freedom to meet ourselves? If life has been good to us, if we have patiently accepted our self-knowledge of these dangerous or nasty or depressing aspects of our selves, we may have found that we could live satisfying lives without satisfying ourselves in these respects. If we have been really lucky, we may have found that somehow the strength has gradually seeped out of them. If we have been as lucky as this, we will also have been lucky in not being too overbearing or righteous overmuch, for we know that though we are indifferent honest, yet we could accuse ourselves of such things . . .

This is really a counsel of perfection. More usually, in the midst of our struggle, what most exasperates us in ourselves we find most exasperating in others. We can fight it in others. This makes it possible for us to dislike one set of strangers for being too hardworking and too close to their families, and another set for being too unpunctual and too casual in work or in their child-rearing. If a distinguishable set of people—of another sex, another class, another colour—shows more temper than I, more greed, more sense of being-hard-done-by, more malice, more depression, more interests in dirty things, then the energy of frustration by which I have banished my own expression of such things can become a self-righteous self-justifying wish to banish others. I cannot bear to be near them.

But if I do repress these others, or alienate myself from them so that I do not and cannot meet them, what else happens? Other people represent not only the disowned parts of myself, but also my uncultivated potentialities. By not knowing them, I am limiting myself, I cannot come to enjoy capacities not cultivated in my circle but brought to the fore in theirs. If I dare let myself be open, to learn from others, I will benefit. Though I may have to keep revising ideas I would prefer to take for granted, I do benefit. When I am estranged from you, I am impoverished, and so is the world around me.

My mind goes back to the 1950s, when many of us were disconcerted by the failure of a process that we had expected to make opportunities for educational advancement available to all, dependent only on performance and not on the financial situation of the pupils' parents. It was found however that on average the better-off children still tended to do better at school than the less well-off ones. Research began to look into this. As a result we learnt a good deal about our society which is obvious now but was simply not known then. One interesting set of findings provides me with my example, though I do not suggest that this was the most important thing we learnt about the workings of society.

Imagination and distance

Basil Bernstein, then teaching evening classes at Goldsmiths' College, wrote a paper, later followed by many others from him and from others, which showed the many different ways in which the language of some working-class parents and children differed from the language of parents and children from the managerial and professional classes. What they said to each other was different, and why and how they said it was different. At that time, school-teachers tended to use language in the same way and for the same purpose as managerial and professional parents tended to: for naming facts and situations and events, classifying them, accurately describing certain aspects of them, evaluating them, forecasting from them, controlling them and using them to order and control other facts, situations, events, and people. And, as Wittgenstein had already said 20 years before, "the limits of my language are the limits of my world". Ease in these skills made school-work easier, gained the approval of teachers, enabled children to take examinations with less strain and more success, and generally helped them get on.

Not Bernstein, but some of those impressed by the work he and his associates were doing, then began to talk in more general terms about the "impoverished language" of the working classes. This has been rightly criticized on a number of grounds, but my point is that, given this lead, no one turned the tables and made a comparable study of aspects in which the language and the lives of middle-class people might be "impoverished". Remember what the people of Hunslet said: "Just fancy." A whole range of feeling for others (sympathy), imagination for how others might feel (empathy), and awareness of their own situation, seems to me to inhere in that story of Hoggart's. Could it be that professionally trained people would, on average, show less empathic feeling and imagination about others, less effortless consciousness of the emotional reactions of others, and less knowledge about their own emotional ebb and flow? Could this partly account for the growth in popularity of such movements as encounter groups? Note the word "encounter" here—there are people who need help in being able to meet others and themselves. Encounter exercises are attempts to remedy a fearful impoverishment that could perhaps be more prevalent among the more educated classes, whose language structure and so on is exactly what helps them to go up promotion ladders but may perhaps keep them remote from other people's feelings and their own.

This may all be great nonsense, for no such studies have been made. My point is, why have such studies not been made? It is because we who make studies cannot see what *we* lack, only what *others* lack. The people of Hunslet knew—but they do not control who does research into what. Those who do control are liable to see the impoverishment of others, but not their own. What is especially worrying about this is that it may be exactly those who get on in life, who get to controlling, service-providing, decision-making, policy-making, planning positions, who lack this sense of fellow-life and fellow-feeling. So they never make provision for its conservation. You cannot preserve what you cannot see. It is as though the tone-deaf and the colour-blind were responsible for the arts. And this is what has actually happened. Communities have been uprooted and dispersed over huge geographical areas; even now, office blocks are being built, destroying the community life that existed in the less highly rated areas of our towns. The generations have been dispersed, so that young and old are cut off and alienated from one another. Hospitals are even now being removed from populated localities, so that patients cannot receive visits from their neighbours. What a loss of mutual support is implicit in all this! Children's schools are huge and far away from where they live and are known. The destructive potential of the unimaginative is everywhere visible, but perhaps especially to those without power, who live in segregated places.

The loss of feeling on the part of those who destroy, however inadvertently, the old styles of living—a loss of feeling into which they may have been educated—is in my view as important as the erosion of our natural ecology. Once you lose such talents as empathy and feeling and intuitive concern for others—once these are called "wet" and are scorned—once these are leached out of a culture and called unprofessional, how can they be restored? And because the decision-makers' education was perhaps deficient in these talents, they do not miss what they never had and are astounded at the destructiveness of a people whose containing culture they destroyed.

Too often, an architect or town-planner is called imaginative because of what he does with bricks and mortar. He may be quite unimaginative and ignorant about the people who will use what he builds. Too often, an imaginative syllabus is imaginative about a field of study, but not imaginative about the people who are going to have to learn about it. Our problem—foreshadowed by the dictionaries—is that we have, in one sense, too little imagination and in another sense too much—too little in that we don't feel what it is like for others; too much in that we imagine we do know.

About other people and their world, we need what the *Shorter Oxford English Dictionary* called the "reproductive imagination", which accurately presents what is absent—not the productive imagination, which attributes to others what we believe to be characteristic of them. In this sense, imagination has more to do with scholarship than with lateral thinking. An effort has to be made, to know rightly, to imagine rightly. Otherwise we fall into stereotype and cliché.

So how do we keep our imagination about other people alive? In many ways, but the one indispensable is surely that we must meet them, and we must be imaginative about meeting them, or we shall be more ignorant after the meeting than before. This is the only check we can make that we are imagining them rightly. Fiction about other people is an enormous help—I used Aunt Dot to get a point across. But it presents a selected view of people, and novelists, too, are in danger of stereotyping unless they continually open themselves to meeting new people. Non-fiction reading about other people helps. But it is one-way and selective: the people I read about have had no say in what I am reading about them. Statistics put people in useful contexts and perspectives. But again it is one-way and selective: the statistics are collected by people whose imagination is only a little less limited than ours at best, but whose imagination at worst may have become, in Veblen's telling phrase, professionally deformed. Television makes some things come alive—again, selectively. Perhaps, since public figures have taken to employing agencies to groom them, television is the most unashamedly selective of all.

How are we to imagine accurately the thoughts of a member of the National Front, the preoccupations of a Cabinet Minister, the ideas of a member of the IRA, the life of an unemployed single woman of 47, the concerns of a choreographer, the hopes and fears of a Bengali woman living in London . . . how do we do that?

It is only by meeting you that I can know exactly where and how I agree with you and where and how I experience you as in the wrong, and where and how you agree with me and where and how you experience me as in the wrong. We differ, and we must talk, and we must meet.

How does one meet strangers?

For decades, in science-fiction, when humans met strangers, the aliens were invariably bug-eyed monsters. This has not been so in the more literate type of science-fiction since 1945, and there is a reason for this. Bug-eyed monsters went out of fashion because we had to recognize that we were monsters— the human race was monstrous. I am not saying we are not angels—I am saying we are monsters as well as angels. We have an enormous range of potentiality.

The human race, we found when we looked around, was capable of systematically rounding up and torturing and exterminating Jews, Gypsies, military enemies, political opponents—anybody who was different. We found we could use terror in our defence and bomb civilians to break their morale, we could destroy beautiful ancient cities and modern industrial towns. We had used two atom bombs.

It is difficult to explain our shock to those who were born after us, who have had to take this knowledge more for granted. We had thought that systematic impersonal cruelty belonged to the Middle Ages and went out with the inquisition. And then we began to find that it was not only imperialist Japanese, Nazi Germans, and some military establishments in the United Kingdom and the United States who could do these things. There were the communal riots upon the separation of India and Pakistan. Now we know that peaceful Buddhists, newly liberated Africans, people in Central and South America, Jews with two thousand years of persecution behind them, in fact, anyone, can be monstrous. Read the literature from AMNESTY. According to their 1984 report, one hundred countries torture their prisoners. The human race is a bug-eyed monster. We don't need to imagine Martians or Venusians to clothe our nastiest phantasies in. We only need to read the newspapers.

So science-fiction writers began to imagine the human race as not acceptable to the good aliens from outer space—they usually choose another galaxy now for the origin of these good creatures—far enough away not to stretch our credulity too much.

We may use our imagination defensively—indeed, destructively. It can lead us to imagine aliens as bug-eyed monsters from whom we have nothing to learn, who should learn from us, who should be avoided, who can be pushed around, regulated, and if necessary destroyed.

But if we are all capable of being monstrous, then we have to meet our fellow monsters in a less rumbustious frame of mind. We have to remember that though we/they may be monstrous, yet we/they may be angelic as well.

How do we meet strangers? When interviewing people who wish to be admitted to various study-courses, I regularly ask them to describe someone for me—a colleague, a client, someone they know. More often than not, the candidate is unable to make the person they are describing real to me. A typical unsuccessful attempt would be:

"A has had a very deprived childhood. His mother was an immature personality. At fifteen he was sent to a detention centre. He displays marked psychopathic features, his ego being very weak."

By the end of five minutes I may know more about that person's mother, or economic circumstances, or criminal charge-sheet, or psychodynamics, but the person is not yet real to me, and perhaps not to the candidate either. I do not feel that I would recognize him if I met him, and though I am familiar with the clichés, I do not feel close to him or to the person describing him. It is as though one alien were talking about another alien to a third. A monster talking about a monster to a third. There is no sense of what is at the core, where a person lives and whence actions and reactions spring.

So, at the end of five minutes I stop the candidate and say, "No, I did not so much want to know about that person, as to know him". Some candidates then light up and start really telling me, with zest:

"He's a bit of a moaner, goes on and on about his griev-ances. The funny thing is that he is right—he does have a lot to put up with. I mean, he's crippled and can't move about easily and his wife is not always around to help him. But then he takes no account that she has to see to the baby and brings in some money from when she's out, cleaning. He just doesn't think, he doesn't realize. He's blinkered. I get irritated and say to him . . . but he just goes, 'You don't understand', and, of course, I don't, really. I find it hard to imagine how he doesn't see how he's helping to make him-self miserable. I can see he's not doing it on purpose—he really doesn't see . . ."

This seems to me a very fascinating description. I can begin to think myself into the mind of the person being described, into the candidate's mind, even a bit into the wife's mind. This candidate moves easily between the man's way of experiencing life and circumstance and his own. It is not by chance, I think, that the language he uses is "impoverished" in Bernstein's sense of the word: he has clearly not yet been educated to analyse others; he is relatively unaffected by the distortions shown by many who have been trained professionally not to meet people but to classify them in ways that will fit them for their profession.

Some candidates really relish the chance of describing people as they experience them. Others, alas, do not know what I am getting at, and they experience me as difficult. For all that, they may go on to become educators, social workers, psychotherapists, whatever, though they may never know another person by direct apprehension.

So how do we meet a stranger? That is to say, how do we meet a person not for the purpose of classification or manipulation, but for the purpose of knowing them?

How open we have to be, how willing to learn even the simplest things anew! We have to discover what are good conversational manners between a person like me (as the other experiences me) and people like the others (as they experience themselves). What is good manners in an encounter between two Ascot habitués might make some people laugh in a Welsh Working Men's Club, and vice versa. What feels fine to many a Briton with a Caribbean background would feel upsetting to some from the Indian sub-continent, and vice versa.

We need a lack of presumptions and a lack of presumptuousness, a willingness to stay unsure of ourselves, a willingness to attend to other people's reactions to us, and a willingness to adapt our responses, a mind more apt to embrace than to contrast, a secure identity to give us the confidence to stay open and vulnerable and imaginative. We need many things. I dare not say much on this subject.

What is it like to be a Cabinet Minister, a choreographer, a Sikh? Lectures will not teach us much. Large numbers of people cannot for long have even roughly identical responses to what is put in front of them. Inevitably, some listeners lose touch, then more and more lose touch, diverging according to their own experiences and their own lines of thought. When students cease to listen and think and relate and understand, when they get lost in someone else's train of thought, they get estranged from themselves and from the subject, no longer following the thread of any argument. What they do instead is to try to memorize it. They cease to be compeers of the teacher, they begin to feel inferior, passive, and dull. (They also feel imposed upon, and more evil consequences flow from this.) I think this matters even in solid factual topics like geology or entomology, because we need imaginative geologists and entomologists, and you cannot get those from students who have had to learn by rote.

It matters even more when we consider fields of knowledge that directly involve understanding human beings—in the areas of psychological, social, and educational studies. The habitual use of a wait-till-I-tell-you approach, with the teacher insisting on students following the teacher's train of thought, is deeply detrimental here. The cultivation of imagination requires contact and give-and-take and interchange—it is about human beings and depends on human relationships. Over a sustained period of time, even the more devoted or gifted teachers, if isolated from the concerns of the students, will wander away from them more and more; we need to be kept in touch by actual verbal give-and-take. Otherwise we are either teaching by rote (imagination by rote! insight and understanding by rote!) or else we turn into demagogues, seducing our listeners away from their own knowledge and experience instead of building on it, creating falsity in their very personalities. Professional deformation.

We must not however cast blame on the teachers as individuals: teachers, too, have had to submit to this very process; they, too, have had their thoughts and experiences and knowledge cauterized by a syllabus imposed on them—both in their own training and in the institutions they now serve (for yes, they do serve institutions more than they serve their students, little as they may wish to do so). I was teaching at the University of Sussex in the 1960s, when some students threw a pot of red paint at the American Ambassador who had come to give a lecture to which some other students had invited him. The whole campus was buzzing with reactions—the strain was so great that the Health Centre had an increase of students feeling anxious or depressed, and a noticeable number of students left Brighton for a few days and went home to their families in order to be away from it all. What did they need to learn? And what was I teaching? I think it was Japanese family structures. It was in the syllabus. I was behaving like one of those "idiots savants" who can do logarithms in their head but don't know enough to come in out of the rain. I was an idiot teaching my students to be idiots in turn, in a structure that was idiotic—what people commonly call "academic". F. R. Leavis says somewhere: "It would be foolish to be surprised whenever the academic mind behaves characteristically."

How can I help you to be imaginative?

As I come to the end of this discussion, I feel I must say something about the conditions that help or hinder the development of an empathic and creative imagination, that will allow us to meet as strangers and not as aliens. Yet how do I do that? I am now involved in an impossible situation, for I have cut the ground from under my own feet. To tell people how they may become more imaginative is in itself . . . anti-imaginative. It implies that there is a class of people (to which I belong) that is more imaginative and that can teach another class of people who are less imaginative (to which you, whom I am addressing, belong). I don't even know you! I think it likely that I could learn a lot about imagination from you, that you are imaginative in areas where I am not. You can learn from me, but I don't know you, so I cannot know what you can learn from me. The difference that we know about is that I have been asked to address you and you have not been asked to address me. But that is a dimension of power. Can you answer me back on equal terms? The toad could not.

So there are pitfalls. Yet, if we are to move along, I cannot dodge the question either. What helps, what hinders the development of imagination? I take refuge in considering what we know about children in this respect. In nursery terms, the desiderata are security, stimulus, and flexible relationships.

(1) *The environment has to provide security* and physical safety if children are to feel free to explore, construct, create, innovate. This—as some of us may remember—leaves us free to invent our own dangers. Not only physical security is needed,

Free your imagination!

but also freedom from too much social anxiety: we must not have too many worries about what is pleasing to others, too much anxiety about praise and blame, about conforming or being different. A lot of bad poetry gets written because children copy models, and a lot of bad poetry gets written because children are under pressure to be original.

(2) *The environment has to be stimulating*, with opportunities for different kinds of play: dolls and teddies and team games and sing-songs and wooden spoons and saucepan lids and . . . playmates! There must be others—real, uncontrollable others—to play with. True, many people's biographies are about a solitary childhood in woods or in city streets full of adventure. But this does not cultivate an imagination that is accurately imaginative about other people; this we must learn from other people. The solitary child cultivates an imagination that is a refuge and a consolation, but it remains a solitary world. Our interest is in the empathic imagination.

(3) *We need flexibility in social relationships*—there needs to be give-and-take, no permanent inequalities. Different children, at different times, should be initiating activities for others. If one member of a group is always saying "Let's do this" and the other is always saying "Yes, alright", however contented both may be with the arrangement, damage is done to both parties. If the same members are always "teacher", the teachers will have no chance to learn to solve puzzles that are not of their own choosing. And, similarly, the "students" will have no chance to learn to give their own thoughts free play in

the company of others. Unless the status-structure is fluid, some children begin through experience to classify themselves as permanently dumb, or as natural leaders. If there is no turn-and-turn-about, the imagination of both parties becomes impoverished.

I am not talking anarchy here, or laisser faire. Good things do sometimes happen of their own accord, but often they do not. I am talking about what Winnicott called the "facilitating environment" needed for healthy development, and for Winnicott, as for me, the facilitating environment is largely personal. There has to be thought, forethought, vigilance, organization, and this is done by people. It does not just come about; it comes about by people who create and maintain the conditions in which everyone is safe from impingement, and in which sufficient stimulus is available for everyone, as well as a variety of opportunities to learn initiative and to learn cooperation with other people's initiatives. There have to be people whose responsibility it is constantly to keep an eye on situations as they develop, assessing them and intervening if necessary, though not continually busy doing something. Ideally, this is not a specialist function. I prefer the creation and maintenance of such conditions to be something that we all should be able to learn to facilitate, to watch for, and to do. We learn it from example, and we teach it by example, beginners and seniors alike. And we have to keep in mind that, when we are in that role, we need backing from others to help us not to become too fond of our routines, and to remain open to new

learning. Conversely, when others are in that role, we should hope to give them the backing that enables them to continue to be open to new learning.

These are the conditions in which the good things happen to which I referred at the start of this chapter: people opening themselves to the stimulus of new ideas, becoming more able to take in more, make use of more, bring more to, the riches that life has available.

CHAPTER TWO

Depression, disadvantage, and the creative response

S ome topics present an in-built paradox. People talk about them who are not qualified to do so, yet if those topics were not aired, they might never get public attention and that might be worse. An invitation to address a conference of counsellors on the subject of Depression and Disadvantage brought this home to me. "Depression and Disadvantage" is one of those topics not often publicly addressed by those most concerned, but rather by the undepressed and advantaged. In the same way, adults often talk about children who are not invited to answer back, men set up specialists to tell the world what women really want, whites have met to discuss the problems they perceive blacks to have, and generally the relatively powerful and educated have tended to talk about, rather than consult effectively with, the relatively less powerful and less easily heard. There is something shaming as well as paradoxical about people like me making general state-

A version of a lecture given at the Annual Conference of Counselling Services at Hatfield Polytechnic in February, 1992.

ments about people who may be too discouraged or too disadvantaged to speak for themselves.

It is worth considering what can be done about this, if one is one of the advantaged. Listening to what the others have to say is an obvious must, as is training oneself to hear what the other people are actually saying, "where they are coming from", as a telling piece of jargon has it. So is accepting that other people come from a different starting-point, and so is working hard to get a glimpse of what the world looks like from that perspective.

This checking-out process is quite laborious: I have to try to translate my ideas into the language of people who normally have no voice, and I have to check with them that I have got it right; and then I have to try to translate the outcome into the language of the advantaged for it to be taken seriously by them. The languages of advantaged and disadvantaged are different. I refer not only to vocabulary, but also to meaning and what is between the lines. All this has to be cleared before I can start on the next operation, which is to consult and check out how I sound to other people, in fact, and in tone, and in emphasis. And I have to check whether I am saying at least some things the other person wants to have said. Somewhere near the end of this process comes confronting other people with contrary ideas, arguing, and so on, which can be a form of respect but can also be a form of bullying of the kind that all who have had a bullying teacher or a bullying boss are familiar with: the advantaged, with the language and the power and the confidence of the strong, can easily out-argue the depressed and disadvantaged. I have not been through this elaborate checking-out process for the present purpose; what I have done, therefore, is not to attempt a coherent and definitive presentation, but to offer some possibly useful concepts in a list of considerations that can easily be added to, and from which damaging or pointless concepts can easily be deleted.

Loss

John Bowlby is our great exponent of loss and what happens thereafter. Bowlby initially had in mind the loss of a loved person through death or other permanent separation. With his full support, other people expanded the concept of loss to include other losses, and thus what he had to say was also applied to people who had lost a limb in an accident, or who had had a part of the body removed because diseased, or who had lost a faculty and gone deaf or blind, or who lost their employment through being sacked or made redundant or through retirement, or who moved house and lost their familiar surroundings, and so on. Bowlby (1969, 1973, 1980) lists some frequently encountered reactions—people can have one or all of these:

1. *Denial:* I just cannot believe that I have lost this person loved, my job, or my ability to move about in my usual brisk fashion. I seem to recognize my loss, I am not pretending I don't know about it. But in my actions I go on as before, buying the same quantities of groceries, not reconsidering plans for the future, and so on. Underneath this there is a great deal of pain, which breaks through at times.

2. *Grief:* an endless awful pain and yearning, a sense of wound that will never stop bleeding. This is DEPRESSION, which often alternates with

3. *Blame and shame:* self-reproach at having somehow brought the loss about, and reproach of others who should have prevented it somehow. Obviously a lot of anger is involved in this. Anger and depression alternate easily in a lot of people, and I think that that is a good thing. When the pain becomes too much, which I suffer passively, my rage for a while is good and active, but then my guilt at being unkind, and my common sense, stop my rage and I go back again to pain and so on.

Anger has very positive effects, when it leads people to challenge the fates. "WHY?" I shout. Not just "why did he have to die?" but "why did my lover leave me?", "Why did I have to lose my job?", and so on. This can get me interested in the deeper and wider cause of things and eventually make me more powerful, less helpless. Why did I have to lose my home and flee? Why war? Why the inequality that makes people's homes not safe? Why no education? Why did we have to emigrate? Why does it make a difference being black? and so on.

Because of this:

4. People are often able to take reparative steps—sometimes a
    rather compulsive caring for others, sometimes a searching
    for causes, perhaps with the idea that someone else might
    be saved the pain they went through. From this much new
    energy may be generated.

Deprivation

Just as the concept of loss was extended beyond the loss of a
person, we might take a further step to include also DEPRIVA-
TION—people's discovery of something they did not lose,
because they never had it, and which they now see they ought
to have had. So people might discover that they were deprived
of good schooling, that the schooling they had was bad and
shaming, and so they rebelled against it and lost what good
they might have picked up from it. Perhaps, they think, in a
different school they might never have needed to rebel. Then
people are faced with the consequences of what they
now discover to have been a disadvantage; they discover their
deprivation and may feel all the reactions listed as reactions to
loss: denial, grief, anger, blame and shame, and reparative
steps.

Not that I want to blame deprivation only on the school.
Plenty of people never took full advantage of the schooling that
was given to them, the reason being that their parents reacted
against schooling with anger and denial, because their own
lack of good schooling hurt them and angered them so much
that they could not come to terms with it without help, and so
they transmitted their attitudes to their children.

Or I might discover that the family and culture I was born
into was boring and sterile, discouraged love and tenderness,
promoted hardness and self-denial. (Again, do not blame the
parents—they themselves may have had to engage in denial
and anger to cope with their own deprivation and loss.) Or,
conversely, I might discover that my family and culture was so
soppy, sentimental, self-indulgent, and short-sighted, that I
was never helped to postpone a current impulse for the sake of

a future greater benefit, so that now I feel I cannot be bothered to make an effort even in my own interest for what I want for myself—my habit is to blame others.

Or a person might discover, perhaps over and over again, that the lack of white skin at each stage of development brings disadvantages to career and life-chances. And so on.

These discoveries of deprivation might be so like experiences of loss that one reacts to them in the same way as one would to a loss. It seems a possibility worth discussing.

Depression and mourning

It is now generally thought that the low, restless, tired, worn-out, tearful, gnawing anguish that we call depression is grief at the bad thing that has happened to us. I believe that these feelings arise not only after private personal losses and deprivations but are also a consequence of the sense of loss and deprivation that comes to people when they contemplate the effect on them of social inequalities: unequal schooling, unequal understanding, unequal know-how, unequal personal or social or economic resources. Denial—i.e. ignoring the bad feeling or pretending that I don't feel bad, or even convincing myself that I am over it—is no good. My vitality continues to seep away, like an indigestion of the mind, a toothache of the heart. In addition to the pain of loss or deprivation, I feel the pain of self-reproach, of a sense that I should have known better, done better. Then there is the pain that comes from blaming others, which inevitably involves me in the pain that I was unable to stop them hurting me or those I love. Further pain comes from the shame of knowing I am behaving badly right now, thinking unkind thoughts about others, being envious and even wishing them ill, being impatient with them, unreasonable in my expectations and demands. And so on.

These are normal forms of mourning. It is tiresome for ourselves and for those around us, but if we just let ourselves get on with it, we do eventually regain our balance. I am bound to say, though, that in my view losing someone really close and dear, like a parent or a long-time partner, makes a person unreliable in mood and judgement for at least a year.

Prolonged denial of pain, with detachment and indifference, are characteristic of a badly mourned loss. Bowlby (1969) likened these reactions to scar-tissue that prevents and distorts the development of later healthy growth (*Loss*: chapter 2). People who have not mourned their loss enough are left with a deep sense of helplessness and vulnerability. Small wonder. What chronic mourners feel so terrible about is the impossibility of ever finding again that which they have lost, ever finding again who or what made them feel loved and safe—the important person or thing having slipped from their grasp without their having been able to prevent it (*Loss*: chapter 14).

The generally accepted remedy against chronic mourning is to help people mourn—i.e. to help them express what they feel, including the feelings they are hardly aware of, or quite unconscious of, and which will seem very unreasonable to them when they first find them rising to the surface, like resentment against the loved one, or self-reproach. But these feelings need to be recognized and understood and accepted by the sufferer and, indeed, by those around the sufferer, as part of accepting and not denying the loss. It is because of this that Bowlby and many others warn against the dangers of preventing people from expressing the anguish they feel. Children, particularly, are really almost forbidden to grieve—they are told not to cry, or told they need not cry, that there is no point in crying, even that they will be given something to cry about if they don't stop it at once, or that they should stop crying in order to spare other people's feelings. People all too easily engage in conspiracies of silence—the more so if they have been made to deny their own fears and griefs. Once again: these considerations are as relevant to the suffering of economic and social as of private and personal losses and deprivations.

Vulnerability to depression

There is a kind of depression that is not attributable to unmourned loss, which is important for counsellors and psychotherapists to recognize. So far we considered people who are in trouble because a loss or a deprivation is impairing their joy and vitality. But there is another kind of depression that seems not to have to do with this, but with what went wrong in earliest infancy, when the first ideas of self (me, who I am, myself) and of others (those around me and how they are towards me) were just beginning to crystallize—ideas of "I" and "me", "you" and "us". If the sense of identity, of "I", "me myself", is too defective, proper defences against later distress cannot develop. The idea of "us" is similarly important. Pain is much harder to bear when recourse to "us" is not available. Sympathetic sharing can be a great consolation in distress. Certainly its absence is an added burden. This has nothing to do with social or economic or educational advantages or disadvantages. We are here considering early relationships between the infant and the environment—usually the mother or whoever is in her place—early relationships that allowed things to happen that the infant could not bear. The child feels "I wait for her and she never comes", "I need her and she is not there", or, worse, "They do not care what happens to me", even "They do not care if I die", even "They are killing me". Such experiences leave lasting traces of pain and vulnerability that cannot be removed by mourning their absence. Something, rather, has to be done in a very slow way, about support and acceptance, which creates the secure conditions in which a good sense of "I" and "us" develops. (For more on that, see Klein, 1987, particularly chapters 16 and 20.)

We can start by thinking what it must be like to be a fortunate baby that feels nice and secure even when the mother is not actually holding it. It has something like a memory of being nicely and securely held by someone whom for brevity's sake I will call the mothering person and even in his or her absence the infant can hold on to that niceness and security until that person comes back. This becomes possible because of those moments when the baby actually was with the mothering person but did not have to take notice of the sheltering presence—that is how secure the baby feels, it does not have to worry about whether or not there is protection. Where there always is protection, a wonderful feeling of invulnerability ensues. In those circumstances the baby has the proof that its trust is justified because when it does remember the mothering person and looks up, there she or he is, still there—absolute safety and security. And the mother or other stands for the whole world at this time, so this baby experiences itself in a totally secure world.

People who have not had enough of this good experience are very very vulnerable to even the slightest loss of support. They are chronically over-dependent—on people if they are relatively lucky (although no person will put up with this clinging for long without exacting quite a price)—and chronically over-dependent on alcohol or other mood changers if they are less lucky still.

This chronic dependence is a genuine compulsion that sufferers cannot extinguish by effort or will-power or intellectual understanding. Their only hope is to find someone who can understand them and help them grow out of it. Psychotherapy can do it sometimes, perhaps with a group of others like them also around, or a residential community around them. We have to recognize that insight and other intellectual aids of that kind are only marginally helpful: the need is more emotional than that—it is for relationships in which people can be securely held while they venture to be in touch with thoughts or feelings or parts of themselves from which the fear of pain and annihilation has long kept them estranged.

Advantaged people

Fortunate people often do not think of themselves as fortunate: they tend to think of themselves as natural, normal, ordinary, deserving what they've got, which they can be proud of because what they have is the proper reward for being well analysed, clever, hardworking, clean-living, determined, or whatever. They are tempted to look at the more disadvantaged and think them to blame for not being as clean, clever, determined, undepressed, and so on. "We don't smoke, so why do the homeless smoke?" . . . "We don't drink, so why are these beggars drunk?" And they attribute the difference to their own virtue. "Why are those others always so depressed?" . . . "Why do they eat junk food?" . . . "Why don't the aged wear knitted hats in winter to keep themselves warm?" The assumption is that they are just not as good as me, so no wonder they haven't got what it takes: "Let them make an effort." What many fortunate people have no conception of is what it is like to be depressed. You cannot just snap out of it and not be damaged. Nor do many have a conception of what it is like to be living day-in–day-out in a disadvantaged situation, what it has done to one's parents, one's love-relationships, oneself, one's children. This results in a form of denial: "It is their own fault; nothing can be done because it is their own fault". It used to be, "Don't give the poor bathrooms, they'll only put coal in the bath." Now we say: "Don't give to charity, it will only produce more problems." We say, without checking the facts, that it all goes on administration. We maintain that it is only a self-indulgent gesture and that famine relief is no solution. In my view these denials, the immense flaws of imagination I have attributed to the quotes above, are often due to the speaker's own pain, which has been repressed. It is due to repressed chronic mourning. In that sense, we are saying: "We have repressed our pain and become successful, why can't they?" It is an interesting position to consider. But a society run by people who have repressed their pain is a very heartless and unimaginative society, in my view. I do not like to think of living in it.

The internalized oppressor, shame and blame

If we look at this from the point of view of the less fortunate, we need the concept of the internalized oppressor. This concept was first formulated by theorists from among the gay people in our society. It applies to many kinds of people who believe, deep down, often in spite of surface denials, that they are not as good as others, not as good as heterosexuals, or not as good as men, not as good as rich people, white people, successful people.

According to Anna-Maria Rizzuto (1991), we have almost always an unconscious idea, an unconscious phantasy, that generates the shame or aggravates it. In that phantasy, I have a picture of myself as unappealing, unattractive, unable to evoke a respectful or admiring response from anyone. Ashamed, I have a notion of what a right person would have been like, or would have said or done, and I give myself the message that I have not done what was expected—eventually, that I am incapable of doing what is expected. So my sense of myself as a worth-while person is more and more damaged—I increasingly see myself as not deserving a serious response to my wishes and needs.

Alternatively, people with a social disadvantage or a depression may blame not themselves, which is a very depressing thing to do, but others: it is his fault—the teacher's; it is her fault—the boss's; their fault—the system's. They are keeping me down, and it is no use trying for worth-while goals. This anger at others can go so deep that people can unconsciously disadvantage themselves further, just to spite the more fortunate. Their envy of the more fortunate is turned destructively inwards, instead of creatively and ambitiously outward.

Defences

What can we say about how people defend and protect themselves from these damaging messages they get or send to themselves? First of all, we need defences; we need defences to protect ourselves from the sudden full knowledge of the pain of our situation. But while some defences help us to survive and grow, other defences hinder and restrict our well-being. Useful or useless, I shall be cautious of attacking other people's defences: they may still be needing them.

Next, let me say that shame can be a useful reaction if, as soon as I realize I feel it, I feel a sort of pressure to become active and do something. That is a useful reaction for both advantaged and disadvantaged to cultivate. But of course there are dangers—shame at belonging to an unvalued or shameful category can be crippling. Not being a graduate haunts numbers of people. Not being confident or well-dressed or with the right haircut or sure about how to behave in a new setting like a committee, or an interview, or a party—all this can cripple a person's performance.

Pre-eminent among the defences against shame is denial: staying in ignorance—"Everything's fine" . . . "No problems." This suits the advantaged. If there is no problem, the advantaged need not feel any concern at being more fortunate, they need not re-examine their situation vis-à-vis others, they need not sacrifice advantages for the sake of social justice. Ignorance suits us also when we are disadvantaged, though really only in the short run. Ignorance is then a useful defence, because it can stop us from succumbing to despair when faced with an overwhelmingly bad situation. Ignorance is bliss. Denial, playing dumb, has saved some of us from being murdered, as well as from committing murder and other extreme self-destructive acts. This is why denial is so often the defence of childhood—children are so helpless. A child in a family where he or she is hated really has to deny that fact to itself—it could not survive otherwise. The danger of denial and ignorance is of course that it can easily shade into useless passivity, harmful lassitude, pointless resignation, laziness.

We have to remember, next, the extent to which victims fight each other. The disadvantaged are just as good at shamefully stereotyping people as the advantaged are. The oppressed also oppress one another. It makes me feel less ashamed if there is someone else around I can despise and shame. So there are people originally from the Caribbean Islands, or parts of Asia, who give in to the temptation to despise others with a different immigrant background, just as much as the whites do. And, similarly, so do subgroupings within these very large geographical categories.

Similarly, some poor people despise others for being poor. Plenty of gay men make fun of women, and vice versa. Among children—very generally shamed for being powerless—there is a great deal of bullying and harassing. The fact that victims fight each other has also to do with the tendency of the harassed to identify with the aggressor: the very group or person that makes one feel bad or small is admired as strong, good, and in the right. That makes one passive.

The alternative is to be always alert to the oppressive element in others and in oneself, and, if appropriate, to challenge it. I have to be alert to the way in which shaming and stereotyping is used in my own group, against whoever is picked on in my group as not as good as we are. And I have to be alert to the way shaming and stereotyping is used in the groups that my own group uses as positive reference groups, which my group sees as better—maybe even rightly in some respects. But even if rightly seen as better in some respects, those reference groups, perfect they are not, and infallible they are not, even the best of them. And they and we do what it is in the nature of groups to do—we find ourselves a group to feel better than, and we do them down, we stereotype and shame them. And to the extent that I use a reference group, I have to be alert, lest, for the sake of belonging to it—or appearing to belong to it, or for the sake of resembling it—I stereotype and shame the groups that they stereotype and shame.

It is important always to question the pull towards helplessness—the feeling that nothing can be done. At the very least, we can clean up our own act and attempt some cleaning of those within earshot. It is useful to have some righteous anger. Which brings me to Pride, the opposite of Shame: "Black is Beautiful", "Gay Pride", all those slogans. "Women do the real work" . . . "Men do the real work" . . . And so on.

Creativity, marginality, originality

Creativity is the best of all boosters of self-esteem, the most powerful anti-depressant. If one can just find the energy, like the frog in milk, it repays a hundred-fold and cumulatively. The story, which I have been unable to trace to its source, is of a frog that fell into a bowl of milk. There was too little milk in the bowl for the frog to be able to swim with enough force to jump out from a swimming position. But there was too much milk for the frog to be able to sit on the bottom without drowning, so he could not jump out from a sitting position either. Did that frog give up? No. It swam, and swam, and swam . . . stirring up the milk with its powerful legs. Stirring . . . stirring . . . stirring . . . until at last the milk turned to cream, and the cream turned to butter floating on top of the milk. The frog climbed onto the butter island and jumped from there out of the bowl.

Creativity is effortful. You have to slog away at it; you don't get a poem, a tune, a painting, a game, right first time. But it repays. Fortunately, energy of the "I'll show them" kind is available particularly among those who are being done down. And why not? It is a healthy reaction to a superior sibling, a bullying parent, a sarcastic teacher, a general prejudice against my kind of person, against forever being less than others, not as good as they are: I'll show them!

I am not saying to depressed and disadvantaged people, "Get on your bike, be creative". I am stating a fact that is as relevant to the fortunate as to the unfortunate. Creative people have hardly ever found that a fairy godmother put a silver spoon into their mouth at birth. They are mostly people who have made a lot of effort, and why? Because they wanted to get away from where they did not like to be. Often they were not born where money, time, work, or respect were available. They had to move away from there. The result is that they are original as well. If there is no one around to copy, you have to be original. There are advantages to marginality.

Warning: to some extent, the dominant culture always tends to adopt new good things for itself, even creativity, and this tends both to tame the originality of what was being created and to impoverish the marginalized cultures. Also, there are, as it were, permitted channels to be creative in. Black people used to be channelled into sports; and they used to be channelled into spirituals and jazz, and more recently into steel bands. Sports and the performance arts are where the disadvantaged find it easiest to make their way, against least opposition, partly because in these spheres the social structures are not such that you get real political or economic power from them, at least until recently. I think the time is coming when sports stars and the performance artists get political power because of television chat-shows and such. There is now an M.P. porno pop-star in Italy, and in India there are several film-star M.P.s. With increased P.R. grooming, there will be more. The flip-side is that this process trivializes the nature of power, and that it is a power dependent on the media. Less insecure and less trivial power is to be found in the higher reaches of politics, in higher-level administration, higher-level educational institutions, and I think that it is more difficult for the initially disadvantaged to get these positions and to use their creativity there.

At this point it becomes relevant to note that there are certain kinds of important creativity that are undervalued by the dominant culture, because to value them would have social or financial consequences that are hard for us as a society to face. I have already mentioned the taming of originality and creativity, and their siphoning-off into the leisure-sphere, sports and the performance arts, where they are less threatening. Another area where the creative response is undervalued, in prestige and in respect and in financial terms is—surprise! surprise!—the domestic sphere, still largely the woman's sphere.

This is the sphere of crafts, not of High Art but of the crafts of homemaking, child-rearing, non-commercial dressmaking, upholstery, and so on. I wish we had a society in which it is possible to get more respect for these sorts of creativity. Further, I wish that—in addition to the opportunity for us all to earn our keep—there were also the opportunity for us all to live creatively in other spheres: writing, partying, playing with and educating children, walking in the countryside, making music, making love, making jewellery, jumping about on trampolines and tennis courts, and so on. We do not give each other respect for this kind of creativity. Nor do we give it to ourselves. Internalized oppression. We have taken in the values of dominant cultures that shame us.

What safeguards can we find against such internalized oppressions, and against being oppressors ourselves? I do not give advice about this. It would be presumptuous. But I remember from when I was relatively less advantaged than most of my contemporaries, as a little (immigrant) refugee girl, how lost I was, how dependent I felt, and how I hated myself a little for being dependent and for having no clear standard to judge anything by. And how I hated myself for behaving in the way in which people who are dependent have to behave, if they are to get what they want. However, I also remember the story of the frog in the milk.

My advice is for us to be aware of the ambivalence with which the less safe come to us, and to be aware of our own ambivalence towards them. And to be clear that the greater the intelligence, courage, and honesty everyone puts into the situation, the more promising the outcome. Without intelligence, courage, and honesty, we get nowhere.

PART TWO

CONCERNING
THEORIES AND TECHNIQUES

Entirely

If we could get the hang of it entirely
    It would take too long;
All we know is the splash of the words in passing
    And falling twigs of song.
And when we try to eavesdrop on the great
    Presences it is rarely
That by a stroke of luck we can appropriate
    Even a phrase entirely.

And if the world were black and white entirely
    And all the charts were plain
Instead of a mad weir of tigerish waters,
    A prism of delight and pain,
We might be surer where we wished to go
    Or again we might be merely
Bored but in a brute reality there is no
    Road that is right entirely.

Louis MacNeice
Plant and Phantom, March 1940

CHAPTER THREE

Psychotherapeutics:
what makes people better?

Psychotherapeutics considers what makes people better. But first we need to decide what we mean by "better". Thinking about it in a common-sense sort of way without much conscious reference to what others have said, I come up with three—or three-and-half—sets of criteria.

The first set of criteria is around the general idea that people who are "getting better" are more able to talk appropriately about themselves and their world, at appropriate depth, with appropriate depths of feeling, and—very important—they are able to do this outside the consulting-room, as well as when they are talking to a psychotherapist. It is part of this set of criteria, too, that they do not only talk more appropriately but also act more appropriately (within fairly wide limits, and don't let's quibble). By "more appropriate" I mean some mixture of what they and I consider more appropriate and what is considered more appropriate in the society in which they normally participate. These are *criteria of appropriate behaviour*.

The second set of criteria is around the general idea that people who are "getting better" are more familiar with, and more tolerant of, a wider range (again, let's not quibble) of their own thoughts, feelings, and experiences generally. They have more of a sense of what they are experiencing and thinking or feeling, and they are not too frightened by that knowledge to be able to hold on to it in their minds, to reflect on it, and to consider its implication for action. They are less impelled to get rid of it by acting impulsively without thought, or translating it into physical symptoms, or repressing it, or otherwise somehow disowning it. Necessarily accompanying this ability to be familiar with their own feelings and to contain them is also that they have more of what Fonagy (1991) and others are calling a "theory of mind"—familiarity with and tolerance of the fact that others, too, have an inner world, have thoughts, feelings, experiences. (Kernberg, in a 1992 discussion in London, suggested an interesting and quite challenging further step in this direction—namely that people who are "better" might be better able to accept that their own view of reality may not exactly match that of others. This is sanity indeed.) These are *criteria of proper containment*.

A third set of criteria is embedded in what has already been said: there has to be a capacity for intimacy. People who are "better" are more intimate, both with their own feelings and with the feelings and expectations of others—a *criterion of proper accessibility and intimacy*.

Then there is a half-criterion. I have put it in a minor position to counteract a tendency to inflate its importance. It is what we require from psychotherapists in training—to be able to talk in a consistent fashion about their own and other people's psychic processes. I think this is necessary for psychotherapists, and nice for anyone, but not required of those who are not going to be therapists, any more than a doctor would expect the rest of us to be coherent about chickenpox in order to avoid it. So this is a half-criterion.

So much for definitions of "better". The rest of this chapter is divided into three main sections:

A. elementary constituents of therapeutics;
B. the role of the other in psychotherapy;
C. the role of the ego in psychotherapy.

Elementary constituents of therapeutics

Helping people to talk

Some people get better just by being allowed to talk. It helps to put things into words—to make conscious a lot of things that may have been vague in one's mind but have never been given proper attention. Just getting this vague muddle into consciousness and into properly organized form may be all that is needed. It helps people to both feel and be more weighty and stable. Good counsellors are trained to do this.

This way of helping people goes back to Freud's dictum, *"Wo Es war, werde Ich sein"*. This is usually translated as "Where Id was, there shall Ego be"—a correct translation, but one that has tended to obscure other equally valid but less daunting versions, such as "Where there was just an emotional muddle, I now have a sense of myself and of my world".

This process tends to happen very naturally from the beginning of a therapy, and it is sometimes all that is needed. In my opinion it is a pity to make people delve deeply into their minds, at great cost of time and money and emotion, and to make them live in the consulting-room rather than in the world outside, if they don't have to. Some sessions with a good counsellor may be all that is needed. Unfortunately there is as yet a problem in diagnosing at the outset what it is that a person in trouble needs, and there are problems in shifting from the counselling mode to psychotherapy and vice versa.

The fact that a person begins to feel much more sorted out after a spell of talking should not be confused with what is called a transference cure, which refers to a temporary improvement in patients' well-being when they feel less lonely because they have someone to love and feel loved by— namely the therapist or counsellor. The effects of speaking one's thoughts are more permanent: conceptualizing their experiences helps people to know themselves better and contain themselves better, to be more intimate with themselves and others, and so on, in accordance with our stated criteria.

Helping people to find the words to say it in

Putting things into words makes people aware of what was previously unconscious or pre-conscious. Being conscious of something gives meaning and dignity, because once a thing has meaning, it is, in principle, either controllable or not controllable. If the thing is controllable, the person is not helpless; if it is not controllable, the person is not responsible. In one way or the other, there is less anxiety and/or guilt. And either way, the person may feel less confused and less unable to manage, confronted now with something that has a clearer shape.

What is it about words that is so helpful? Words are what we are conscious with. When we have the words, our inner world becomes less ego-alien and less chaotic. But if that is so, then the therapist's words themselves should not be too alien to the patient too often, and the concepts the words embody should not be too alien too often. Unfortunately, sometimes the therapist cannot help astounding the patient, because people can at first be quite amazed to discover that they do things without knowing why they do them, or even without knowing that they do them. The very idea of unconscious processes is sometimes alien to a person and astounding, as are the ideas of ambivalence, unconsciousness, and other such. That cannot always be avoided. But where it can be avoided, it is quite important not to create a layer of ego-containment or superego control couched in language that does not belong to the language in which that person normally experiences life.

How do therapists and counsellors prepare themselves not to offend in this respect? By learning the language of the patient, and this they can really only do when they themselves have so thoroughly understood the nature of common psychic processes that they do not have to use the language and metaphors in terms of which they first encountered the phenomena under observation.

Helping people to accept their feelings

> It may be that only genuine emotion, necessarily spontaneous, can penetrate the autistic barrier and lift the compulsion to repeat. . . . One of the principal difficulties

of difficult patients concerns the ability to share emotions.
The patient may learn that certain emotions can induce
positive changes. Crying is a relief. Tenderness softens and
may sadden. Indulgence in wishful thinking creates a desire to live. . . . [Badaracco, 1992]

We live in a world where many people do not believe in being
intimate with their feelings. They are offended by the very
existence of certain feelings: they believe these feelings should
not exist, or if they do exist, they should not be acknowledged;
they go in for all sorts of devices to disown them. It is here that
acceptance as a basic constituent of the therapeutic process
can begin to make itself felt: the therapist's recognition that
the patient is as he or she is and that there is nothing that need
be left out of the consulting-room as inappropriate or uncontainable. The first lesson of therapeutics (as far as the patient is
concerned) is: everything can be contained here. A later lesson
is that there are appropriate and less appropriate ways of
expressing what is there (but first we have to have a look
at it).

With time, as the intimate relationship with the therapist
gets more established, the ban on prohibited feelings may be
weakened. With luck and skill, the therapist will come to be felt
as so accepting that patients can hope that they will not be
penalized for having their feelings. In time, also, the therapist
may feel free to confront and challenge a patient's unconscious
assumption that a particular hidden feeling does not exist or is
not acceptable.

Helping people to make conscious connections

Similarities, parallels, or recurring themes may crop up in the
course of talking. These may be noticed by the speaker without
any help from the therapist, or they may be accepted the
moment the therapist points them out. These virtually spontaneous connections are usually not very unconscious: they are
just connections that have not been conceptualized till now.
But they are very helpful. Such new connections are therapeutic because they help make sense of one's universe. A person
may say: "I suddenly thought! The reason I don't like dinner

parties is because I hate sitting round the table eating with other people. It takes me back to all the quarrels around our dinner-table when I was little."

Why does making connections conscious help? It helps people to contain themselves better. Words help us to contain ourselves. Concepts help to contain us. A word is a concept—or, rather, it embodies a concept. It conceptualizes an experience. Take the word "tiger". Take the words "elephant" and "spear". Now consider the word "tiger-hunt". It connects the simpler concepts of tiger, spear, etc. into a more complex concept. "Tiger-hunt" embodies an organized pattern of concepts. A sentence is an even more complex pattern of connected concepts. A paragraph even more so. Patterns of connected patterns of connected patterns.

Words, and concepts, are patterned ways of summarizing experiences. Experiences may connect with each other in meaningful patterns. The more an experience can be consciously seen as part of a pattern, the more meaning can be seen in the experience. If several patterns can be made to fit together in a bigger pattern, it means that more experiences in a person's life are felt to be coherent and meaningful—the person ceases to experience life as a flow of unrelated experiences following one another in a senseless way. Thus the experiences are more contained, and the person feels to that extent "better".

Helping people to cut unconscious connections and be open to new experiences

Our past experiences live on in the patterns of our minds, and these very nearly determine how we experience the next thing that comes along: "All the people who ever came to our house have been nice to me, therefore people are (always) nice to me, including this person now approaching." Our established framework encourages us to meet new experiences in a pre-determined way. But there are obvious dangers to this. On the one hand, a person who does not learn from experience is bound to behave in inappropriate ways. Helping people to make conscious connections helps them to a more complex way of understanding the complex world, and helps them to be closer to it and contain it more appropriately. Equally, though, we need insight to perceive when past experience is not an appropriate guide—unconscious connections between thoughts may need to be weakened.

How can we help people to feel less identified with inefficacious ways of being and behaving and relating, based on their past experiences? How can we help them overcome their resistance to new insights? How can we help them to face what they have been unable to face? How can we help them to live more in the interpersonal world—not just in their private fantasy world—and how can we help them to bring the interpersonal world and their inner hopes and wishes more into line with each other?

Interpreting: helping people towards new insights and towards overcoming resistances

Because of long-established habits of mind, or because the connection is unusual, or because the connection is an uncomfortable one, some experiences are not consciously connected spontaneously—not even when people are given the chance to talk. It is no use waiting for these connections to just arrive. It may be the therapist's responsibility to help to bring them about. This is necessarily a slower business, since there is some resistance in the patient's mind—otherwise the connection would already have been made conscious, or abandoned, or accepted as soon as it had been pointed out by the therapist. Interpretation is needed.

By interpreting I mean what the dictionary means—putting something in different words or in a different language, translating it. Thus it may be necessary for the therapist to translate a patient's sentence such as "he gets on my nerves" into the pattern "I am afraid he will make me feel inadequate" before the connection is seen. Or it may be necessary to establish that what in the patient's language is "I hate dinner parties, they are so much work, shopping, cooking, cleaning" has nothing to do with chores because the speaker usually likes these, and it has to be translated into "I dislike sitting with other people round a dinner-table". The language may have to be clarified before the meaning becomes clear enough for new connections to be made.

It is at this point that counselling skills and psychotherapy skills begin to diverge. Many people turn out to need more help than is provided by the freedom to feel and talk in the presence of an accepting and skilled listener. There may be an unconscious reluctance to recognize the right—or wrong—connections between events: there may be deeply unconscious resistance to be overcome. Sometimes it is possible to achieve this just by talking in an accepting atmosphere in which connections can be reconsidered, but more often interpretation is needed of what is happening: therapists taking the initiative in re-evaluating the connections and the meanings in a way that the patients have been unable to do on their own.

This is the more interesting because of what it requires from the therapist. The meaning may be so deeply unconscious that it is not obvious to the rational part of the listening therapist either, who must then involve his or her own deep inner workings so as to arrive at an understanding of the patient by non-rational intuitive means.

The focus now needs to shift away from what happens when the therapist allows a relationship to develop in which patients feel that there is space and permission for their mistaken or inhibited or repressed thoughts and feelings to emerge and be reconsidered. Shifting the focus allows us to see how a therapist can use this relationship so that the interplay it creates can itself become a source of change.

The role of the other in therapy

Helping people from the delusional private world into the interpersonal

Helping people to live in the interpersonal world and not just in a private world of their own is a way of helping them to be open to new experiences. It is much easier to let go of tightly inward-looking connections and to be open to new experiences when one is already in an at least to some extent trusting relationship with other people. Sometimes there is only one other to relate to: the counsellor or therapist or analyst. The great Harold Searles gives us dozens of examples. People in a private world of their own are in fact lonely and deprived. We are born into relationships with people "out there", and we do from early on always somewhere know the difference between a person "out there" and a person in our heads. To have no one out there to care for, and no one who cares, no one to quarrel with, is a deprivation even when it appears to be the only escape from the fear and pain to which people out there expose us. The therapist may be the only person with whom a relationship appears possible and who thus might alleviate this loneliness. And with this a whole new set of therapeutic processes becomes more available. Even the rather cognitively based processes so far focussed on are less efficacious when coming from someone who means nothing to us. Why should this be so?

Generally, as soon as we relate feelingly to someone, our past crowds in to give further meaning to the relationship. And past experience accounts both for the accuracy and the distortion of our perceptions. An understanding of these distortions is a tremendous advantage in helping people towards an understanding of themselves.

Badaracco (1992) uses a characteristically psychoanalytic theoretical framework, which assumes that all our concepts come to us from those people around us with whom we identified at one time or another, the earlier identifications being the more deeply significant. That sounds interpersonal, but it is not. These people have become "internal objects"; they have become people in our heads. They may have been there for years, often unconsciously and hence even more powerfully. To the extent that this is so, we are likely to feel whatever we feel— grief or shame or guilt or contempt or contentment—not interpersonally with reference to what is going on now as seen by an uninvolved bystander, but in terms we internalized from those earlier identifications "in our heads". And this makes it much more difficult to make good new connections or to lose existing bad ones; it makes it harder to learn from experience.

If we had friends around us, they might help us question these internalizations and identifications. Other things being equal, honest people with honest friends are less likely to need a therapist to help them live in the interpersonal world. By definition they are there to some extent already. People without friends are more likely to live in a world of their own—a world of fear, grief, resentment, numbness, self-satisfaction, or whatever, derived from past identifications. Sometimes the current circumstances are such that those old meanings would still appear appropriate also to an uninvolved bystander, but sometimes not: the danger is that they may have become delusional. Honest friends not only sympathize with us and listen, they also contradict us and adduce information that puts our perceptions into a new context and gives them new meaning. They prevent the slide into the uncontradicted solitary delusional world. (See also Klein, 1987, pp. 166-168, 314-317.)

Without friends, people may withdraw further and further into an inner world of their own, especially if contact with others points up grating contradictions. Once this has happened, insight and awareness are not enough, for important areas remain unconscious, unquestioned because unchallenged.

The therapist (or the good honest accessible friend capable of intimacy) helps us move out of our isolated phantasy-world not only because of the inevitable confrontation with new ideas. That is the cognitive aspect of the benefits of human contact. The other aspect is more emotional. Blatt and Behrends (1987) have an extensive paper on this, starting with a good historical perspective on how the theory of psychoanalytic technique has moved its weight from emphasizing the more interpretative/cognitive aspects, to balancing these with more libidinal, interpersonal, and emotional forces. Blatt and Behrends have a very neat theory that involves this balancing act, drawing at the same time a parallel with theories of child-development. In fortunate circumstances, the relationship of patient with therapist (or of child with parents) starts as a gratifying one. The patient (infant) feels safe with the analyst (parent) because the analyst (parent) at that early time is not confronting but accepting: confronting might shake the patient's (infant's) sense of security. But a point comes when the patient (child) feels secure enough to be able to discover that there are at times differences of opinion and of viewpoint between the two of them. Blatt and Behrends call these times "experienced incompatibilities", wherein people begin to feel threatened because of their discovery that there are other realities than their own, and other demands on them than they might wish. The analyst's interpretation of the patient's wishes or resistances or conflicts can bring this discovery about, for it is at those moments of incompatibility that patients discover a separateness from the analyst which they had hoped never to experience. But, say Blatt and Behrends, painful though this discovery of separateness is, it also makes for individuation and growth, and this can be gratifying too, especially in its effects outside the consulting-room. So patients take in the new idea, and also the experience of separateness, and make both of these their own. Thereafter, the sense of togetherness is restored between patient and analyst, which in the course of time is then ready to be disrupted again, at a new level. Each level of gratifying involvement with the analyst is eventually disrupted by an experienced incompatibility, and "the analysand oscillates between two poles in the analysis, between seeking gratifying involvement with the analyst and experiencing incompatibility with this gratifying involvement in its current form". So the patient experiences that it is possible for two people to remain in contact although they do not agree, time and time again. And, each time, this experience gives the patient another boost of courage to permit changes in ideas, feelings, and behaviour, and thus risk differing from the therapist yet again. This is how we grow. In the example that follows, the patient did not like it when the therapist put forward a point of view different from her own, and she felt momentarily let down, but the incident ended happily:

A patient with little self-esteem felt humiliated when, in a traffic tangle, she had allowed a very assertive taxi-driver to take up her space in order to reduce the risk to a third car. After the taxi had driven through the gap she had made, the third driver had shrugged and made the sort of gesture you make when indicating someone is stupid. The patient had felt that this driver was ridiculing her for giving way to the taxi, and she felt very hurt. She was amazed at the suggestion the therapist made—that perhaps the third driver had meant her to join him in ridiculing the stupid assertive taxi-driver who had nearly involved them all in an accident.

The incident was discussed in length and detail, and eventually helped this patient to clarify also her suspicion that the therapist was contemptuous of her, and, indeed, her tendency to be suspicious of people.

But people who cannot bear the experience of incompatibility, who feel that they must have either uninterrupted gratifying involvement or nothing at all, are in a serious plight. Such people have no trust that difference and separation can be temporary. In sheer self-defence, they stay in their private world: they do not let themselves give meaning to relationships or to other people.

Helping people to regain appropriate trust in the interpersonal world

People in his plight, and their therapists, have a problem here. Without the ability to take another person seriously, the patient cannot break out of the private phantasy-world into one shared with the therapist and others—but the distress attendant on taking another person seriously is exactly what keeps people in their private world. A vicious circle.

Challenge and confrontation are necessary skills for a therapist faced with a person living in a private world, or, rather, therapists need the skills that allow them successfully to challenge and confront what goes on in there, in a way that arouses the serious attention of the patient without too much antagonism. But before the therapist can be admitted successfully into someone else's world, trust has to be established, trust that the therapist's world is reliable, seriously concerned, not exploitative—in short, very like a friend. Also, trust that the therapist can understand and see how it is (Betty Joseph, 1992). People living in a world of their own do not have this trust, or they have it only intermittently, and this makes life more difficult for them and for the therapist. In these circumstances, what is needed is accurate interpretation of what is happening between patient and therapist then and there, put in such a way that the patient can recognize that it is indeed a dilemma for both of them. Typically, a therapist in this situation might say something like,

> "I am thinking of what we were saying just now, and how it leaves me in a dilemma. If I leave this silence for too long, you may begin to experience me as having lost interest in you, as you have often said this worries you. But if I do start talking, you may find that you experience me as exploiting you for my own benefit, because it so often feels to you that I talk for the sake of hearing my own voice. . . ."

This containment, by increased intimacy with what is going on, does often help the patient to establish more trust in the therapist's understanding and concern. At times it is an impossible aim, at least in the short run, because of the vicious circle. But in the long run the therapist's honest sympathetic recognition and discussion of what appear to be the ups and downs of the patient's trust and mistrust can be a powerful means by which such trust grows. Sometimes it is the only way in which a patient can be reached.

The therapist here acts as pioneer. The therapist may be the first person, for many years, to be admitted into the patient's private world.

Helping people face what was unbearable:
the repressed, the split-off, and the unthought known

Sometimes we experience the unbearable. It sounds like a paradox: how can we bear the unbearable? In one way or another, we do not take it in. But we bear it in three rather different ways, requiring rather different techniques to help us eventually repair at least some of the damage done.

• *we may not conceptualize* the experience at all, so that no meaningful pattern is formed,

or

• we may conceptualize the experience, but, finding that the meaning of the pattern contains much suffering, we may not allow that pattern to be part of how we experience ourselves: *we keep it split off* from the rest of what we are conscious of,

or

• we may allow it to be a working part of the self, but not in a way that allows us to know about it: *we have repressed the experience.*

These three will now be considered in reverse order.

In the case of repression, the unbearable experience has in fact been integrated as part of the patterned framework with which new experiences are encountered, but the experience as an event in itself has remained unconscious. Then people find themselves doing unaccountable things, and they cannot give a convincing account of what they did and why. And neither can anyone else, because the unbearable event—the unbearable part of the pattern—is not mentioned, not known about in a conscious way, not available to be taken into account in a conscious explanation.

> An ordinarily good-natured male patient begins to talk eva-
> sively in an analytic hour when he describes seeing me at a
> concert the night before. It is clear that he is embarrassed
> and anxious. After this point is acknowledged by the pa-
> tient, we explore the underlying reasons and we discover
> that he felt jealous and resentful that I seemed to be enjoy-
> ing the company of a young man. In subsequent hours we
> uncover the fact that this rivalry situation mobilized in him
> a tendency to a terrible rage outburst. He had suffered
> from frightening temper tantrums as a child when his
> younger brother seemed to be favoured over him. Part of
> his later neurotic character deformation was an unreason-
> able rigid good naturedness. [Ralph Greenson, 1967, p. 81]

Greenson goes on to say that this example demonstrates two layers of what was repressed: the jealousy and the violent rage it provoked were repressed, and the embarrassment that covered the repression was itself repressed. The analyst notices the embarrassment and waits to see what comes up by free association. Jealousy appears, and a previous experience of jealousy, and what is associated with that—rage. Simple, really. Certainly simple compared with what we look at next.

When the unbearable event causes a *split in a person's consciousness* rather than a repression, the meaning to be attributed to what a person is doing at any time is clear enough, and the pattern in terms of which its meaning is perceived and understood is clear enough—what is unaccountable is that on different occasions the person is quite different and acts according to a different framework of meaning. To take an everyday example, some people, "splitters", are able after a serious quarrel in which terrible things have been said, to behave cheerfully when their friends come to dinner an hour or so later. They have been able to put it out of their minds. People who do not split in this way find themselves unable to enjoy themselves after a quarrel; they cannot shake off the mood. Some seriously splitting people do not believe after such a quarrel that they said what they did say. What has happened is that the original unbearable experience, and some of the framework of meaning to which it belongs—including part of people's sense of themselves and their self-imagery and self-awareness—has split off from the rest of the framework in such a way that the person's sense of self is now sometimes experienced in one framework, and at other times in the other. When this happens, the person concerned does not at any moment feel that he or she is doing anything unaccountable at that moment. But the onlooker, who can remember the whole sequence of events, feels it. The person does not think so because his or her sense of self has temporarily withdrawn from the framework within which the events were experienced.

Thirdly, we have what Bollas (1987) calls *the unthought known.* For example, one of Bollas' patients, called "Helen" for this purpose, had a habit of beginning a sentence or a story and then stopping in the middle and becoming silent. So Bollas never got to the end of anything. He tried all sorts of ways of understanding this—how hard it must be for her to talk to a stranger about herself, or that she might be waiting for him to finish her thoughts for her as her previous therapist had been experienced as doing, and so on. He felt very confused by her and found that he would wander off in his thoughts during her silences, and that he only vaguely experienced her as a person. After several months of this, he told her how her long pauses left him in a state where he felt he lost track of her, and that it seemed to him that she was creating a kind of absence that he was meant to experience: she seemed to him to disappear and re-appear without warning. Helen felt immediately relieved by his having said this. She said she knew she did this, but she did not understand it either. There they left it for the time being. Quite a long while after (in the second year of the analysis), Helen began to be able to talk to him about her mother—how distracted and out-of-this-world she was, and only able to relate to people for short periods. Bollas concluded that he had experienced Helen's silences and absences as impinging on him in a disruptive way, much as Helen had experienced her mother's episodic ways of relating as impingements that disrupted her sense of her self.

Helen was haunted by an experience that was neither repressed nor split off. It had simply never been conceptualized at all, never put into words. This may occur either when events happen so early in life that the conceptual apparatus is not yet in place or not yet complex enough to incorporate the experience into meaningful patterns, or it may happen when an experience is so traumatic that the fragile barely established young framework disintegrated in the stress of it. Then the unbearable is somehow there in the mind—Bion might perhaps say that its beta-elements are there—but it is not incorporated into a pattern. It is the unthought known, and its effects show up later in life as general callousness, general stupidity, or other diffuse overall incapacities. Encouraged by child psychotherapists and child analysts, we have begun to try to work with adults in this state.

What therapeutic skills are required to help people face what they have been unable to face?

Helping people undo repression is the simplest and oldest psychoanalytic technique. When patients talk about how it is with them, either in relation to the therapist or in relation to people outside the consulting-room, strange unaccountable inappropriate behaviour and emotions show up, as in the example with the taxi-driver. The strangeness can then be confronted in a sympathetic and unsentimental way, and the unconscious connections—or the unconsciously determined lack of connection—can be explored. This is what Greenson did with the man who saw him at the concert. So the meaning of the strange bit of behaviour comes to be explored. In this way, simple repressions dissolve, and often the event that had originally been so unbearable that it had to be repressed, is much more easily borne by the adult personality now aware of it.

The therapists in those examples used the classical psychoanalytic techniques that encouraged people to explore their irrationality. Undoing repression involves the patient's rationality, will-power, self-image, common sense, and so on. Therapist and patient cooperate in the exploration. There is a therapeutic alliance acknowledged by both, a rational cooperation involving the common sense of both. But this does not always clear up troublesome symptoms, or it only partly clears them. Sometimes it even seems to create further symptoms. Then we may suspect that there are other factors at work besides repression, and then enlisting the patient's rationality, will-power, etc. will not help. Helping people to mend splits caused by unbearable experiences, and helping them to put into words what has never yet been conceptualized, requires more.

Mending splits involves the connecting of two or more hitherto unconnected rationalities, will-powers, self-images—what Kohut (1977, p. 177) calls independent centres of perception and initiative—each apparently self-sufficient within one person. This is what makes it possible for people to deny that they stole something, or that they said, or meant, the terrible things they may have said in a quarrel, in the heat of the moment, when their consciousness was split; they excuse themselves by maintaining that they were not themselves. Talking with people about their feelings or their troubles is not really the whole answer then.

Addressing just one isolated part of a person's personality does not do enough to mend splits. Kernberg (1984) recommends drawing a person's attention to both sides of the split, and this is of course a sensible thing to do, but it is perhaps most useful when there is only one split, between two sides of a person's ambivalence. However, my experience seems often to be with people who are not just split into two, along some ambivalent line: they are split into a number of fragments along all kinds of lines (see Klein, 1987, Chap. 10). Kernberg also assumes that the bit that is hearing his comments is in some sort of control over the other bit(s). My experience seems often to be with people who do not have a permanent controlling bit of this kind.

At a simple experiential level, what makes the difference, therapeutically, is the steadily containing regard of the therapist. Where part of the patient's experience has been split off from the rest, only part of the patient will be with the therapist, from the point of view of what the patient consciously experiences. But from the point of view of the therapist, of course all of the patient is there in the consulting-room. The therapist becomes familiar with and relates to all the ways in which the patient knows himself or herself, while the patient's consciousness moves from fragment to fragment. To the extent that the therapist experiences and relates to the whole of the patient, splits in the patient's way of being conscious can begin to mend. This is not just a cognitive but a total, experiential, repair. In consequence of being treated as a whole person and in consequence of the split not being acted upon by the therapist, patients become more able to experience themselves coherently—more coherently than they had allowed themselves to be before (Klein, 1987: chapter 9 and chapters 16 ff.).

I think this aspect of therapeutics is grossly underestimated. But we can do more. In this situation the use of the transference work comes into its own. The collaboration between therapist and patient changes its nature. The consulting-room becomes a laboratory, or a test-tube, in which we can study amazing processes.

Think for a moment of those children whose grown-ups have allowed the boundaries of what is acceptable behaviour to become obscured. The children then do not behave in normally acceptable ways—they become noisier, ruder, more spiteful, more withdrawn, dirtier, and so on. When we do not insist on polite behaviour, we can see what lies below it at a more impulsive and feeling level. Similarly, many patients, allowed such freedom, begin to behave differently. It is generally thought that older or earlier wishes and relationships are being re-enacted—wishes or relationships that are more appropriate between the infant and its mother, or perhaps the toddler or the child. It is from these experiences that the word "transference" is derived, meaning the transference of a previous relationship onto a new person. Also derived from such experiences is the word "regression", meaning a relaxation to a level where considerations of rationality and civility do not obtain.

Casement (1990) epitomizes an experience many of us know when he says that patients come to us with an unconscious hope that we will be able to recognize something they themselves are unable to grasp, although they sense that it is there.

What is experienced in the consulting-room, when a patient is allowed to regress, illuminates, as in a test-tube, what is happening at a level of the personality not normally open to inspection and discussion. What appears, sooner or later, in these conditions, is a relationship that involves the split-off personality—or even that part of a person's experiences which has never yet been conceptualized and found words for. The conditions of the therapy are now allowing those things to be acted out in relation to the therapist. It is then the therapist's role to discern what is going on, conceptualizing it and communicating it back to the patient—sometimes at the time, sometimes much later, as seems appropriate. This may be the first time that various split-off parts were available to become parts of one whole meaningful pattern, and all available to consciousness for the first time.

Working with the unthought known calls on all these skills and, particularly, also on that part of the therapist's understanding which derives from the use of countertransference phenomena. The unthought known is what we call those experiences that never got as far as being sufficiently conceptualized to be capable of repression or splitting, and which nevertheless exist. They can cause distressing symptoms in the present, and of course they cause reactions in other people— they make other people feel things. This is what happened between "Helen" and Bollas. So here the use of the countertransference comes into its own. What the therapist is made to feel by the patient's behaviour may be the very thing that the patient never got conceptualized. It was never organized into a meaningful pattern. But there it is in the therapist, who is being made to feel it by the patient. The therapist needs to be alert to this: it may be the only avenue by which we can be in touch with a past unknown unconceptualized relationship. Surprisingly often the patient is at the inflicting end rather than at the victim end of the relationship. Bollas, who invented the phrase "the unthought known", gives many examples of gradually understanding what was happening to him in an analytic session. When he was able to put his experiences into words, his patients were often able to recognize that these were, indeed, like the experiences that they had suffered in the past, without ever being able to arrive experientially at the concepts in terms of which they could have been contained.

The role of the ego in therapy

So far the emphasis in this chapter has been on one person helping another. In the final section let us look at a person's own resources and how the person in the patient-role contributes to the therapeutic process.

Who looks after patients at non-session times? and after they have finished their therapy? The current orthodox response is to say "the internalized therapist"—a concept easy for many patients to accept and use. But it is not for all patients the whole truth, and there is an arrogance in it. Is there no way in which patients can take care of themselves except via the therapist? My own view is that many people in the patient-role do get much from their therapist, but that they may have other resources besides, which enable them to look after themselves, just as other people do, to an extent that depends on the nature of their disability.

There are theories which hold that we are all managed by our inner and/or internalized objects (Meltzer, 1973, presents a very extreme example of this view). But I belong intellectually and emotionally—although not ethnically—to a Protestant pragmatic positivistic tradition, and I like to believe that it is I myself who looks after me a good deal of the time, and also I prefer the company of people who can believe this about themselves. Where does this sense of self-reliance come from psychologically? Agreed, in part it comes from what I internal-ized from people around me. But also, this sense that I can cope comes from my knowledge that I have coped with difficul-ties in the past, and that I can rely to quite an extent on my ego-functioning (see also Klein, 1987, index on "skills"). So I am bound to feel that while, on the one hand, we need to give weight to the importance of patients' interpersonal emotional experience with the therapist—transferential and other—yet, on the other hand, we need also to give due weight to the importance of people developing their ego resources. We need to consider the relative therapeutic importance of (1) the thera-pist's ability to manage the relationship, and (2) the patient's ability to use the experiences of psychotherapy. The latter depends on who the patient already is, on the patient's ability to see straight, on the patient's ability to endure the discovery of imperfections and errors (their own and other people's) in an honest way and without feeling too disabled to carry on, and so forth.

There are those who maintain that only through experience in the transference can any real change be brought about. To go to the other extreme, I believe that people who have not had enough honest relationships with other people for a good length of time, for fear of losing face or for more deep-seated reasons, cannot work in the transference in a way that will be useful to them therapeutically. They may produce plenty of transference phenomena, but are they benefiting? I deal with this question in chapter six.

However, battles about the relative values of the two ap-proaches generate mainly acrimony. What we need to do is to define the issues more closely and make them more practical—thus: in what circumstances, at what stage in the therapy, for people of what cast of mind, is it probably better to encourage work in the transference, and when is it less advisable and we should, rather, encourage the patient to develop strength in other ways to deal with the discoveries to come?

So this section must consider what to my mind is the major non-transferential factor determining how people get better: ego-strength. By "ego" I mean that part of the framework of linked thoughts, feelings, concepts, memories, and so on, that was built up over the years and has to do with our subjective experience of identity—our sense of who we are. I have no quarrel with Anzieu (1987, but quoting his earlier work in French), who uses a different metaphor very felicitously. He thinks of the ego as a kind of psychic skin, noting the similarities between its functions and the functions performed by the skin that covers our physical being. The skin/ego is a shield against stimuli and a container for all our psychic processes, and the part of us that rubs up against other people, both as a boundary and in pleasurable contact, and so on—nine functions in all. In any of these ways people might feel relatively more safe or more vulnerable, according to how well their skin/ego functions.

The ego can be relatively "strong" or relatively "weak". A stronger ego enables people to admit painful events without too much injury to their proper self-esteem and also without too much distortion of the realities involved. People with a relatively weaker ego might evade integration of these realities and/or suffer a heavier and more disintegrating blow to their self-respect.

By "ego-functioning" I mean those processes of perceiving, conceptualizing, understanding, making patterns, giving meaning, remembering, comparing, planning, and so on that, between them, build up the general framework of meaning of which the ego is a part.

We need to be aware of two aspects: (1) The role played by the ego and by ego-functioning in holding a person together and integrating his or her experiences so as to allow further growth to take place—by adapting, learning, developing, and other such. (2) The role played particularly by that part of the ego which involves people's self-image, their self-esteem, their self-respect. (I am using simple English here, to avoid so far as I can the controversies around narcissism.)

Getting better has to do with integration and with the healing of splits and wounds. Ego-psychology and self-psychology have contributed to our understanding of these processes, and also, I hope, the recent greater tolerance of therapeutic forms of holding (see chapter four).

Kernberg (1984) relies on characteristics of the ego and of ego-functions to differentiate neurotic personality structures from psychotic ones, and both from more borderline configurations. In his system, the relatively greater ego-strength of some people shows in their greater ability to control their impulses to action: they can tolerate more intense anxiety; they can live more easily with contradictions; they are better at accepting themselves and other people as they are, imperfections and all. With all these blessings, no wonder they can get help from others more easily, including help from psychoanalytically based psychotherapists, who sometimes require a good deal of abstinence from the patient.

Kernberg also relies a great deal in his diagnostics on what he rather infelicitously calls reality-testing, by which he actually means a person's sense of reality. This shows in the greater or lesser ability of people to recognize whether an impulse to action has come from within themselves, or whether it seems to them to have come to them from outside (at worst by rays from Mars or whispering devils), and with that of course their ease in distinguishing the boundaries between self and others.

Kernberg is so persuaded of the importance of these characteristic ego-manifestations that he advocates different forms of therapy as particularly appropriate to each. According to him— and he relies on many years of experience as well as a good deal of systematic research done by others—those with neurotic personality organizations (i.e. those with sound ego-strength, relatively speaking) do best with the more interpretative and unyielding techniques of psychoanalysis or psychoanalytically oriented psychotherapy. People with "borderline" traits, with a rather shakier ego, do best with the kinds of psychotherapy that allow a great deal of talking and abreaction, but they do badly in the full rigour of the classical American-style Freudian analysis of drives and their derivatives. Those with major psychotic traits, with very faulty ego-functioning, do best with less challenging counselling and support. Needless to say, the practitioners of all these techniques will themselves need to be properly aware of, comfortable with, and in touch with transference and countertransference phenomena.

I find Kernberg's a helpful lead, but I think he raises problems too, mainly because his system could be misused when applied in a cut-and-dried fashion by practitioners in a less imaginative, more rigid, and less perceptive frame of mind.

People do not come in three packaged sets of personality organization, really. Rather, the structures themselves fluctuate, sometimes rapidly, sometimes very slowly. On some days, or for some minutes, Mr X seems is neurotic; on other days or at other moments he seems to be more psychotic, or on the borderline. Sometimes his ego is weak—he cannot tolerate the slightest frustration; sometimes his ego is strong—he is in a position to weigh things up seriously. The therapist has to consider almost from moment to moment how best to help X's ego gain greater strength. In one session this may mean unconditional acceptance, in another it may mean interpretation of what X has said, in yet another it may mean interpretation of what is going on in the session. Psychotherapy is more like painting than like engineering.

Mr X's ego-strength fluctuates, just as ours does. We need to be in touch with how much a person is able to bear at any moment. Our patients' ego-strength is usually less than ours, and so we must be tender with them in this regard.

Looking through the literature, a gratifying increase is noticeable in the warnings that we must not impose burdens on the patient that the patient's ego is not strong enough to bear. What happens if you do? Either the patients leave, if they have strength to do so, or they split in the way described in a previous section, and the part the therapist deals with is the part that is allowed to exist. Thus Sandler (1992) quotes with approval a paper by Fonagy and Moran (1991) in which they advise that there may be a "need to devise strategies of analytic intervention aimed to support the child's ability to tolerate conflict". I understand them to mean that the child's ego needs strengthening before the unconscious inner conflict that led to the child's distress can safely be made conscious. Cooper (1992) goes further, and also quotes Greenspan (without reference, unfortunately) in his work with young children, that "better mothering or removal from an abusive situation produces powerful and lasting changes in the child, even though the child is not helped to develop insight into what is going on." (There are numerous other important references in this very useful issue of the *International Journal of Psychoanalysis*.)

Conclusions on how people get better: something borrowed, something new

To sum up. People get better by cleaning up the framework created by their past, in terms of which they experience their current life. Right connections are made, wrong connections reconsidered, new conclusions drawn, new experiences greeted in a less distorted way and integrated into a healthier context. Through this, and through close connection with another human being, people are also connected to others in a better way, better able to receive the love and hate and fear of others, and better able to handle their own. They can come closer to other people than was possible before, and they are able to get away from them more easily when they need to. They can feel for others more accurately, and also more freely so that they do not get trapped in them but can move in and out of their identifications as seems best to them. Our capacity for this depends on our ego-strength, which is what allows us to identify without too much fear or idealisation.

The capacity to empathize and identify in this free way brings new riches to the personality, as people try out new roles and new perspectives to test their consonance with the already existing framework. The imagination is freed. Much of this can happen while a person is in therapy and on the way to "getting better" but needing the safe relationship within which new personalities can be voiced, tried out, modified, discarded, or accepted, as seems right. These new identifications come from the people we meet, the books we read, the memories we have, in new combinations and permutations. I do not go along with those who believe that it is all "already there", like archetypes or like Meltzer's (1973) internal parental couple whose harmony has to be found before we can have our own. There may or may not be something there already, but it seems important to maintain that the human personality is able to make a new thing, even of itself, given the right circumstances.

CHAPTER FOUR

Holding: recognizing, accepting, understanding, containing, organizing, integrating, metabolizing, and other such

I wonder why our theoretical interests have, for nearly a century, allowed us as a matter of course to refer back and forth between adult and infantile forms of love, or hate, while ignoring so much of the adult's and the child's need to hold and be held? The infant's need for holding does not vanish as it grows older, leaving no residue behind; common sense suggests that the need transforms itself into more and more mature forms, just as other infantile needs do. Of course, generations of psychotherapists have been conscientiously taught to use each holiday-break to explore their patients' dependency-needs. And for decades we have had the inspiration of Bowlby's painstaking work on attachment, and a great deal is being said about "containment". Yet I think there must be a gap in our perceptual apparatus, which prevents us from seeing infantile dependency-needs in our adult patient's longing to be held. Partly we may explain this gap in theory by noting that Freud's mother does not seem to have been much of

---

A version of a paper given *In Memoriam Cyril Richards* at the Association for Group and Individual Psychotherapy in June, 1991.

a cuddling woman (Freud Research Group, 1991). Also, Freud was a man, and it can be argued that the male's need to be held moves to some extent from a whole-skin experience to concentration on the penis.

One way or another, theory rather missed this area out, and this is now being remedied. A whole range of concepts has come into being about processes that bear a family resemblance to one another: recognizing, containing, understanding, metabolizing, integrating, and so on. I propose to look at some of these processes, distinguishing characteristics they have in common, and others that make each special.

I should perhaps also say at the outset that these processes, which are kinds of holding, are not, in my view, particular kinds of intervention—rather, they are aspects of many of the interventions and interpretations that we make anyway. I am not advocating that we should do something very different from what many counsellors and psychotherapists and analysts already do. I am saying that there are aspects to what we are doing that are worth looking at in more detail.

Sympathy as a kind of holding

Here is a story of a student therapist, after six weeks with her first patient, who comes twice a week. This patient, a woman of about 40, was a useful patient for a rather insecure and not especially well-founded student. The patient had had a difficult life, and she used these early weeks to unload a vast quantity of passing thoughts about her past and current life, not pausing for reflection or for breath, and certainly not giving the student easy chances to say anything. "Good", I said, "she'll give you time to get used to the situation." She was the sort of patient who has a marvellous time at first, just from having someone listen to her while she talks. The therapist, when she could, said things like "Oh dear", and "How sad", and "How frightening", and so on. To my mind, these are the simplest forms of holding. The therapist was doing some holding simply by listening with feeling, and some more by sympathetically voicing her interest in what her patient was saying, her concern for her and, yes, her sympathy. In a crude shorthand that does not do justice to the delicacy of the process, I call such evidence of sympathy "dear-dearing". In these ways, the therapist was able to give this patient a good experience of being allowed to do what she needed to do in the presence of someone willing and able to let her do that. This is the interaction that Winnicott calls ego-relating (Winnicott, 1965, chapter 2, first published, 1958).

The therapist noticed that there was never any affect in her patient's voice, nor did she ever cry, although what she had to say was often harrowing. It is important for my argument that the therapist—and I—were harrowed. In the sixth week of therapy the patient was talking about her first husband, who used to come home drunk and who would take her by force if she did not agree to have sex with him. The therapist, harrowed, said, "It must be terrible to be made use of against your will". The patient was silent for about five seconds—a long time for her—and then said, "I suppose I have always made use of people"; she then paused for another instant and then began to give examples of her mother's reproaches to her about her making use of people.

I was pleased with the therapist for having said, "It must be terrible to be made use of against your will". I had been saying to her that there was a split in this woman's awareness: her awareness that she was feeling terrible was split off from her awareness of what was happening to her. If the therapist could find opportunities to notice what the patient must have been feeling during the events she was describing and could express her feelings at that instant, this could be the first step in reconnecting two aspects of the patient's life.

The holding function of understanding, acceptance and recognition

But let us look again at the exchange, "It must be terrible to be made use of against your will" . . . "I suppose I have always made use of people." Everything was new to this therapist. She had a bad shock when I pointed out that her patient had turned round the meaning she had intended, turning her expression of sympathy into a reproach (or, as I shall put it later, not accepting the metabolizing of her experience). By not understanding her, she had to some extent failed her patient in some other very simple forms of holding that we often do without even thinking about it, but worth focusing on for a moment before we put them back in the general context of what it is like to do therapy. Those simple forms of holding are: recognizing, understanding, accepting. It was incumbent on the therapist at that moment to recognize, understand and accept what the patient meant. What the patient needed was a therapist who could recognize that she thought badly of herself as an exploiter of other people. She needed a therapist who could let her know that she understood the patient's badness, thus allowing her to discover that she could accept being with someone who did things neither of them approved of. For instance, the therapist might have said things like, "You are telling me about what you did and I can see you are sorry about these things. It will be good for us to look at them together so that we can understand more about how it was for you at the time. I think I know you feel badly about it, because—without noticing—you turned something I said in sympathy into a reproach. You condemned yourself and took it for granted that I would too", etc. etc. When patients believe they are reprehensible, they need evidence of holding even more than at other times.

Such holding often leads very naturally into more complex processes like metabolizing and integrating, discussed below, where I shall be returning to this example. But it is worth lingering here in order to emphasize that just being recognized, just being understood, just being accepted, are in themselves therapeutic processes. They do not sound very spectacular. But, especially for people with splits, to have someone to relate to who can see not only the one side of the split that they are aware of, but other bits as well, is very comforting and very therapeutic. Acceptance, recognition, understanding are comforting and help to make connections across splits. Good counsellors have known this for decades, but I believe it to be still controversial in some more psychoanalytically oriented circles. I may be wrong, but I notice how little discussion there is of it that would validate it during students' training, in lectures, for instance, and in supervision. However, to show my lack of bias, I take my examples from analysts who understand very well about recognizing, understanding, and accepting, and who remark on it. My first example comes from a child analysis by Eleonora Fé d'Ostiani (1980, pp. 57–79).

Pietro's mother was a very anxious woman. When Pietro was three or four months old, she began to worry that he was not gaining weight properly and went to see a series of paediatricians to see if he was normal. She dared not share her worries with anyone, but she did not feel attracted to this sickly, thin, crying baby, her first. She felt she could not mother him properly, and when he was 4, she brought him to d'Ostiani, to whom he also appeared stunted: smaller than most children, very withdrawn, refusing almost all food. The mother had phantasies of getting rid of this ugly child, especially as she had since had healthier children. Once analysis began, Pietro began eating and gaining weight almost at once. Within 18 months he looked like the beautiful healthy 6-year-old he was, and was relating in a much less defended way. Then he stopped developing and stopped relating to the analyst, becoming more like an autistic child, disregarding people and relating to bits of paper, etc. This went on for months, and now it was the analyst who began to think perhaps he was handicapped, just as the mother had thought. Now it was d'Ostiani who took him on a round of specialists for tests, none of which was conclusive of anything. Now it was she who wondered if he would do better with someone else using a different technique.

> At this point it occurred to me that the behaviour pattern repeating itself between me and the child was identical to the one that had taken place with his mother when he was three or four months old. . . . Once again Pietro was having to accept that his anger at being unacceptable was not accepted by a maternal figure, but that it upset her and caused her to reject him and search for external solutions. I therefore prepared myself to accept Pietro as he was, with no attempt to interpret this refusal of his to "grow" . . . and with no further attempts to explain, understand, or overcome the "obstacles". My thinking to myself "I am taking you as you are, even if you don't grow, even maybe if you are retarded" provoked an almost incredible change in Pietro within one session. As though wanting to make up for lost time, he began a series of most beautiful and profound sessions, mainly about how terrible it had been

when he felt so isolated from maternal acceptance and loving support. He had been down a dark well. . . . [p. 61]

This example shows the importance of accepting, and of the acceptance being accepted by, the child-patient, who then began to be able to communicate again, having regained trust in being held and helped.

What happens when the therapist holds by accepting, recognizing, understanding? Two kinds of things. One is that the experience does get held in a pattern or context that enables the patient to stay with the experience instead of being so horrified by it that it stays unacceptable, i.e. split off. The other is that the patient has a chance of looking at what the therapist is holding, from various points of view, until it is integrated.

Enduring as a way of holding

In this connection, one might extol the therapeutic usefulness of enduring the behaviour of a patient who is being very annoying, very demanding and plaguing, or very attacking and irritating, without flinching, retreating, or retaliating. It is a useful quality for a psychotherapist working with very disturbed people. It is hard to do in a genuine way, to not even wish to retaliate or cut off, but fortunately it is not the wish but the behaviour that makes most of the therapeutic difference. Disturbed and disturbing patients are likely to be intuitively aware when the therapist feels like opting out or dotting them one, and they are likely to use this perception to engage in further persecutions. But that does a disservice to the poor therapist rather than to the patient. It does the patient good to know that, whatever the therapist very naturally feels like doing, the therapist will not actually do it. Good therapists contain their rage or repulsion, and to the extent that the patient can take that in, it is therapeutic. Slochower (1991) has some splendid examples of this, both as regards the therapist's endurance of the regressed patient's dependency-needs, and as regards the therapist's acceptance of the patient's despair, cynicism, and fear.

Sometimes the therapist can do more than simply endure. Sometimes the therapist actually understands what is going on for the patient in these phases of the relationship so well that acceptance and recognition are the context in which the event takes place. The patient will know this with great relief. Then, later, the two can talk about what has been going on, enabling the patient to feel not only accepted, but also recognized, understood, and perhaps even integrated within.

Integration as a form of holding: introducing ego and superego

Integrating, structurally speaking, is the making of connections between one experience and others. Structurally, integrating an experience is the opposite of isolating an experience or splitting it off. Splitting off and isolating an experience prevents it affecting anything else that has happened or may happen. (For more on structure see chapter seven, and also Klein, 1987, chapter 10.) It is taking an experience out of context or not putting it in context—keeping it apart. We isolate an experience when we do not allow it to be affected by what we already know or by what we learn later—as, for instance, in my not forgiving someone for coming half an hour late, even when I subsequently learn that they had been stuck in a lift at the time. Integration is an undoing of isolation. To integrate is to make connections between one event and others, and so allowing an experience to derive some of its meaning from the context in which it happens. In experiential terms, when we integrate an experience we accept that what happened really did happen. When it is something we feel badly about, we are often able to accept it and integrate it, if we are lucky enough to be in touch with other, related, things about which we do not feel so badly. Usually these are happier memories, or maybe loving arms, or something that the future promises. For some of us it helps when a line of poetry comes to mind which expresses beautifully our own ugly experience, or if we can rest our mind on a piece of music or a painting. Of course, there are less fortunate versions of integration, when events habitually integrate themselves into gloomy, painful, angry, or terrifying contexts. But we can at times manage not to be overwhelmed by a painful event if we are able to stay in touch with a happier context. It is this that gives us the necessary ego-strength to endure painful events without going to pieces. In other words, this is how we find the ego-strength to tolerate uncertainty, ambiguity, and frustration (see Kernberg, 1984, passim), and to resist impulses to actions that are not in our best long-term interest. So both ego and superego can play holding functions.

This ability to hold the pleasant and the unpleasant in one pattern both requires ego-strength and encourages its further development. Before the child can manage it for itself, it is a parental function. It is what good-enough adults do when responding to a child's distress—its rage and terror, for instance when it falls and bangs its head. We sympathize and kiss it better and surround it for a few moments with love and praise and comfort to enable it to accept the event.

It is also what therapists do: receiving a patient's distress, terror and rage, or pleasure, and eventually relating it to other events in the patient's experience (or in the shared experience of patient and therapist together). Here "integrating" shades over into metabolizing.

Some cautionary considerations

I believe that isolating an experience (splitting) is too easily assumed to be always an undesirable thing to do. The disadvantages of splitting can be great: splitting interferes gravely with the growth-processes of understanding meaning, reflection, and control. Yet isolating an experience, not integrating it, sometimes makes pain bearable and sometimes keeps terror or guilt or shame within bounds. It may be an appropriate defence while the personality is so weak and fragile that pain would cause too much disorganization.

On the other hand, there can be holding that is bad for a person. Mostly this chapter is about insufficient holding. But there can be too much holding—holding that is too constricting, and basically a misuse of power—both in child development and in psychotherapy. Take, for instance, the kinds of parents and the kinds of psychotherapists who become anxious when the child or the patient goes off in an unanticipated direction and who bring them back to what they had in mind for them. "Don't explore, go where I say", or, "Don't be anxious, don't be unsure or uncertain", leading the child to hide and disown those emotions, like the therapists who say "You must be feeling angry", or whatever they "must" be feeling. All who insist, "Feel as I say, see it my way", are engaged in malign forms of holding.

Metabolizing as a holding process

In the process of integration, experiences become changed, metabolized. The nature of the experience is changed by virtue of the context in which it is placed. An event can first be experienced in one context, and get its meaning from that context, and then, in the course of reflection or conversation, it can be placed in another context and have its meaning changed. The context affects the meaning of the experience. The student-therapist in our example could have indicated to her patient that she was understood and accepted with her bad things. If she could have heard what her patient actually said, I am sure that she would have accepted her, and then she could have indicated that she could see more than her badness, that her badness could be put in a context which gave it meaning and logic. She could have put it in a light where something other than the badness could be perceived, and this would make manifest a hope that, though the bad thing was done and remains a bad thing, it has not made her a bad person through and through for ever, because she and the therapist can see how she came to do it, and that thus she can become more free either to do it again next time, or not, as she chooses. As an example of the extent to which meaning can be made to depend on context, consider this drawing (Klein, 1987, p. 402):

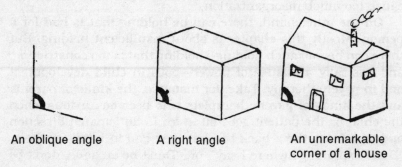

An oblique angle   A right angle   An unremarkable corner of a house

Taking another metaphor for the same process, I once amused my small nephew, while putting down a saucer for the cat, by saying that a cat was an apparatus for turning fish into puss. Metabolizing means digesting. And what does "to digest" mean? It means to break something down into its elements, which the body can then use in new combinations to build itself up with. Catabolizing (breaking down) followed by anabolizing (building up) is metabolizing. Metabolizing is assimilating. It is taking something that had been alien and not-self and making it available for use by making it part of oneself. I think this is very like what Bollas (1987) had in mind when he discussed the transformational process.

Then, in the slow process of psychotherapy, we enable people eventually to hold the experiences they have taken in, and to metabolize them better than they did before, so that they can contain and integrate and give more appropriate meanings to what happened to them, and use their experiences in new ways.

What I call "metabolizing" may, I think, be very like some of the processes that have come to be called "containing" by those who draw their inspiration from the writings of W. R. Bion, but I prefer my own terminology.

Kinds of terminology for kinds of containing

Different writers have different terminology and imagery for the containing function. Sometimes the containing is called *limit setting*, and then it has some quite fierce and sometimes self-righteous overtones. The speaker has children in mind or generally awkward people who are wanting something that, in the speaker's view, it is inappropriate for them to have. The speaker sets the limit, or provides the containment, by refusing to give in, and may accompany the refusal by explanations, rationalizations, or interpretations.

Others seem to think of a container as *a skin* or *a bag*, holding together things that belong together inside there, providing identity and unity and continuity for the things inside, which might otherwise be an unintegrated collection. To yet others, a container seems to be more like *a stomach*, transforming by digestion the things that are in there—the fish-into-cat metaphor comes to mind. Bion, for example, seems to think mainly in terms of undigested unmanageable bits of experience generated by an infant that cannot manage any of its experiences until they have somehow moved out of the baby into the mother, who does something to what has been moved into her and then moves it back into the baby, who can now manage the experience because of what the mother has done. The mother, in Bion's model, is a very active container of a very stomachy kind (as is the analyst in that model). And the bits of experience moved into her seem to be minute events, particles of experience. Bollas has a variant on this that I find easier to work with, less inert than a skin bag, but less overpoweringly metabolizing than a stomach, altogether a more mutually cooperative model. Bollas' baby is expected by and large to develop and integrate its own meaning at its own pace, but it cannot of course do so by itself—for instance, it cannot arrange to procure food for itself, or change its own nappies. There are many things a baby needs an understanding and active mother for, and an intricate process of communication goes on which enables the mother to understand the nature of the infant's needs at a time when the baby can neither conceptualize nor voice these needs. R. N. Emde, Daniel Stern, and Colwyn Trevarthen, among an increasing number of psychologists observing infant development, would recognize this baby, which would seem an ordinary though fortunate baby to them. This is a baby that gives cues to a sensitive, willing, and experienced mother, who then responds appropriately. Note also that we are not talking about particles of events here, but about meaningful sequences of action on the baby's part, which produce meaningful sequences of action on the mother's part (or the analyst's). When this baby gets upset and panicky, this mother recognizes, understands, and accepts what is happening and takes the necessary steps to deal with whatever caused the distress in the first place. In these ways she physically and emotionally holds and comforts the baby. And the baby, the original cause of its distress alleviated and almost back in the intimate contact with the mother that it had in its unborn days, feels safe and ceases to be upset. The mother in this story is active, but note that it is not she who metabolizes the baby's feelings: she provides a context that enables the baby to re-integrate its feelings in a way that makes the baby feel alright.

Impulse barrier, skin bag, preponderant or cooperative stomach, and *mirror*. There is also a characteristically Winnicott kind of containing, which he called mirroring: the baby sees itself in its mother's face and in the mother's re-actions, and gets a sense of its own identity and personality because to the mother the baby already has such an identity and personality. Here we see, not bits of a baby, but a whole little person contained and transformed by virtue of feeling contained in a loving frame. So may a therapist see a patient as the patient may become.

No doubt we can find parallels in the consulting-room for each of these kinds of containment, and for others, too. There is a more elaborate discussion of these issues in the final section of *Our Need for Others* (Klein, 1987).

Searles' version— therapeutic symbiosis in potential space

My own understanding of these processes is probably very near to what Searles calls "therapeutic symbiosis" (Searles, 1979, passim)—not a felicitous term, since he does not mean sym-biosis as this is conventionally understood: it describes a particular phase of his work with very confused people diag-nosed as schizophrenic. He finds that he does not always experience clear firm ego-boundaries between himself and these patients (e.g. p. 32). He does not precisely think of the patient as intentionally if unconsciously communicating with him when the ego-boundaries blur, as is currently imagined by many Kleinians and some others. Rather, he has in mind a process by which he, the therapist, allows himself to be open to non-verbal cues provided by the patient's body-language and by what he gets intuitively from reading between the lines, letting his unconscious inferences, based on his own life-expe-riences, come into consciousness (chapter 22). To the extent that therapists block these inferences, they cannot operate at this level. To the extent that we are afraid of our own violence or hate or other feeling, we cannot pick up accurately or confidently what other people are feeling, and we cannot help them. For this kind of therapy, therapists have to hold on to their awareness of their own love or fear or boredom, and to be accepting of the knowledge that this is the sort of person they are.

Eventually, after a good deal of work, the patient can see that Searles accepts and acknowledges his own inner world even at these alarming levels, and that he is living with it in a relatively anxiety-free way—in short, that Searles can contain what he is within himself. *This is what the patient internalizes* (p. 532): Searles' ability to live with his badness and contain it. This process seems to be Searles' version of metabolizing.

In the interval from first acquaintance with the patient to this crucial internalization, there is a phase where the feelings and the inner object relations and what Searles calls the figures from the past which the patient has in the foreground of his psyche and those which the therapist has in his, so overlap and resemble each other, that each understands the other at a deeply intuitive, not necessarily spoken level. These feelings, figures, relationships, symptoms, etc. may be thought of as in a space shared by therapist and patient. Searles explicitly names this space a "transitional space", and the phenomena in it are "transitional phenomena"—a valuable connection with Winnicott's way of looking at things.

By the way, Searles contrasts his own experience also with that of Rosenfeld (Searles, 1979, quoting Rosenfeld, 1952). Rosenfeld seems to Searles to be aware of some such process as Searles is describing, but to be experiencing his patients much more as imposing their symptoms on the analyst. It seems to Searles that Rosenfeld, in reaction to his patients, strives to keep his cool and be less involved—disowning the feelings in himself as it were—whereas Searles believes that the analyst's owning of them, and living comfortably with them, is an essential part of the patient's cure.

I find this difference interesting. Searles' language is quite clear. The analyst has feelings, symptoms, figures from the past, etc. So has the patient. The feelings, figures etc. are alike, but each clearly has his own. Searles' language does not suggest that the patient "puts his feelings into" the analyst and gets rid of them that way. And, indeed, we know that one cannot get rid of these things that way—the transmission is not a material one but via intuitive understanding.

In Searles' way of writing there is not that slight blaming note that seems to me to creep so easily into the language of those who use the putting-feelings-into-the-other metaphor. And this is largely because Searles understands the communication process differently. But it is also partly because, as Searles sees it, the therapist's reception of the patient's communication is more voluntary and hence less resented. The therapist has not had to repudiate his own inner world, but holds it and is on terms with it. Blame very naturally creeps in when we do not welcome what hits us at a deep level.

Holding by ego-functioning

As we consider these more and more complex and demanding forms of holding, identity becomes more important, and all the processes by which the personality is able to hold itself together to stay integrated and unique. Some of these processes, in my view, are functions of the ego.

When using the term ego-functioning, my emphasis is not on what the ego is. The emphasis is on certain processes such as putting into words, combining concepts or ideas, remembering, reflecting upon, making connections between, making sense of, understanding the meaning of, etc. It sounds intellectual because that is what much of ego-functioning largely is: many ego-functions are cognitive functions such as planning, remembering, drawing conclusions, making comparisons, allotting priorities, making sense of, understanding the implications of, patterning, and so on. This is the case largely, but not entirely—a tradition from Winnicott through Bion to Donald Meltzer warns us that the disciplined rationality that these processes suggest and indeed require, must not be isolated, but must be integrated and suffused with all the rest of us, even with our most unconscious and incorrigible dream-life, if they are to be appropriate and original, not stereotyped.

How does this ego-functioning kind of holding work? Let us consider the "making-sense-of" ego-function, drawing on an example from Bion (1970, chapter 10). Here Bion describes his sense of what the container does with the contained.

> . . . a man wishing to communicate his annoyance is so overwhelmed by emotion that he stammers and becomes incoherent. . . . The *forms* of speech that the man uses to convey his meaning, these I regard as being *intended to contain* what he has to say. . . . The annoyance he strives to communicate I regard as being *what should be contained* in his speech.

While the man is stammering and raging, he can do nothing with the feeling—it just rampages around in an unintegrated way. When he finds words to fit and express what goes on with him, he will find meaning in the experience. *The words are the form* with which he can now hold on to that meaning.

Words help us to be conscious. Words enable us to make patterns and to hold on to patterns. It is the patterns that give events their meaning and significance. They provide the context in which experiences get their meaning. It is their metabolizing function to do so. Patterns, we have already seen, can change an obtuse angle into a right angle, and a right angle into a corner of a house. Patterns of words interpret experiences and give them further meaning. Patterns of words enable us to reflect, to communicate and elaborate meaning.

If the patient finds the right words first, in which to give meaning to something that has happened, we say the patient has shown insight. If the therapist finds the right words first, that is an interpretation. It is the ego-functioning of patient and therapist together that allows interpretation to have a holding function.

Thus Rosenfeld, one of the most sensitive and helpful exponents of work with psychotic processes, wrote of a very disturbed patient:

> This patient needed a very special holding environment which could be created only by an analyst who could hold the material of the patient very clearly and logically in his or her mind. The analyst would also need to give it back to the patient in such a way that she could follow the logic of her own way of thinking and feeling, and also understand

the anxiety preventing her from holding on to the logical
state of mind. [Rosenfeld, 1987, pp. 58–59]

Therapies that rely less on ego-functioning

At this point we may glance aside from our focus on psychoanalytically oriented psychotherapy to the more expressive
therapies: Psycho-drama, Psycho-synthesis, Gestalt, Bio-
energetics, Co-counselling, and so on. I admire and envy these
for the varied array of delightful techniques they can employ
to bring feelings and phantasies to overt expression. Some
patients go through phases in their therapy during which I
wish I could sub-lease them to therapists of a different persuasion. With the expression of previously unconscious
feelings that some of these techniques facilitate so well and
directly, old memories and phantasies may be brought to the
surface, and a good deal of inhibition and splitting can easily
be mended—a good deal of integration takes place effortlessly
in the process.

On the other hand, these are less interpretive therapies,
less affected by a theoretical framework. Because of this, where
there is strong resistance against integration, in general or
along the particular boundaries, the affects or the phantasies
remain isolated, and then there is no integration. I have on
occasion been fascinated by the difficulties I have had in encouraging people who had come to me after making a good deal
of progress in the course of other therapies, to work through
what they had got. Some of them had no previous experience of
holding on to the feeling or phantasy they had just expressed,
and hence no experience of the benefits of working through and
consciously integrating, getting a fuller meaning of, what had
just become conscious. It is especially difficult where patients
have accustomed themselves to acting out something very like
an evacuatory phantasy. Just as some people believe that
faeces will poison them if they do not have a substantial daily
bowel movement, so there are those who believe that their
feelings will poison them if they are not promptly and feelingly
expressed. Then they are reluctant to stop and reflect—to

employ ego-functioning and understanding. They consider holding on to their feelings the equivalent of constipation. Also, sometimes, the expression of an emotion, or of a phantasy emotionally expressed, is so gratifying that there is consider- able resistance to reducing it to understanding, sorting out motives and misunderstandings, and recognizing what it has all been about and how it relates to their past and their present relationships. I am then left with having either to analyse the negative reaction brought about by my efforts to make them look at and understand something (and thereby losing the thing I was trying to get them to look at), or trying to hold on to the thing at issue while ignoring the negativity I am generating.

The two aspects of integration

Kohut sees integration as a two-part process (1977, p. 88). The first part is about acceptance and recognition; the second part is about ego-functioning, about explaining, about fitting the experience into a context that makes sense of it. "The analy- sand must realize that he has been understood. Only when this is secure can the ego-functions be properly engaged and an interpretation made which explains where the piece of behav- iour fits the patient's life." The explaining has to be done in order to facilitate integration, to help undo the damaging isola- tion in which the previously encapsulated bit of experience had been held. The experience which therapist and patient are now talking about might slip back into isolation again, unless they engage the ego-functions, for instance by putting it all in differ- ent words in different ways. This enables them to firm up its integration into a living here-and-now experience, referred to again and again in the process of working though.

Kohut sees integration taking place in two modes—inter- personally and intra-psychically. Interpersonally, people's isolation from other people is undone, because they feel recog- nized, accepted, and understood by another person: the thera- pist. And, intra-psychically, there can be an integration within each person of experiences that might be in danger of being left isolated from people's general experience of themselves. People are helped to understand more of their own nature and their own life; life and their own nature gain more sense and meaning.

Kohut puts the two aspects of integration into a right perspective. The kind of personal integration that relies on ego-functioning is pretty important, but not uniquely so. The kind of integration that relies on interpersonal relationship-processes like acceptance, recognition, etc. is equally important. (See also Blatt and Behrends, 1987, and all together in the same issue of the *International Journal of Psycho-Analysis* on psychic change: Blum, Cooper, Pine, Pulver, etc.) So the therapist or analyst, in Kohut's view, does two sorts of holding, one intellectual, one interpersonal. Eventually our patients will be holding themselves: a therapist will not need to do that sort of thing for them any more. And then the patients will be doing two sorts of holding, some via their intellect—their ego-functioning—and some via their friends.

Holding on to a person, holding on to meaning

It is useful to remember that the experience of being held is equivalent, for our purpose, to the experience of holding on to something—this something may be a person, as it undoubtedly was in our infancy, or it may be a meaningful concept. There is a nice story Patrick Casement tells from his social-work days, when he was training to be an analyst. He had undertaken to help a little girl (aged between 6 and 10) with her lessons. She was difficult. Her mother could not relate to her, could not hold her emotionally, and therefore had to try and contain her by bribing her into good behaviour. The child was impulse-ridden, and when thwarted would kick and scream and throw herself about. One day, when she had become too beside herself for anything of Casement's to reach her, he wrapped his arms around her. She screamed "Let go. Let go." Casement said "I will as soon as you are ready to hold yourself". And, a little later, "I think you are ready now to hold yourself, and for us to do some constructive work". And it was so (Casement, 1990).

Casement had to hold the little girl physically. In something like the same way, the therapist's holding is needed in the case of some people who come to us for therapy, so that the patients can relax their hold: their grip has been too desperate and too limited, or it has been a grip on second-best objects. When they can relax, secure in the knowledge that they won't fall apart because someone is holding them, they have a chance to re-organize. Integration is, after all, about how you hold together or how you are held together.

Joan Symington (1985) gives two examples, of which one is given below and one in a later chapter, which show the child/patient's need to hold on to something in order to survive and not dis-integrate, and the parent/therapist's holding of the baby-patient. In both examples, the analyst's interpretation is at first not taken in (i.e. not integrated), because it is not complete enough to allow the patient to feel understood, accepted, and held. In each case, when the analyst later shows that she understands the patient more, the patient does feel properly held, and relaxes.

In the first example, a patient at a Monday session had said that he felt utterly miserable at the weekend, in despair of even getting through life. In this state he had opened a book by Freud, and had started to get things into perspective again, and felt less despairing. This was interpreted as a turning away from the analyst: "I don't need you, I've got something better, Freud himself, at home." This interpretation may well have been true, but it did not take into account the patient's desperate need to do something for himself, *in order to hold himself together*. Thus the interpretation resulted in silent hurt and increased defensiveness. When the destructiveness and the feeling that he had to hold himself together were both interpreted, the patient felt contained and understood.

Without interpretations that strengthen the ego-functioning of patients so that they can eventually *hold themselves together*, one is in danger of the sort of interminable analyses that counsellors can get into whose only skill is holding. On the other hand, we psychoanalytically orientated therapists need to be careful of the timing and the dosage of our interpretations. There can be interventions, aimed at ego-functioning, which are premature or incomplete. These cannot hold the patient securely, and we thereby create the effect we see in people insecurely held by parents in their early years: we create a false and premature ego in our patients, who may well report feeling better, and who may talk psychoanalytic sense, but somewhere one feels a lack of depth and truth in them—their deepest feelings have not been recognized at the holding level.

The sense of self as a holding function

In order to complete our discussion of holding we need one more concept—that of the self. There is a moving and interesting passage in Kernberg's *Borderline Conditions and Pathological Narcissism* (1975, p. 213), in the chapter called "The subjective experience of emptiness". Kernberg there reminds us that when there is an absence of normal connections between the self and the other internal objects—that is, when these are isolated from one another and unaffected by living experience—"pathological subjective experiences of a painful and disturbing nature develop. Predominant among these experiences are a sense of emptiness and futility, chronic restlessness and boredom, and a loss of the normal capacity for experiencing and overcoming loneliness." For, he says, "the normal integrated self and its related integrated conceptions of others guarantee a sense of belonging to a network of human relationships that makes life meaningful", and this guarantees "self-feeling".

The self is built up from a slow process during which experiences are integrated and metabolized, and successively, with further experiences, re-integrated, re-metabolized. At each moment in time, the current self performs a contextual and holding function for the next inflow of experiences. So we cannot do without some such concept as the self. Different people call it "ego", "sense of identity", "self image", etc. It is not my purpose here to differentiate between such words. I have in mind that sense of oneself, based very much on remembered experiences, albeit often unconscious, which has become part self-image, part ego-ideal, part consciousness of one's own ego-functioning and other processes, without which one would feel lost and unintegrated.

How is it acquired? Kohut is relevant here, Winnicott, many writers, myself included (Klein, 1987, pp. 406 ff).

The mother has a phantasy of her baby. She has a phantasy of the baby as a person who can experience and reflect and intend its responses just like anyone else, sometimes like herself or her friend, or her husband, sometimes like her sister, sometimes like her father or mother. What the mother's phantasy is about does not matter just now. What does matter is that a whole person is being imagined. The baby is *potentially* a whole person, with conscious purposes, directions, and intentions, but at this stage it is not functioning as a whole person except in the eyes of some of its grown-ups. Its behaviour is related to by, say, the mother as if it were a whole person's, and in this way the baby is contained by the mother's imagination.

Parallel to this, in therapy we see and relate to patients not only as patients think of themselves, but also as possessing split-off and repressed bits known to us but not to them. Here and there we see more of the patient than the patient does. And this has therapeutic effects.

The first holding that babies know about is an embrace that is physical. By this means, through its skin, the baby learns the outlines of its more or less loveable body-self. For the lucky ones, this physical experience of itself develops almost imperceptibly into a sense of itself as being understandable and understood, respected and validated in the process of being taken care of—a more psychological sort of embrace. Physical embrace turns into psychological holding embrace, into psychological recognition. At first, someone else has to tell the baby of its existence. "Now there's a baby", the curates used to be taught to say. At first, someone else has to hold the baby, and the baby's image of itself, just as at first the therapist, holding patients who have relaxed their defences, may have in mind an image of the whole person-to-be, holding and mirroring, not what the patients are, but what they may become. Gradually, babies and patients are able to do their share in holding and taking care of themselves. Fortunate people can embrace themselves and recognize themselves without hassle and with respect: they have little trouble in knowing themselves, understanding themselves, recognizing themselves, accepting and loving themselves, having hopes for the future.

But still, someone else had to do it for them first—parents, friends, psychotherapists.

The same gradual progression holds for the development of adult ego-functioning: attaining concepts, fitting concepts to words and words to concepts, making connections, understanding meaning, seeing implications from the past, reflecting upon events, making plans, and so on. First the psychotherapist does it; then the patient begins to do it. It is what we do in psychotherapy, and it is what we do in life.

CHAPTER FIVE

Patients who are not ready for interpretations

"P atients who are not ready for interpretations . . ."—a friend criticized this title on the ground that it implies some unreadiness *on the part of the patient* not to be ready for something. As though patients ought to be available for interpretations, as though interpretation is what psychotherapy is about. This is not what I believe. Psychotherapy is therapy: it is about enabling people to explore their processes, conscious and unconscious, so that they can understand better what they are doing in their lives and gain some control over the alternatives that are in principle available to them. We know that it can be helpful, in pursuit of this goal, to interpret to people the unconscious meaning of what they are doing or feeling or thinking. But we also know of people we are not able to help by this means, and therefore a more accurate if clumsier title would have been "Patients for whom interpretations are inappropriate". Or, even more accurately, "Patients for

A version of the Annual Public Lecture given for the London Centre of Psychotherapy in June, 1990.

whom interpretation of unconscious material is inappropriate".
What I find inappropriate with particular people is for me to
bring in aspects of their experience of which they are unconscious, which are ego-alien to them and sound strange to them.

I shall give two long examples of my experiences with people
for whom interpretations were inappropriate. My first example
is of someone who could not tolerate what she experienced as
my intrusiveness. My second example, at the end of this chapter, is of someone who had no objection to interpretations, but
also did not benefit from hearing them.

I saw "Rose" for more than ten years, from her early twenties onwards. She came twice a week for personal therapy,
and once a week to a group I run. She was dreadfully
depressed, anxious, and generally unalive, living most of
the time in what she described as a grey fog. In the first
couple of years I interpreted in the normal way what I
thought was happening to her or between us. She seemed
to listen to what I said, often agreeing, and we got nowhere
much, except that she did keep coming. I cannot take much
credit even for her continuing to come, for early in her third
year she was able to tell me that she had not really come
for therapy exactly: she had been sent by an unfortunate
alliance of her boyfriend and her mother, who had said that
she needed it because of her sexual unresponsiveness. I
then got a glimpse of how much had been invasive in her
life. I also saw the validity in my feeling that I was being
kept at bay, but discussing this led nowhere. She mainly
talked about current problems and distresses, and I
mainly listened, sympathized, occasionally putting forward
alternative possibilities. It was to be years before her resentment at what she felt to be my advice surfaced in the
sessions. However, she put up with it and kept coming.

Late in her third year she was able to confide an even
more difficult thing. In her eyes I at times turned into a
witch, as, in a horror film, a character's face would suddenly reveal itself as evil, she later said. So all this time she
had been coping with the fact that she was in therapy with
an unaccountable woman (closely modelled on her early
experiences with her mother) who at unpredictable times

turned into something vile. At other times she felt some hope that I meant well, and that if she did conscientiously what I told her to do, then I would make her well, in a magical way, rewarding her for being good. I was more or less ignorant of this too but was fond of her, listened to what she was telling me, interpreted when I could, and gave what support I could by being in fact a steady predictable presence who at times accurately reflected back what she had just said to me, thus making her feel that her judgement was valid. I put up with her rages when she began to show them in her fourth and fifth years, and I put up with her absences, which were much more frequent, when she felt unable to show her anger.

She and I were also helped by her being in my therapy group. Rose felt safer from me in a group. While she had few memories of good adults in childhood, and no brothers or sisters, she had had friends at school. In some ways it helped her that the group members were not frightened of me as she was at that time—they did not see a witch when they looked at me. In other ways she saw them as more frightened than she was—she felt that, unlike them, she, at least, could see through me and stand up to me for them all. In the group she could at times be very angry with me, or defiant, and still feel safe. The group was useful because it enabled her to split the transference at need. I do not think she could have managed if she had been made to contain the split within the one relationship, the one with me. Her mother had in terrifying ways threatened to take her over completely. She could not cope with me on her own, and it helped her to feel she had the group at her back when facing me. So a lot of negative feelings about me could find consciousness and expression in a relatively safe setting. She was at times very unkind to me in the group, coldly contemptuous or mocking, often in little asides, especially when I made a mistake. At other times the split went the other way and she felt protected by me from the group, for instance when returning to the group after an angry absence. (For more about this group, see the appendix to this chapter.)

Meanwhile, say in the fifth, sixth, and seventh years, in the individual sessions, though from time to time the witch still appeared, she began to talk to me rather more freely and in greater depth, and also to take more in from me. Of course, I had learnt meanwhile what would upset her to no good purpose. I continued to make occasional interpretations, and she was now able to show her annoyance whenever I did so, repudiating what I had said, often with a malicious cold anger that made me see her mother in her. Transference interpretations, being more intimate, made her most angry. However, she increasingly worked things out for herself, and with increasing success and security. Terrified by things she suspected in herself, she nevertheless allowed herself, inch by inch, some looks at her inner processes. Some people can get splinters out of their fingers themselves when they could not bear another person to do it for them. My function was partly to be an Aunt Sally, partly to recognize and contain, and partly to float ideas for her to take or reject.

In the next two years she became much more often able to take in interpretations, though she did not like them. Mainly we concentrated on two things. One was her unconscious sabotage of what would make for her happiness "out there" in her current life—this knowledge she quickly made entirely her own, voluntarily indicating when she realized she had been sabotaging her happiness or success. The other was her unconscious sabotage of the therapy: she was often late, often had to cancel, usually with what appeared to be valid reasons, but the frequency with which this happened in the end enabled her to have a real blinding insight into her unconscious resistance. During this time there developed an earnest endeavour to grasp and hold on to the interpretations I made, and not run away or fly into a defensive rage. She would see that what I said was true (if it was true), but still she could not help feeling persecuted by my saying it, as she used to feel persecuted by her parents' hostile remarks. Also I think she struggled with an unconscious sense that I should have arranged the world so that she would not have to suffer this.

I am sure I made mistakes in my work with Rose. I daresay someone else might have helped her more, and faster—but not, I believe, through the use of more accurate interpretation.

A re-examination of the status of classical interpretation is of professional, scientific, and social interest. It is of *professional* interest because we lose patients who should not be lost. I know this is partly a matter of experience and skill—it can be assumed that the more practised psychotherapists lose fewer patients than do beginners. But we have to remember other factors: the more established practitioners are freer to take only "interesting" or "promising" cases, and of course they take psychotherapy trainees, who are highly motivated to stay. It is a matter of *scientific* interest because to the extent that we take "analysable" patients only—i.e. ones who can take interpretation on board from the start—we lose the opportunity to learn how to help the others. It is, after all, standard practice to do a trial interpretation in the diagnostic interview, which allows prospective patients' responses to be used to determine whether or not they should undertake psychotherapy. There is, thirdly, the *social* aspect: there are simply too many disturbed people whom we are not even trying to understand how to help. Some of these are helped by alternative methods, but there are methods and insights that psychoanalytically based practitioners have, which could be useful, if we could make up our minds to learn how to use them.

The concept "analysable" was created to sum up the sort of people we can confidently hope not to lose if we work with them in strictly traditional ways (N. Coltart, 1988). It excludes most of the people I see.

An interesting paper, called "The Lost Ones", appeared in the 1988 summer issue of the *British Journal of Psychotherapy*, based on the remembered experiences of three of the authors—Ingrid Coltart, Coline Covington, and Arthur Sherman—at the time of their training with the Society for Analytical Psychology. They had formed a group for mutual support while they gathered more experience; for the time being, income was not a priority, usually a very relevant consideration. What occurred was the experience of most trainees and newly qualified analysts. They were referred "the most technically difficult and unpromising candidates". Don't we know about this! Most of us lost them in the first year, and mostly we blamed ourselves while saying aloud that the patients were unanalysable, could not take our interpretation, and so on. Our traditions give us permission to attribute to our patients the unfortunate fact that they are not amenable to the techniques we have learned to use. Most of us, as our practice increases, cease to take them on, and so we lose a source of knowledge; indeed, a valuable field of research is lost to us in this way. Moreover, as we get more experience, especially if we also get more eminent, we get more psychotherapy students as patients, and these tend to behave as they are supposed to, not like "the lost ones".

> . . . in spite of having seen many psychotherapists, these patients often did not have much idea of what would be most productive to bring to treatment, so that a process of educating them to be patients had to come first. . . . It took time, causing a large amount of frustration and resentment which on occasion led to the treatment ending. [Coltart et al., 1988, p. 381]

"Also, these patients were marked by extreme psychic and physical pain. Indeed some had no history except of pain." Some people are so dominated by their pain that they cannot concentrate on much else, not even on explanations of how psychotherapy is meant to work, and certainly not on discovering appropriate techniques without help from us. They need to complain to us until they are sure that we mind about their pain, before we can educate them into taking an interest in its unconscious meaning. People in pain cannot concentrate.

This is aggravated by a third factor: "The patients understood their heroic search for a therapist not as a search for themselves, as we thought. For them it was a search for someone who could remove their pain for them, making it vanish in a magical omnipotent fashion." *We* know that a long process is needed in which only what the authors call "normal channels of consciousness" can be used, in which an ego may slowly be strengthened and integrated, and finally a self found which can cope with what was unbearable and hence unconscious. But *they* don't. "Labouring under the expectations of a magical cure, the analyst was a sad disillusionment."

Fourthly, and particularly hard to bear for students in training and newly qualified people, all the patients had marked feelings of hopelessness, which were easily passed on to the analyst.

Ample case-illustrations were given by the authors. I, too, have seen many patients over the years, for whom interpretations were inappropriate. The variety of them is bewildering. There was the young woman who only came because the psychiatrist at the university where she had been, and whom she had a lot of love for, made her promise to find a therapist when she left. She fulfilled her promise by finding me, but she would not talk to me after this explanation. Nevertheless, we got on quite constructively, with me doing the talking and she doing the contradicting if I got it wrong. In her case, reconstruction freed her to lead a more normal life.

There was the text-book schizophrenic whom I saw for over four years, who for the first year addressed me once a week on the subject of women's liberation, but did gradually become more aware of me as a person in the world of shared reality, whom I (and his very supportive family) certainly kept out of hospital, and who got tremendously more in touch with himself and others during our time. ("Anders", in chapter seven). He left me, alas, because I failed to manage, in a sufficiently bearable way, the transition from what I was doing (mainly paying attention to him) to the more orthodox techniques. I have found it very hard to do these transitions well.

A different category of people for whom interpretation is not appropriate, at least not to begin with, is not necessarily as disturbed as that. They just do not come from circles where psychotherapy is known about or psychological matters talked about. They come to the initial interview because some present distress has led them to consider psychotherapy as a solution to the pain of bereavement, problems with delinquent offspring, or whatever. Some do have an interest in interpretation from the beginning—they have some sense that their trouble can be alleviated when they understand themselves better. Others do not really believe this: they think a therapist will help them in a direct way to a solution involving the disappearance of the problem. Often these are as able to be helped as the others. But if you try an interpretation on them in the assessment interview, they will assent, without interest, out of courtesy: they do not see that it has anything to do with anything. They need time. If they go to a therapist who concentrates on interpretations from the beginning, there is a chance that they will catch on: "Yes, this is how I will learn to understand myself and the situations I can't handle." But it is also possible that they are simply caught in a net, thinking they have to believe what the therapist says in order to get better. Rose tried to be like that, but fortunately she could not make herself believe in me. Fortunately, because the risk is that such patients will try to ape the personality they think the therapist requires of them. Other people just get unhappy and leave. Between a third and half of our referrals do fall by the wayside in the first few months. What, for instance, will happen to Mrs Z? I quote from my own assessment report.

Assessment interview with Mrs Z aged 38

Dress and demeanour of a depressed, angry, downtrodden middle-aged woman. "Caricature of a bad teacher" was my first reaction, later confirmed. One of those for whom everything is either her fault or else not her fault. Already over the phone we had difficulty fixing a date because neither daytime nor evening, neither weekdays nor weekends, suited her for an appointment.

In Hinshelwood's terms, a neglected frightened child coping with her pain by disregarding herself ("putting herself last") and coping with the subsequent anger by destructively fussing others in a "caring" way. [Hinshelwood had given a lecture on diagnostic interviews, saying, look for the core of pain or conflict.]

A picture of an unlovable-feeling, angrily dependent woman emerged from her personal history (which is not given here).

She started the interview with not knowing where to sit (hardly possible to have doubts about this in my small room) and then steering, in spite of my indications to the contrary, for the one chair where I would obviously sit. Then she challenged me: "What kind of therapy do you do at the Centre?" I told her a bit, and then asked if that helped. "Not very much", she said, unaware of her hostile tone.

I let her talk on. She relaxed, began to trust me, and it began to feel like one gawky 16-year-old talking to another. It was visibly doing her good to be talking on this unburdening almost counselling level, and I think she will need a lot of it. Three times I tried the same interpretation: "You're telling me about your father (or mother, or daughter—never husband, incidentally) and I cannot tell how it was for you when that happened. Do you notice how you are blotting yourself out of the picture you are painting for me?" Twice she went straight on. The third time I said it very firmly indeed. She said: "Well, I'm coming to that", in a slightly aggrieved tone.

This woman needs to talk and talk before she can listen, let alone cooperate in understanding her motivation. However, she can listen, and she is intelligent and educated and, though deeply hurt, not deeply disturbed—neurotic, not crazy.

Psychodynamic formulation: "Of course you are right not to love me but you really should do this or that for me." A Fairbairn type: Anti-Libidinal Ego siding with the Rejecting Object, but the Libidinal Ego glued to the Frustrating Exciting Object.

This woman would be highly motivated to stay in therapy if the initial anger at having to be in therapy at all (which she sees as other people's fault) is tactfully dealt with. She would make a good training patient for a student inclined to listen a lot and go easy on interpretations for the first six months. It would need to be someone who can work with a patient who is not going to lie down for a good while (fear of being abandoned).

She should be seen not less than twice a week.

Where interpretations are not taken up creatively in the assessment interview, we need to look for a therapist who can value and maintain the holding function, for this may be a patient who requires a good deal of latitude in finding his or her way, with only an occasional attempt to judge the patient's readiness to respond to an interpretation. We lose so many who get as far as the initial interview. . . .

* * *

Our imagination has now been directed towards the kind of people I wish to be talking about, whom we have all met, I dare say, in our own practice. They are very varied—the only element so far noticed as common is that they could not do with interpretation and would have left therapy if it had been insisted upon. But leaving therapy prematurely is hardly a diagnostic category. What concepts can we apply to make theoretical as well as imaginative sense of the facts? The only other common element I found was that conditions were not propitious for establishing a therapeutic alliance. I think that the reasons for this relate to three or four other factors that between them seem to me to account pretty well for the whole range of people for whom interpretation is inappropriate:

1. *No understanding of what therapists and patients do together.* This is a simple factor, but not a negligible one. It has to do with not being psychological-minded, in the sense of never having had enough contact with things psychoanalytical to know what to do. Maybe there is also a naive resistance to such contact. Stuart Sutherland (1987), the professor of psychology who had a breakdown, wrote a comical but determinedly charitable account of how contact with psychoanalysts feels if you are not accustomed to it. People don't all know our funny ways. If tactlessly handled, they leave after a few sessions saying "She's crazier than I am". No therapeutic alliance can be formed in these conditions.

2. *No trust in the object-world.* A world experienced as untrustworthy or dangerous negates the possibility of a therapeutic alliance. People cannot communicate with a therapist if they do not believe it to be in their interest—if they believe that, given a chance, you will do them down. And what you as a therapist say to them cannot reach them because they are waiting in a paranoid way to see what you are *really* after. Their powerful bad inner objects are projected. What you say to them in this mood is not heard as it was meant, and your interpretation about not being heard as you intended is also not heard as you intended, and so on down the line. It is a waste of breath.

Your first aim must then be to create an atmosphere in which trust can grow.

These people are often what I call skinless, and that is why I say "atmosphere" rather than "relationship". An atmosphere is required in which people can grow, and can grow skins (see chapter four, as well as Klein, 1987, chapter 19). Here are people who cannot cope with anything as concrete as objects, cannot cope with people as persons, cannot cope with you if there is too much of you, since practically everyone and everything is potentially dangerous. But an atmosphere, painless, unnoticeable, a pre-object matrix in which relationships have a chance of crystallizing gradually, may be less tainted with the fears and distresses associated with the object-world. Do not mistake me: I am not saying that a silent therapist is necessarily less intrusive than one who talks.

3. *Ego-weakness—two factors: faulty ego-functioning and faulty ego-integration.*   Ego-weakness can be attributed to two different but related elements—faulty ego-functioning (i.e. faulty thinking), and faulty ego-structure, (i.e. a faulty sense of self). These interlinked elements go a long way towards explaining how some people come to be overwhelmed by their bad inner objects, to the point where interpretations do not reach them. People need an ego of a certain strength to contain their feelings and not be overwhelmed.

Faulty ego-functioning—the inability to think—can be crippling. The capacity for thought seems to me a prerequisite for allowing some analytic space to develop. If you have people in therapy who cannot hold on to ideas, cannot reflect on ideas, cannot reflect on themselves and their situation, you cannot expect them to contain what is happening to them. I am not referring here to the kind of people Bion (1967) had in mind when he wrote of attacks on linking. The disability I have in mind does not seem to me mainly due to attacks on links that exist: it is more like an inability to make links now. To the extent that you cannot think, you do not have an ego. And the therapeutic alliance is between one ego and another, so we are here thinking of people who cannot make good alliances.

The inability to think seems to me due to a variety of causes. Bjorn Killingmo (1989) draws a powerful contrast between a deficiency pathology, which I think accounts for some lack of linking, and conflict pathology, which I associate more with attacks on linking.

There may also be something in people, or projected out, which tells them that they must not think, that they are not supposed to think, must draw no conclusions nor show any initiative—a superego sort of thing. "Ken" (at the end of this chapter) illustrates this. A domineering parent, or something phobic, may be at the back of this.

The inability to think may also be due to an experience where some early link between events, some faulty conclusion come to in childhood, has so hurt or terrified the person that the dangerous activity, of putting two and two together, has been given up. I suspect sexual abuse in those circumstances.

Or there may be so much noise going on in a person's head, either due to this very inability to think and thus process and contain incoming stimuli or due to a maelstrom of feelings that upset them, that there is simply no room to think—like being at a loud disco, I imagine.

So we may have people before us who cannot think, or fear to think, or are out of practice. We may have to guide them to better ways, after perhaps decades of denial and avoidance. This disability may not appear in very dramatic form. You just find, after a while, that with this patient nothing you may have said has sunk in. "I see", such a one will say, "Yes". But nothing happens. Such a person will wait patiently until you have done speaking, and then go on doing their own thing. They may even pick up the words you use, but not to any purpose. I think it diagnostic that I get a sense of superficiality, of lack of grip, in the sessions. I lose the sense that I am talking to a person.

I think this is symptomatic of people extremely lacking in ego strength, and particularly characteristic of *faulty ego-structure*. It feels as though there is no person there. At worst I feel a blank—what Tustin calls a hole. There is no integrated person there to address myself to, only bits. No therapeutic alliance, therefore. At best I feel in touch with an inchoate mass of feelings: a heap of terror, a clump of resentments. My first draft had "a wall of terror", but you can only have a wall if there are objects on either side of it. Some people do not have even that much psychic structure, nothing that coherent or permanent. They are skinless. You get a sense of immense pain sometimes but, equally sometimes, a sense of no one at home. There is no core, no identity, only ego-nuclei. If you have a patient without identity, no alliance can last. You are just talking to today's bundle of fears, hopes, angers, and so on, with little organizing principle and little continuity.

What does all this suggest by way of action, of changes in our behaviour as therapists? I am a little embarrassed now because this mountain is about to produce a mouse. I have nothing to recommend that we are not already doing. I just think that if we did it in different proportions, or more confidently, or more appropriately, some people would be better off, who are now turned down as unsuitable for psychoanalytically oriented psychotherapy, or who leave prematurely, or who have an unnecessarily hard time of it. So, with some embarrassment, I put before you my recommendations, first in three rather broad sweeps, then with some follow-up implications and detail.

- *Broad Sweep A.* People have to experience themselves before they can think or talk about themselves. With the rider: they may need a therapist's help before they can experience themselves in a way that allows psychoanalytically oriented psychotherapy to proceed. I think that those who started out as child psychotherapists may be much better at this kind of help than the rest of us.

- *Broad Sweep B.* People who are not used to experiencing themselves will need to establish trust in their therapist. Without this trust they cannot relax enough to experience themselves. Instead, they watch and experience the therapist. There must be at least moments of trust and alliance. I am talking of the condition Winnicott calls "ego-relatedness", and Balint "guilelessness". It antecedes even what, following Bollas, I may call the transformational experience.

- *Broad Sweep C.* Sweeps A and B are conditions for sound ego development, both in childhood and in the consulting-room. Without an ego, you either experience your feelings in all their unprocessed uncontained violent immediacy, or you split them off. In my view, people should not be put in touch with these split-off feelings until they have a strong enough ego to contain them. In some cases, therefore, therapists must first help the patient to develop this ego-strength; they must not lay feelings bare before they are sure that the person can cope with them.

To look at practical implications, let us follow up the factors I have noted as adverse to the therapeutic alliance. Incidentally, they indicate what we might do to help an ego develop. Looking first, then, at the situation in which there is *no understanding of what the therapist and patient are supposed to do together*. What does this suggest by way of action? We have to remind ourselves that people need explanation and containment and reassurance, sometimes repeatedly, before they can reflect upon themselves—before a potential space is created, let alone an analytic one. Without that, you can create major silliness. You say "You are upset", and the patient says, or thinks, "I know I am upset, now shut up and let me get on with telling you about what upset me". Or you say, "You felt he was rejecting you just like your father did when you were a little girl", and the patient goes, "But that was 40 years ago". Or, if you interpret the transference, they go home and report "She kept talking about herself".

What is it like to talk to people whose feelings are a foreign country to them, as Patagonia might be? Either they are not aware that Patagonia exists (they do not know that they have these feelings or that there are unconscious aspects to the feelings they do know about), or they know that Patagonia exists but not that it matters, or it frightens them. The first and most obvious point to make is that they do not understand Patagonian, and so this is not a good language to address them in. The language of psychodynamics is foreign to them. This is not resistance—they just don't speak it. The second point to make is that we do not speak their language very well either. I conclude that one of us has to give way if there is to be communication and, at least to begin with, it had better be us.

In general, interpretation is like translation. Here is a person for whom feelings are a foreign and perhaps a hostile territory. So it is an interpreter's job to point at things going on in that country and give their names in that language: "that is a cow" . . . "this is an oak" . . . "that feeling I think you are now having is what we call *anxious*". Often interpreters have to give some background to help make sense of the phenomena. A Chinese may have to explain to us that in her country white is the colour of mourning. Not told that essential fact, there will be misinterpretation of the phenomena. So we may have educational things to say in the early stages of therapy: "In matters of feeling, it is possible to feel something and not know about it. It is possible to be anxious and not know it" . . . "People can get upset when contradicted, and I have been contradicting you and now I am wondering if it has upset you"; and so on.

I think there is what one might call a technique to learn here, certainly a mental attitude, a discipline to be acquired, particularly by those who wish to work with people who cannot do with interpretations. Good hosts and hostesses have it. I did not learn it from my training as a psychotherapist. I learned it before then, as a youth worker with touchy young people in a setting where I had reason to talk with them, and they had no reason to talk with me. They were free to walk away if I bored or annoyed them; they would not lose anything by it. In those circumstances you learn fast. In their reactions they were very like some of the people I have been describing: skinless, hurt by a breath, rude, crude, tough, uncommunicative, threatening, fragile. Many were easily bored, either because they were so cut off from everything that they could not cathect, or because they could not think or reflect on anything, and so needed constant engagement—which I had to provide or they were off. A special variety of holding, this. It was easy to trigger paranoid responses. The trick was to keep in touch with them without raising their antagonism to the point where they left the party prematurely.

A non-interpretative intervention I am interested in is the kind where we communicate to people—if necessary over and over again—that we are interested in them and in what happens to them. If need be, we are good hosts and hostesses, getting people to talk, asking interested questions: "Who was standing next to you?" . . . "Did you worry about it?" . . . "What do they want you to do next?" This is one concrete way of conveying to people that what they say does not have to be impossibly deep or important or whatever, as long as it matters to them.

Supposing we do find a way of engaging with hurt, skinless, wildly mistrustful, never-heard-of-psychoanalysis people in a way that holds them, then the next task becomes, "Can we create an idiom in which we can converse with them in ways that they find useful?" If we follow up the factors noted above as adverse to the therapeutic alliance, they point to things that help an ego develop.

Patients and therapists have to work together to enable the patients to experience themselves in a new way. There is nothing new or out of the way about that. Patients tell us what they said, and what uncle said, and what they said, and so on, and we make our interpretive comment. But we need to keep in mind that *there are people who lack ego-strength* to a degree that makes therapeutic cooperation unlikely. About these it could be said that they cannot experience themselves, because there is no experiencing person there—hence also, no observing ego, no reflecting ego. The processes that mostly go on in most of us, most of the time, which tell us that this is now happening to me, this is what I am now feeling, this is what now goes on and what it means now to me—these processes can be very very defective.

How do we notice this in therapy? Our own feelings about the other person tell us. Why don't we notice it more often? I think the reason lies in too much emphasis during training on defensive behaviour and resistance characteristic of conflict pathology. This prevents us from noticing that our patient is in fact not capable of taking things in. Inappropriate focusing on defensiveness and resistance may make us believe that the person in front of us—like the people in the cases in the books we have all learnt from—that this person has an "I", an "ego", but is concealing it from us. We are taught that it is up to us to get past this concealment. But supposing—scary thought— that there is nothing there to be concealed? We sometimes interpret defences without making sufficient allowance for the possibility that what is being defended is not an "I" in the usual sense of the word. Pain is being defended against. But no clear inner object is being defended. If, then, we penetrate the defences, we have a patient on our hands who is defenceless against his or her unprocessed and now uncontainable feelings! Their ego was not strong enough to contain them! We have allowed them to be overwhelmed.

We need also to deal in a more relaxed fashion with the third factor I mentioned that can militate against the therapeutic alliance: *fear and mistrust of the object-world*. Again, if only we dared more often to put up with that doubt and mistrust without challenging it as resistance. If only we could say, in an inoffensive unoffended way, "I realize that you have a lot of reservations about what I say". Of course, this is not going to be a mutative comment. These people know well enough that they have reservations. They don't trust us, we don't have to tell them that. Though possibly we are letting them know that we understand their lack of trust well enough not to be offended, nor frustrated, nor angry about it, without challenging them to drop it, here and now, as inimical to the therapy. In the long run this could have a mutative effect. But not because we interpreted something they were unconscious of. Rather, because we created an atmosphere, an ambience, which raised the possibility of a safe situation, in which ego-processes can grow naturally, where patient and therapist might possibly meet one of these days: a potential space, precursor of analytic space.

My main conclusion is that *it is essential to create this potential space—our eventual meeting being the potentiality in question*. In that space we may usefully talk together and make a working alliance.

What am I saying? I am saying that we have to take people's conscious experience, their ego-experience, as seriously as their unconscious. It is through our conscious experience that we are aware of our existence. Especially with very insecurely structured people, people with major ego weakness, we have to do a lot that helps them feel we recognize their existence. Because they don't. Because of their ego-weakness, they don't feel as a matter of course that they exist, and they may be touchy about that. But in potential space, at least, they exist.

My concluding recommendations are impeccably orthodox, it seems to me. In fact, they almost mirror the insight-producing procedures advocated by that straight-down-the-line psychoanalyst, Ralph Greenson, as the essence of psychoanalytic technique. Only, where he uses the more aggressive term "confrontation", I say "recognition" or "validation".

There are four things we need, to work with people for whom interpretations are inappropriate:

1. We need to *recognize* their existence, or at least their potential for ego-development.

2. As well as recognizing and validating their existence in potential space at least, we need to *clarify* what it is like to be the way they are here and now, at a conscious as well as an unconscious level.

3. When we have recognized and clarified what is going on, we can try to reformulate the experience in the succinct form that belongs to a theoretical framework capable of embracing all phenomena. *Interpretation* puts experience into an intellectually meaningful and coherent context.

4. *Working through:* when we see how the behaviour we are interested in fits into a more general scheme, we still have to trace its implications for this particular person's life.

By way of a final summing up of my argument, I present "Ken".

Ken was 31 when he first came, and, like "Rose", he took more than ten years to come to a good resolution. He had read in a magazine that there is such a thing as psychotherapy, and he hoped it would help him to mature and, in particular, to make relationships. The only relationships he had had were hostile ones with his parents and his sister, and a somewhat ambivalent one with an old school-friend. Until the year before he came to see me, Ken had lived at home. His immature Oedipal father had throughout Ken's life been jealously hostile, with a good deal of physical violence. The mother was also hostile, in a more phobic sort of way; her wish was to have nothing happen, ever. This included "don't make your father angry", although she seems to have enjoyed the strife between the two males, in an Oedipal sort of way. The parents had common ground in a taste for belittling, especially anyone who was "notice-able"—a trait which they suspected in everyone. Not sur-prisingly, Ken was very afraid of his father and of all males and, further, terrified of being noticed. He tried not to do things, because to do anything or to learn to do something he could not already do met with the parents' envy, with his father's verbal and occasional physical attacks, and with his mother's phobic fears as to his adequacy in coping. Also, Ken felt it was presumptuous and, as it were, wrong to do anything, let alone to do it well. As far as he could, he tried not to do or to be: "It is easier not to bother." You may imagine what an obstacle to the therapy this could be.

To aggravate this, Ken lived in an isolated London sub-urb, where much of the male culture was yobbo, which he hated but which he necessarily subscribed to; no alterna-tive had been available to him. Too beaten down to be a yobbo himself, he was the victim of others at work, seen as slow and stupid by his superiors, the butt of his fellows, who teased him grossly about having no sexual experience, and so on.

At first I saw Ken once a week, later twice, just getting him to talk. He could not talk about his feelings at that time, but with encouragement he could talk about events at work, and what happened at home, where he still spent his weekends, and with his friend Reg. He *had* feelings, he said to me later, but he felt he was not allowed to have them and certainly not allowed to talk about them. He liked coming to me. He liked the opportunity to talk and be listened to. After four months he joined the psychotherapy group, where he sat for months not meeting anyone's eyes. He felt hostile to the others there because he experienced them as hostile and as not wanting him there. I interpreted this often, but it had no mutative effect. For a long while he bounced these projections back and forth. It took two years (the twice-weekly individual sessions continuing) for him to realize and volunteer things like, "I know now that I am angry with you and not you with me".

When he had been in individual therapy for a couple of years, he developed something we called "basking", which I later recognized to be analogous to being safely and lovingly held.

> *My soul is an enchanted boat*
> *Which like a sleeping swan doth float*
> *Upon the silver waves of thy sweet singing.*
>
> Shelley, *Prometheus*

This man could not remember having ever felt accepted as he was by anyone. He felt accepted by me and held on to this feeling. It may be the feeling an infant thrives on. Note that it is not conducive to thought, reflection, or awareness. It antecedes ego-development. It is being-at-one-with, as Winnicott (1971), and of course others, have seen it.

It seems to me that during this time I allowed a symbiotic relationship to develop in order to give him the courage to "thrive", to persevere with looking at himself and talking about what he saw. A lot of his work with me was entirely passive, but increasingly at times also a bit like metabolizing Bion's (1962b) beta-elements into alpha-elements. He did not bring what I could detect as unmanageable feelings; only a depressed and inadequate-feeling tip of the iceberg showed. I did a lot of low-level, what I call "dear–dear" interventions: "Dear, dear, you must have hated that" . . . "Oh dear, that must have hurt" . . . "Dear me, I wonder how you felt". During this time, his emotional awareness developed in pace with his growing security in talking about his feelings. He hardly ever contradicted my interpretations, but he rarely took them in or looked at them either. He just did not swallow what could not make him grow at that time. He never had any strong negative feelings about me either. Everything went very slowly, as it does in real life, but there was a definite sense of development and a very marked decrease in his misery and his sullen hostility to the whole world of people. He himself noticed it and was pleased about it. His social life expanded slightly, and over the years he got several promotions, including the important one from manual to clerical/managerial. He detached himself further from his demoralizing parents.

For the first three or four years, he suffered no more than a withdrawn and cut-off depression during my holiday breaks, rather like Eeyore. Then he began to feel more clearly let down by me. Though not yet directly reproachful, he did begin to feel he had rights in me. Being able to lay claim to me, who let him down, gave him more of an interest in other people (freed his libido, one might say) both as a substitute for me and to pique me. Finally in the fourth and fifth years, he began to be able to feel and notice anger against me. But basking was the context in which he grew, in a particular mixture of what *he* detected of his feelings and what he thought *I* would wish him to feel or think or do. He began to be able to do things "because you told me to". And I did tell him to. I encouraged him to go away for his annual holiday, and he did so for several years and reported enjoying parts of it. I encouraged him to go on evening classes. He, himself, not on my advice, tried dating agencies. Concurrently, his experience of my non-phobic acceptance of his guilty and very inhibited sexuality allowed him gradually to integrate these drives in more wholesome ways, in potential space if not yet in practice.

The next stage—in his sixth and seventh years—came when he began to say to the group, "Jo told me to go to evening classes" or whatever, evoking in the group the same disapproval the reader may be feeling. I took this to mean that he was strong enough to attack me and to try to withstand me, or at least strong enough to experiment with so much separation. The time was coming for him to stand on his own feet.

My response was gradually to behave more like an ordinary therapist—less help with the basking, more interpretation of his material, and especially more interpretation of the kind that became relevant around then: "You are doing nothing to change your life because you are waiting for me to do it for you" . . . "You are trying to forgive me for not having a (sexual) relationship with you, but only if I provide you with someone else to have a relationship with." After a while he recognized that this was so, but nothing changed.

At this time he floored me by insisting that he did want to take the initiative and to do things, but could not. Other people could. They had motivation. They had strength. He had not. We stuck there for a year. I interpreted what was going on—in terms of his fear of doing things and being noticed doing them, in terms of his Oedipal fears, in terms of his regression—but to no avail. He seemed to agree with me, but most of the time he was just basking. At this time all the preconditions for the development for ego-functioning had been met, but a solid ego had not formed. It was forming, however, through the very process of "defying" me and thus separating from my wishes (viz. that he finally get better and lead an independent life). Eventually, in a marvellous session, he discovered his thinking part, which he described in terms appropriate to the generally accepted concept of the ego, with a few elements of superego added. He also discovered—i.e. became conscious of possessing—a strongly anti-libidinal part, definitely a punitive superego. After this we could move into a process very like a classical psychoanalytically oriented psychotherapy, which carried on for several more years.

APPENDIX
The group

The information sheet sent out to referral sources reads:

> The group meets from 7.45 to 9.45 on Monday evenings. It is run on supportive rather than psychoanalytic/interactive or encounter/abreactive lines. The age range is 24–40. We aim to have six to eight members as a rule, roughly balanced between men and women. There is a regular turnover of members, with people usually leaving before the August break, but some members have been in the group for a long time. New members are asked to try a minimum of three months, and then, if they like it, to commit themselves at least until August. Everyone decides before August whether they want to stay another year. Fees range from £8 per session to nothing at all, depending on a person's financial situation.
>
> People tend to join this group because they feel very depressed, very anxious or very isolated, or very confused, so it is not a very jolly group, but it is a group in which people can feel the relief of genuine human contact.
>
> It is not an intellectual group, and we usually have a balance of more and of less educated people.

I started this group because the way I was working encouraged people to talk about their everyday problems too much, leaving too little time for analytic work. Much of this talking had to do with their pleasure in having someone to share their experiences with. These were people who had become, or had always been, lonely and friendless. They did not know whom to trust or not to trust, they were at sea. So they talked to me about the problems that life set them: there was no one else they could talk to at this level. They were also alienated from common sense and made horrible errors in everyday living. Even though I did not usually give advice, it was noticeable that they did better after what was essentially nondirective counselling, i.e. they just went on talking and listening to themselves. But it did crowd out more psychoanalytic work. I thought that if they could meet with each other, and with someone in charge to protect the group from pathological group phenomena, they might be able to encourage and support each other. And so they did. I am careful not to put into the group anyone whose transference is likely to make positive mutual sibling support impossible, and only once did someone have to be eased out because, in the course of the time, he became determined to destroy the group and I was unable either to contain him or to help him through this phase. I am also careful to avoid what used to be called the hebephrenic: the silly gabbler who just creates noise and takes up time uselessly. I make mistakes, but on the whole it is working well.

Because I avoid those whose transference would get out of hand, I do not usually have to intervene by interpreting behaviour as a way of controlling it, and so I am able to make it a ground rule that no one interprets anyone else's behaviour. (Though we all sometimes do, but always with a sense that this is dangerous ground.) No one can tell anyone else what that person is "really" feeling or doing. This ensures that interpretation is not used by the members as a covert attack on each other.

Another ground rule is that no one is to give advice, though we all, at one time or another, find devious—if acceptable because unoppressive—ways round that, e.g. "If I were in that situation, I think I might well consider moving".

We have also made it a ground rule that, in May or June, people look at their own work in the group over the past year and decide whether they want to stay another year. Thus we control the amount of attention that has to be given to loss and mourning, and to new babies and the disturbance attendant upon them. This does not work terrifically well, but still it is better than being in continual uncertainty.

CHAPTER SIX

Times when transference interpretations are (in)appropriate

C hapter five considered times when interpretations of any kind are inappropriate. The question in this chapter concerns transference interpretations in particular. There have been some interesting discussions on the meaning and efficiency of transference work in the last few years (Stewart, 1987, Reed, 1990, Renik, 1990, Schwaber, 1990, Smith, 1990, Ogden, 1991, Parkin, 1991, and nearly the whole of the second issue of the *International Journal of Psychoanalysis*, 1992, on psychic change), but my focus is narrower. It is on patients who cannot do with transference work at all. Which patients? Why not? When not? And must they have it in order to get well? Is all our life a re-enactment of earlier experiences? Do we all transfer all the time? In the same way? Is life as Meltzer (1983) sees it, in which the reality we seem to share with other people is only an epiphenomenon of our dream life, where the real things go on?

A version of a Public Lecture given for the London Centre of Psychotherapy in June, 1993.

To clear the ground with some definitions first: in chapter five an interpretation was said to be a translation, for the patients' benefit, from a language they do not understand to one they are used to. When interpreting, the service we provide is that we understand the language of the patients' unconscious ideas and behaviour better than they do and can clarify it for them. Broadly speaking, transference interpretations are meant to show the patient that a phantasied relationship, often based on a past relationship, may be being unconsciously re-experienced with the therapist.

In its simplest form, Haessler (1991), basing himself on Hoffer (1956), puts it nicely: a person develops particular ways of dealing with conflict and other distress. These ways get elaborated in the course of life as more and more situations are perceived in those terms and therefore tend to be dealt with in the same way as before. They will then also appear in the therapeutic encounter. From this point of view, transference in therapy is one local variant of a characteristic way of encountering the world. This I can accept. Whether the patient is best helped by concentrating on this characteristic pattern in the consulting-room, or by concentrating on it elsewhere in his or her life, in my view, depends.

This chapter presents first a brief history of the idea that transference interpretations are efficacious, indeed so efficacious that the analyst must induce a neurosis in the patient in order to be able to use this path to well-being. There follows a review of some doubts about this, philosophical, practical, and theoretical. Then we shall try to understand when patients are likely to engage therapists in transference phenomena, and when not. Some illustrations follow of what various people seemed to need in their therapy. Then we try to identify more closely with when transference interpretations are appropriate, and when they should be used with great caution, if at all. As we canter towards a conclusion, we take another look at the relationship we call "space".

History of ideas on transference and transference neurosis

Initially, transference phenomena were an unwelcome intrusion into Freud's and Breuer's pre-psychoanalytic endeavour. Freud's genius showed itself in realizing that they should not be ignored or avoided, but used and interpreted for the benefit of the patient, and this has been the practice ever since these processes were identified a hundred years ago and written up in Freud's *Studies in Hysteria* (1895d). Twenty years later—written up in "The Dynamics of Transference" (1912b)—Freud wrote about transference as a regular and interesting thing that happens between analyst and analysand. By 1915, in "Remembering, Repeating and Working Through", he was writing about the deliberate induction of transference neuroses as the treatment of choice, relating it to the idea that patients repeat their childhood conflicts within the transference. "Provided only that the patient shows compliance enough to respect the necessary conditions of the analysis, we regularly succeed in giving all the symptoms of the illness a new transference meaning and in replacing his ordinary neurosis by a 'transference neurosis' of which he can be cured by therapeutic work" (Freud, 1914g, p. 154).

According to Laplanche and Pontalis (1973), from whom this potted history is abstracted, the difference between transference-reactions and transference-neurosis proper is that in such a neurosis the whole of the patient's pathological behaviour comes to be re-orientated round his relations to the analyst, and that, from this standpoint, the ideal procedure for a cure is that the clinical neurosis is transformed into a transference neurosis whose elucidation leads to the uncovering of the childhood neurosis. (At that time it was thought that making the unconscious conscious invariably cured people of their neurosis.) Laplanche and Pontalis remind us that five years later Freud put forward a less one-sided view of the transference neurosis, drawing attention to the risks run if this development is allowed to get out of hand: "It has been the physician's endeavour to keep this transference neurosis within the narrowest limits: to force as much as possible into the channel of memory and to allow as little as possible to emerge as repetition" (Freud, 1920g).

While many analytic writers have heeded this warning, many others have instead elaborated the transference neurosis as the only way to a cure. Thus Strachey (1934), in a famous paper, insisted that only transference interpretations are mutative—that is, able to make a permanent difference to the personality. But he also allowed that other interventions had an important and at times essential function. He had no belief that analysts should confine themselves to transference interpretations only. To anticipate, my own position is that there are times when only transference interpretations are mutative, that there are even people who do best for long stretches of the therapy if you confine yourself to interpreting only transference phenomena, ignoring everything else. But equally, at the other extreme, there are people who do best with little or no attention to transference interpretations, either just then, or ever.

I find it really confusing, the ways in which the understanding of transference work has changed its nature and meaning in the course of this century. Its early beginnings were simple: "You do this to your brother or to me, the analyst, now, because you are repeating an experience that happened when you were 5", with the main focus of interest in what happened at 5, the theory being that if that is made conscious, the neurosis will inevitably vanish. Though we no longer believe this, we still find it a useful thing to say at times. But the focus has shifted to include other possibilities, also useful at times. We can bring things more into the present: "You are doing this to me now because you are angry with me for reasons that have to do with you and me, and which we can explore (or already know) and whose transference significance in terms of past events we may (or may not) explore now." Or: "You are talking about an experience when you were 5 because you cannot face what you are now feeling towards me, the therapist, in a more direct way." In this last interpretation the time dimension and the causal connection run counter to what had originally been maintained by Freud.

Very popular, currently, are such notions as that everything a patient does in the consulting-room is by definition transfer-

ence-based and/or that all of a patient's problems will naturally come to the surface eventually, if analyst and patient
agree to examine only what the analyst means to the patient.

I should mention one other notion, now more of historical
interest than current practice: that analysts should present a
neutral smooth mirror-like surface to the patient, so as to leave
the patient free to project onto them whatever object-relation
the unconscious is most preoccupied with. At the back of this
idea is something scientific about sterile test-tubes and un-
contaminated research-findings, as well as a laudable wish not
to influence the patient by one's own biases and prejudices. I
think it is more generally accepted now that many people
create whatever they need to create from even the most
unpromising or most distracting data. Nevertheless, we should
take care not to intrude, and so it is a point of view I wish to
preserve though I do not think universally monopolistic claims
should be made for it. It presents two problems. One is that the
theory is incomplete: it is simply not true for everyone that, left
with a blank-screen analyst, the most pressing concerns will
emerge from the unconscious. They will for some; they will not
for others. I would like to know more in advance for whom it is
true. This is the second problem: we do not know in advance
whether the patient now before us will benefit more from one
approach or from another. This we consider when we look in
greater detail at questions of diagnosis. But to return to the
first problem: for every patient who, when left alone, brings up
pressing problematic material from the deep unconscious, I
can produce one who experiences a sense of parental abandon-
ment, of being put under the microscope by a Gorgon (Wright,
1991), of being bamboozled and mystified, and so on. You may
say this will be the patient's most anxiety-laden preoccupation,
but I don't think so.

I shall not keep distinguishing between all these kinds of
transference work, because all of them are useful some of the
time, in my view, and all of them appear to me counter-produc-
tive or even damaging at other times.

Kernberg puts the contemporary version of transference
work as sympathetically as would seem possible. It seems that
he does not think that the transference is actually there to
begin with, but that patients come to analysis with a "transfer-

ence disposition"—a kind of readiness to experience the analyst as a transference object.

> In psychoanalysis, the patient's defences against a full awareness of his transference dispositions are systematically explored, which leads to a gradual transformation of latent into manifest transferences. Transference reactions evolve into a full blown transference neurosis. The systematic analysis of the transference neurosis permits its resolution as a resistance against awareness of the unconscious past. Then the information about the past contained in the transference can be integrated with the patient's recovery of the previous unconscious past through memory and reconstruction. [Kernberg, 1984, p. 163]

An acceptable point of view, perhaps, but still it leaves open the question whether we are not as able to observe and use transference effects in other transactions that patients report to us. Do we have to be ocnophilic about it? Do we have to insist: "You must go through these experiences with ME"?

Is there always transference? Does everyone do it all the time?—or invariably in particular circumstances? Do contemporary psychoanalytically oriented psychotherapists have to confine themselves to transference interpretations? I have doubts, and these are detailed next, first in connection with "analysability", then via an illustration, concretely, then morally, philosophically, and in the light of the history of theory.

Doubts about analysing at all

There are, as we saw in chapter five, patients who are not ready for interpretations of any kind, transferential or other. Among these were noted:

1. people who do not see that it is they who have a problem: others have the problem—their daughter, their doctor, their mother, their boss, or whoever;

2. people so dominated by pain that they cannot concentrate on what appear to them irrelevant intellectual or abstract matters;

3. people in search of something they will not have to work for, looking for a magic cure;

4. people just now feeling too hopeless to work at anything, or so threatened by what the world may have in store that they shrink from any contact with shared reality;

5. people with ego-weakness—either they have not much more than the rudiments of thinking in them as yet, cannot retain ideas, cannot put two and two together, or else they are so split that what happens in one session is not connected with what happens in another.

There are patients not handicapped in these ways. Still it may be inappropriate to work with them in the transference. But not because they are "not ready" in the way in which some people are not ready for interpretations. It is because people vary: some can get themselves sorted out with minimal attention to transference phenomena, and others can only get themselves sorted out with constant elucidation of their transferences. The minimal ones cannot be described as not ready any more than I can be described as not ready for a massive dose of antibiotics. I can do without, thank you, I don't need it just now. In the same way I cannot be said not to be ready to have my leg amputated, or to have a kidney transplant. These things are invaluable for the right patient; on other occasions they are inappropriate but that does not mean that the patient is not ready for them.

Almost by definition, those normally classified as "not analysable" will not benefit from intensive transference work; at worst they can be harmed by it. This can easily be seen if we look at some of the questions Coltart (1988) suggests we ask ourselves in making decisions as to the best treatment for people who come for assessment.

• Is there some capacity in them to stand at a distance from their own emotional experience?

• Can they go on and reflect on themselves as a result of being listened to?

• Is there some capacity to perceive connections between parts of their history, details that are being recounted, and their prevailing sense of discomfort?

- Is there some capacity to recognize and tolerate an internal reality, with its wishes and conflicts, and to distinguish it from external reality?
- Are there signs of a capacity to recognize the existence of an unconscious mental life?
- and so on.

Coltart picks out two criteria for suitability for analysis: psychological-mindedness, as indicated by that sort of question, and the will to be analysed. The will to be analysed depends very much on whether the patient has a strong-enough ego to keep the treatment-alliance going during the more difficult phases of an analysis.

> The will to be analysed is not by any means the same thing as the more random, changeable and drive-motivated "wish for recovery". . . . One should listen . . . for this potential function of the autonomous ego because this will be what ultimately keeps the therapeutic alliance alive. . . . The will to be analysed in the therapeutic alliance will be of vital importance when the transference neurosis becomes active and resistant and opposes treatment, and when the early wish for recovery is forgotten in the day-to-day work of the therapy. [Coltart, 1988]

Namnum (1968), on whom Coltart draws in this discussion, was writing at a time when the use of transference work was neither as pervasive nor as refined as it is now, and so no mention is made of working without a treatment-alliance. It is now better understood that there are times when the treatment-alliance is itself a transference phenomenon; indeed, it is maintained by some that all treatment-alliances are transferential (Sodre, 1990). Leaving that aside, we have to accept that if the treatment-alliance cannot be relied upon to hold the patient stable, and if there is not enough ego-strength to cope with transference interpretations, other techniques have to be used, not based on transference work.

Doubts: an example

A patient is talking about one rotten apple in a barrel spoiling the lot, in a story about a corrupt policeman. Maybe he is talking about me, the therapist. But suppose he does not think he is talking about me? And suppose he is not? Or is it axiomatic it must have been me? If I believe that, I am very nearly believing that patients who do not agree with me about this are not suitable for psychotherapy. Out they go. Not analysable. Hold on. Perhaps there is more to be said, and it will turn out that we can include in psychoanalytically oriented psychotherapy at least some of the people who will not agree that they are invariably involved with me when in my consulting-room, and who yet might need help and might benefit from it.

Let us suppose that this man was indeed talking about me as a rotten apple, and knew he was but just did not say so. I indicate to him that he is talking about his experience of me (i.e. I make a transference interpretation) and the man is relieved that I know what he was taking about and that I am neither frightened nor vindictive. He is also, incidentally, relieved of the necessity of being the person who actually puts this thought into plain words. Now this is a good thing in certain circumstances, but in other circumstances perhaps less helpful, for the man might have needed also to know that he could say such things plainly to me without disguise and without help from me. It might at times be better to give him space to get there on his own. If, on the other hand, he was talking about me, but without realizing it, he deserves a chance to discover me to be, in his world, a rotten apple. If I say too plainly that he is talking about me, much of the strength of the discovery is lost. And it is an important loss, because such a discovery, spontaneously made, strengthens self-respect. Finally, let us suppose the man was not talking about me. Suppose I tell him he is talking about me, and he is not. I say that he is, but that he is unconscious of it. Suppose he is strong-minded and disagrees. We both hold our own. I say he is talking about me, he says he is not. Well, at least that gives him a chance of an identity separate from mine. Not much harm done, though an identity too dependent on contradistinction has some dangers. But, suppose that he is docile and agrees that he must have been talking about me, dredging some stray thought out of the back of his mind and giving it a prominence it does not in fact have. What have I done! I have made a mistake and compounded it with a second error, much more damaging to his well-being and growth! Let us hope it does not happen too often.

Moral doubts

> Provided only that the patient shows compliance enough to respect the necessary conditions of the analysis, we regularly succeed in giving all the symptoms of the illness a new transference meaning, and in replacing his ordinary neurosis by a "transference neurosis", of which he can be cured by therapeutic work. [Freud, 1914g, p. 154]

This provision, that the patient must show compliance, excludes a lot of people who come to see me. This worries me, but also, I have to say that the moral status of the idea of "transference neurosis" worries me. What is the behaviour to which the words "encouraging a transference neurosis" might refer? It must be about getting patients into the habit of structuring their perception of life, their experiences and their understanding of these experiences, all in transference terms as long as they are in our consulting-room. And we get them to this state by speaking to them as though everything they tell us refers to them and us, as in the example of the rotten apple. But if everything is transference, why do we have to induce it? If therapists interpret everything a patient says as relating to them, some patients are bound to get more neurotic, yes, the increment being due to the confusion generated by the therapist's insistence. Of this the patient can then be cured. For a straight-talking evaluation of just how some therapists bring it about that they "regularly succeed in giving a person's symptoms a new transference meaning", I refer you to David Smith's controversial *Hidden Conversations* (1991).

In the last 50 years or so, there has been a swing in the climate of opinion so that we have become very sensitive to the charge of brainwashing—the use of psychological techniques to make people doubt their own senses or their own logic. So what have those therapists done who have come to believe that the only cure comes from working through a transference neurosis and that therefore they must induce one? Brainwashing is repugnant. But a piece of doctrine has come to be believed by many therapists, that everything the patient talks about is necessarily about the therapist and the patient. The neurosis is there all the time, it is said, you only have to uncover it. Therapists who hold this view can use transference interpretations all the time, sincerely unworried by the charge of brainwashing. Yet it is a view based on insecure foundations, such as the experience they themselves have had of analysis. But one instance is not evidence.

I also have moral doubts about aims. What do we want for our patients? It is not unfair, I think, to recall that analysts since Freud have as a matter of doctrine disowned the primacy of aiming to help the patient get better. "Analysis for its own sake", i.e. for the sake of self-knowledge, was the first version of this; I understand it to have been Freud's own. Many interesting psychoanalytic writers since then, however humane they may be in practice or in principle, have not in their thinking and in their writing appeared to ask themselves how what they do relates to the welfare of their patients. I instance Lacan, whose practice I do not understand, and Bion in pursuit of the ineluctable O. I do not think that writers on theory and/or technique should have notions of people's well-being that are too different from the conventional, or from what most people in a patient's circle would consider well-being.

I am aware that many people believe that at least some of the more arcane writers delve into the patient's deepest unconscious processes, that our patients will get more deeply better when we delve like this, and that therefore we had better follow them. But I question that. I have learnt from Freud to mistrust our fascination with the arcane, its nursery origins lying behind the closed bedroom door. More arcane is not by definition deeper or more efficacious. Indeed, I question the assumption that deeper is better for all who come to us for help. More drastic is not always better. In my generation, tonsils were whipped out at the slightest excuse, just in case. In my parents' generation it was appendices. We need to have better *differentiae* to indicate when to go into the abstruse for our patients' benefit, and when to refrain.

The medical profession has for millennia had the rule that, above all, you must not damage the patient. *Primum non nocere.* The equivalent for the psychotherapist must surely be that, above all, we must not damage the authenticity of the patient's experience. *Don't undermine.*

I am a therapist. I am not an analyst. What do I actually want for my patients? Nothing high-faluting. I want them to be less troubled by troublesome symptoms. I want them to be able to go on underground trains. I want them to be less uncomfortable with their children. I want them to wake up in the morning thinking "Oh good, another day". I want them to sleep securely at night. I want their sex loving and rewarding and personal. I want less cruelty. And so on. These ambitions may seem petty or arrogant or optimistic—not worth trying or not likely to be achieved. I think it can be done, though not as yet for all troubled people. But I think we should aim to improve, to increase our understanding and the range of our techniques so that we can be more efficacious, helping more people to feel more love, more safety, less terror, and so on. Whatever may in the end be the intractable residual, we are nowhere near the limit of what can be achieved, and to me it is a moral issue. At least some of us ought to push on in these directions with experiment, research, and depth of thought, so that we can all get nearer the limit.

Philosophical doubts

Philosophically, the question "Is there always transference?" is a question about the existence of the world out there. It is about blue defined as a wavelength, warmth defined as x degrees Fahrenheit, the impact of a brick breaking the skin, twice two equalling four, and the square on the hypotenuse of a right-angled triangle being the sum of the squares on the other two sides.

What is at stake here is the validity of what is conveyed to us by our senses, and by our rational powers. Both are admittedly weak. I also admit that the reality of the world which our senses convey to us has justly been the subject of debate all over the world, in the East and the West, for many centuries.

The conclusion I draw from these debates is not that we have got it right at last, but that it is seemly not to be too wedded to an extreme view, since there is so much to be said on so many sides of the question. Crudely, the question is: is there an order in the world, conveyed to us by our senses and by our rational powers, or do we ourselves create all patterns, all meaning and order? The answer I want is an agreement: Both, to some extent. Yes, there is a world out there, some of it conveyed to some extent by our senses, and some of it ordered by our rationality, however defective. And yes, we do create meaning and order by the way we choose to conceptualize, but we do not create all the meaning and order there is.

If I can get you to agree to this, I think I have got you to agree that people bring some of their own world into the consulting-room, and that not all phenomena in the consulting-room are created by the two people in it.

There is for each of us a world out there, full of beauty and terror and sorrow and perhaps love, just as there is a world in the consulting-room of beauty, terror, sorrow, and love. We live in either world to varying degrees. Personally, I live "out there" a good deal.

> Nothing is so beautiful as spring—
>   When weeds, in wheels, shoot long and low and lush,
>   Thrush's eggs look like low heavens, and thrush
> Through the echoing timber does so rinse and wring
> The ear, it strikes like lightnings to hear him sing;
>   The glassy pear-tree leaves and blooms, they brush
>   The descending blue; that blue is all in a rush
> With richness; the racing lambs too have fair their fling.

Gerard Manley Hopkins, Spring

It gives me great pleasure to read that poem by Gerard Manley Hopkins, called "Spring", and to read it to friends. I want my pleasure to be valid: I want this pleasure to be not merely derived from exchanges more than 60 years ago between my mother or my nurse and me. To share it with people now seems important to me.

Similarly, I want deep griefs I suffered in more recent years to be validated as deep griefs about contemporary events, not reduced to re-enactments of my infancy. It seems demeaning not to take them seriously for what they meant to me at the time, belittling the importance of the event to me.

Also, I may sincerely want to return to events in the past, and to understand them from the standpoint of my present insights. Events that really happened then, whose significance I now want to explore. I mean events when I was 8, 18, 28, 38, and so on. It is my life that I want to understand, not just the dynamics of the infant in me now, in relation to my therapist now. The cause of my wanting to look at these events now may or may not be transferential—it does not invalidate my need to reconsider and explore my past. To understand the meaning of my life seems to me not an unworthy ambition. It seems wrong to have my attention re-directed to how I feel towards my therapist. If that is true for me, who am not currently in therapy or analysis, I think it can be true for people who are.

There are important social and political implications to this view. Mainly, it allows for action in the here and now, outside the consulting-room, outside my head. In working to change the world for the better, in working to change things I do not like, I am not merely acting out old battles. Feeling passionate about this cause or that abuse is not to be reduced to transference merely. I assert that it is worth striving to improve things. The world exists. The world is more than a Nintendo computer game. What happens matters.

I insist that some people bring into the consulting-room their passionate concerns about the world out there. Their experience of life has not been overwhelmed and taken over by life in the consulting-room. What they are talking about may not be transferentially based. Some of them we can train to see everything transferentially. But surely this is a damaging version of creating a transference neurosis. We are training them to deny much of what matters to them.

Theoretical doubts

For me, a world exists which I did not create purely from the stuff of earlier relationships. There is an order in the object-world, independent of my individual invention, an order that is more or less available to most of us, for us to perceive and use, and if we do so, we shall increase the range of our responses and of our creativity. This view contradicts the view currently more prevalent in psychoanalytic circles, that our experience is very severely limited by our inner constructions.

In passing, I must share with you my pleasure that this view is being unobtrusively eroded by the serious interest that British psychoanalysts are now taking in empirical studies of child development (such as Ainsworth, 1982, 1985; Murray, 1988, 1991; Trevarthen, 1984; Stern, 1985).

Interestingly enough, psychoanalytic thought has once before had to debate the question "Is all behaviour a manifestation of some inner realm?" It bungled it rather, but got near to something important. There was a time when the dogma was that all behaviour and all experience derived from instinct. When reading the material from those days, one gets that same sense of an iron hand of fate, of immutability, of everything being derived from something that cannot be altered. Then it was instinct, now it is transference, but you cannot do anything about it, the Calvinism of the day. Whether you are saved or not does not depend on your efforts: it has already been decided—it is only up to you to accept it.

It was Hartmann, in the 1930s, who asked the heretical question of those days: "Is there behaviour independent of instinct?" He decided that the possibility could be entertained, if we reconsidered the nature and development of the ego. In his view the ego had more to it than was attributed to it in his day, when it was seen as merely the outcome of instincts in conflict with the demands of the interpersonal or non-personal world. Hartmann maintained that the ego had a conflict-free area to it: it was an apparatus of perception, memory, and general cognition, and as such could sort through experiences past, present, and anticipated, and could come up with things that did not have their origins in conflict: algebra, sunsets, sonnets, aerodynamics—see Laplanche and Pontalis again, this time their section on the ego. Rapaport, writing in the 1950s, coined the phrase "the functional autonomy of the ego" and refined Hartmann's theory to maintain that progressively greater freedom from instinct could be achieved, as the ego was progressively strengthened by being freed from instinct—a sort of gradual pulling oneself up by the bootstraps into the light of rationality. Eventually, one's behaviour would be only remotely derived from the instincts: it would derive from derivations of derivations of derivations of instinct and hence be virtually autonomous of it.

Unfortunately—does this sound familiar to you?—Hartmann's way of viewing things was not popular. It threatened to undermine the analysis of conflict, which was the central technique of analysis at the time. Nevertheless, the primacy of the analysis of conflict gradually declined in various areas of the psychoanalytic world, in favour of a more object-related approach. Sadly, with that, interest in the role of the ego as freeing people from the iron hand of determinism (whether of instinct or of the past) was lost again in many circles.

That controversy shared an important common element with the one I am now addressing: the function of the ego. The ego is the means by which our senses convey to us something of the world-order we did not create. I think the ego is best thought of not topographically as a place in a personality-structure, not as the single function of a single agency, but as a collective noun referring to a number of quite often cognitive things people do. Perceiving is one such function—that is, the function of the senses, obviously. But also conceiving—making sense of what is perceived, at a higher level, giving meaning to what the senses convey. And this in the light of other ego-functions like remembering, comparing, foreseeing, planning, and so on.

Once again I have to make an excursus to convince you of my even-handedness. I respect and love and praise feelings: their colour, their strength, the depths from which they spring. But as regards feelings *versus* ego-functions, I know the dangers of too much reliance on either at the expense of the other, and do not wish to extol either at the other's expense. On this occasion I wish to excite in you the respect and love and praise that our ego-functions excite in me. It is to our ego-functions that we owe the construction of great theories, for instance—how inspiring, and how useful, their logic, their depth, their coherence and elegance, their explanatory power. Much of this we owe to our ego-functions.

What the ego does is to enable us to be effective in our contact with the interpersonal and non-personal, with what many people call "the world out there". That your patient's grievance against the boss he cannot get on with may be like his grievance against his uncle or against you, and that an old object-relation is being re-enacted, is important. But that the boss is in fact mild as milk or a terrible tartar is also important. What patients need to understand is *both* the re-enactments they are engaged in *and* that their perception of the present situation is or is not accurate. In many circumstances therapists cannot help with this is any direct way. But we hinder it if we do not take an interest in our patients' current experiences because we see their recital as irrelevant except insofar as they are transferential. That demeans people's experience outside the consulting-room, and erodes their confidence in their power to perceive what is in front of their eyes.

There was a remarkable discussion at a recent psycho-analytic conference. Otto Kernberg gave an example of how he worked with a quite disturbed man who accused him of having spat at him when they met, as the man thought, on the street. Kernberg knew he had not been there, said so to the man, but, finding him unconvinced after several tries, used the situation to try to get him to see that there were two realities in the situation, his and Kernberg's. It was all he could achieve, and Kernberg recommended it as worth achieving. Later in the discussion John Steiner took it up as illustrating differences in style between different analysts, and commented that he himself could never have been as sure as Kernberg was that he had not spat at the man. I warm to Steiner's point, and I would not want an analyst who did not warm to it. But for myself I want an analyst who, when the chips are down, knows quite well whether he did spit, or did not. And I myself want to be a person who knows, almost all the time, whether I did spit, or did not. And that is what I want for my patients too.

When are people more prone
to transference relationships?

As far as I know, the question "what kind of person engages strongly in transference phenomena, and what kind of person does not?" has not been addressed. Nor has the even more frightening question "what kind of patient benefits from transference work and who does not?" I need a clean new word to help me think about this: "transference" is too loaded with connotations from nearly a hundred years of use. Also, "transference" is a noun, and thus lends itself more easily to vague and abstract uses than verbs usually allow. I need a verb to give due weight to the fact that being involved in transference phenomena is a thing that people do. The people who do a lot of it also deserve a word of their own. Can we do better than "to transfer" and "being a transferrer"? "To project" often describes well enough what transferrers do, but it seems to me to leave out something essential, which has to do with the feeling I get when I am with people heavily into transference behaviour, a feeling that I have been pulled willy-nilly into their universe, onto their inner theatre, onto a script that they created and over which I have no power. Looking for metaphors that do justice to that feeling, I find myself with words like enrol, abduct, recruit, shanghai, kidnap, impress, indent. In fact, I have opted for "recruit", but my mind is still open.

The tendency to recruit, then, is the tendency to relate to other people in terms of a personally invented world, usually composed of very few figures. People from here and now are recruited into that world, onto that stage, into that script of long ago and far away.

The more extreme recruiters are at times prone to ignore what might seem to the rest of us obvious features of the object world (people, mostly), because they live in a world they invented (of "internal objects"). And what is, then, their relationship to what Winnicott called the world of shared reality—the world they share with the rest of us? They are not much into exploring or even discovering it, and we, the people who live in it, are not discovered or explored as who we are. Instead, we have been invented, recruited, to play the part written for us in the world they invented. And don't they just hate differences of opinion, which they experience as confrontative and humiliating experiences.

It seems significant to me that I got my first insight into "who are the recruiters?" not from a colleague but from a friend whose professional interests lie elsewhere. I had been struggling for weeks with what it might be about some people that makes them more prone to engage in heavily transferential ways of behaving. Without hesitation she said that these must be people who very much needed to have others around them at all times. Ah, I said, much enlightened, Balint's ocnophils (1959), and Bowlby's attachment theory.

The ocnophils (Klein, 1987) are the homebodies, very person-centred, very personalizing. They are not easily bothered into feeling intruded upon, they are happy to drop any task in order to welcome you. When they have something on their mind—grief, hope, upset, good news, whatever—they naturally turn to other people. They are not touchily or strenuously aware of self/other boundaries. Less immediately thought of as recruiters, but just as person-centred, are people who relate negatively to others—touchy about being intruded upon, fearful of contact with others, resentful of their presence. Still, they are recruiters. What distinguishes the ocnophil is being always preoccupied with people, always recruiting, as friends or as enemies. In therapy, they benefit from transference interpretations because relating to people is the stuff of their lives. They stand in contrast to people who have less urge to be so closely involved with others, in affection or in hate or fear, people who are just less preoccupied with others: the philobat persuasion.

Balint suggested in 1968 (p. 175) that there was a danger that the psychoanalytic profession might be taken over by the ocnophils. Even more than in his day, it seems to me that, in the course of the development of psychoanalytic theory, the transference neurotics, the recruiters, have taken over the universe of our discourse, so that there is little room for theories less focused on recruiting. What has got lost is that part of theory which would allow for the possibility that not all our patients are natural transference neurotics.

People who need other people around them much of the time are people whose well-being depends massively on the feelings of others towards them. This alarms the philobats (the spacebats), but the ocnophils (the homebodies) like it that way. To be close, in this sense, is to be willing to put up even with unpleasant feelings arising from contact with another person, rather than not be the object of their interest and barred from interest in them. Presumably most people would prefer to be dependent in a positive way on the goodwill of others, but we all know of instances where the dependence is of a less blissful kind. There are whole categories of people—the recruiters in fact—natural transference neurotics—who want to be in close emotionally significant relations with others all the time, preferably lovingly, but hate or fear will do as long as the needed interpersonal emotional significance is there.

There might be a lot of good in this. To be close might mean to be finely attuned to the feelings of another person. Stern (1985) uses the term "affect-attunement" for this talent and gives some ideas on how it is developed and how variations in the capacity for affect-attunement might come about. But of course there is not necessarily a genuinely interpersonal relationship. The other person, as seen and understood by an outside observer, is not necessarily of great interest to a recruiter. The "other" person may be only a lay figure, a puppet clothed with sentiments from heaven knows where in the recruiter's phantasy life.

Whence this passion for recruiting from the object-world onto a person's inner stage? Why would people want so desperately to stay in their invented world? Why would they not want to look out at the object world? Perhaps it was too frightening? Made too frightening by projected rage? Perhaps the attachment-figure was too dominant and did not allow for a loosening of the bond? Is the thought of a world that cannot be magically controlled by one's thoughts too unacceptable? Perhaps the relationship with the attachment-figure was so insecure that the emerging personality had to concentrate all his or her faculties on studying that link to maintain it and could spare no energy to get a proper hold on the rest of the object-world? Henceforward such a person might be confined to the inner stage, on which new experiences had no hold except in the form in which they were recruited to represent the familiar experiences of long ago.

Whatever the origin, some people's early experiences predispose them in some way to be transference neurotics— obsessive recruiters of other people onto their inner stage. Some may be one-person recruiters, who never separated from mother, the infant/mother boundary having been destroyed for some reason. Some may be two-person recruiters, no one having come between mother and child to represent the outside world. All such people may be condemned to imprisonment on their inner stage, with unpleasant feelings coming from their phantasied interaction with invented actors: they fear to be separated from these too significant others lest they be separated from the source of all their feelings, a double loneliness threatening them all the time.

A different class of recruiters may be trying to catch up. For instance if a baby has been too much out of touch with a mother too often experienced as not there, it might later tend to cope with stress by going for constant recruitment of people in order to eschew that void. Special cases may be found among those who have been traumatized by some felt deprivation in early life and who are now unconsciously always searching for a person who embodies an idealized conception of the parent they did not have. This is likely to be a case of the "unthought known" (Bollas, 1987), not a repressed wish or a split-off hope. I am thinking, for instance, about people whose mothers were not experienced as sufficiently holding, so that the need to be held is there but not satisfied. Such people are likely, whatever else preoccupies them, to be always looking at the object-world with the possibility in mind that the next person may be the one who will hold them perfectly—and so they cannot relate to other people with an open mind but tend rather to feel aggrieved at others' failure to be what they hoped for. In the same way, we may imagine the plight of people for whom, as babies, milk was hard to get and needed a taxing effort to obtain, or who suffered constant impingements into their rest-periods, or whatever—I have in mind any set of circumstances embodying significant interpersonal disappointments or frustrations. We are here considering categories of people who, for one reason or another, are always carrying some hope that the object-world will perhaps now finally give them what they need—a hope that is always eventually disappointed. Nothing and no one in the world is able to continue for long to conform to our infant hopes and phantasies. These are bound to be disappointed and hurt. If the hope cannot be abandoned, such people are likely to continue to recruit, with increasing bitterness and despair.

We need not conceptualize the source of compulsive recruitment exclusively in terms of a re-living of early attachment experiences. While for some people the early object-world plainly still holds that kind of sway, for others this is not the case: what is much more obvious is their inability to contain themselves. There is something wrong with their ego-processes. They dump. Their anxiety, anger, joyousness, or whatever, spills over onto us, regardless of good sense, here and now. Sometimes these feelings do belong to object-relations in the past, transferentially, but the point I here wish to make concerns some people's lack of control over expressing what they feel now, whether the original stimulus came from long ago or from just now. A bus conductor has been rude to them, the bus did not stop for them, and they are rightly furious, and still furious when they come into the consulting-room where they cannot contain themselves. They are irritable in the session, although not aware that their anger started, as it were, with the bus conductor. It spills into the consulting-room as though it had to do with the therapist. Of course, often this works just fine, but I do not think we should expect it always to do so, as a matter of psychological necessity.

In therapy we may have to decide whether this is a good time to say out loud that they have recruited us when their anger was set off by a bus conductor and not by us, or that when upset they just unload their feelings regardless of any connection between the cause and the recipient of their feelings. Similar choices face us with other emotions. Falling in love is quite a complicated process, and we must not take it for granted that the therapist is the focus of it. Or a person may be grieving about a recent loss. To a lesser or greater extent, people's feelings rub off on those around them. Obvious, you say. Of course it is. So we must not unswervingly attribute here-and-now reactions to then-and-there transference processes. And more particularly at this point, therapists also need to explore what it means when people are unable to manage to contain their feelings.

To sum up, there seem to be at least three main predisposi-
tions governing the need to recruit. Two are ocnophilic: people
clinging either to an old object-relationship or to a never-
experienced ideal relationship; the other—dumping—has more
directly to do with a mal-function of the ego-processes. The
ocnophilic options have to do with the tendency to react to
things by staying in one's invented world; dumping has to do
with the inability to process and contain one's strong feelings of
rage or guilt or joy or whatever. In different ways, all three
tendencies seem to have to do with the ability to keep a boundary between self and not-self. What is responsible for the
creation and maintenance of such a boundary? Ego-functions
are. Let me remind you of Freud's sketch of the ego as intervening between what he called "reality" and what he called the
id (Freud, 1923b). You will remember—the sketch looks a bit
like a cloud, or like a potato. The ego-functions are hidden in
the skin of the potato, regulating the boundary between self
and not-self.

Illustrations

It is time to look at some illustrations. Those I have not taken
from other publications I have to some extent invented, based
on patients I have known of at some time, in my own practice or
from cases I supervised or from seminar presentations. All are
modified for the sake of confidentiality.

Illustrations of malfunctioning ego-processes
and concrete thinking: no therapeutic alliance available

Rosenfeld, whose work I respect deeply, always writes as
though transference interpretation is the only cure. "It is my
conviction that the psychotic patient's speech and behaviour
(particularly in sessions) invariably make a statement about
his relationship to the therapist" (1987, chapter 1, second
paragraph). I myself do not believe this is true either for the
fully psychotic or for others. And Rosenfeld does not actually

always proceed immediately to interpret. Rather, he reminds the reader "to pay minute attention to the patient's communications and to seek to conceptualize and understand what these communications mean. . . ." Yes, indeed, though the sentence ends, ". . . in the transference relationship". I am sorry for that last bit. Are we not to be allowed to think what it means except in the transference?

It is to his credit that Rosenfeld then proceeds to give an example where he makes a premature transference interpretation that the patient unfortunately understood to be a seduction. This patient had been showing an unmistakable sexual interest in her therapist, and she had said that she had heard a voice telling her she was going to get married. Rosenfeld told her that he believed she had thoughts that her therapist (himself) was going to marry her. This was too much for her—she had had no such conscious thought. Alarmed, she deteriorated. Rosenfeld reminds us that the therapist has to take care lest people plagued by concrete thinking mistake an interpretation for a suggestion.

On the other hand, I, who tend to underplay transference interpretations and to rely a good deal on that state of mind in which transformational phenomena occur—a transformational transference, if you like—am especially indebted to Rosenfeld for some of his warnings: that very confused patients may not realize that their improvement comes from the therapist's help unless the therapist regularly refers to the relationship; that if people are too little aware that the therapist is working with them, they are more likely to finish therapy prematurely or without warning after a break; and that if you don't discuss anything about the relationship, the patient is apt to idealize you, with all the dangers that entails.

Examples from my own practice confirm to me that there are patients with whom one may actually have to discourage a transference if one can, and certainly not encourage it. A broadly smiling young man strode in when I opened the front door at the start of a preliminary interview, his hand outstretched, saying loudly and apparently confidently, "Hello Josephine!" Throughout the interview he was bobbing in and out of quite delusional experiences, as he was to do for some months to come, so that he was often quite at a loss as to why he was where he was, though only elusively aware of these alterations in his state of mind. In this kind of confusion, he could not cope with any as-if talking on my part. He kept his thinking concrete. When he told me of terrible events in his childhood, his voice sad, his face immobile, I unfortunately said something like "What a terrible time you must have had; I expect there is a lot of crying about it bottled up inside you". (I don't, incidentally, think this was a good way of saying what I wanted to communicate.) He understood this as a promise that he would get better if he cried a lot, and he set himself to cry a lot in my consulting-room for many sessions. Actually it did do him good, but what did him no good was the effort he put into it, for which he paid dearly, for he felt both guilty towards me and badly let down by me when the quality of his life did not improve markedly after he had cried so much. I was unable to repair the damage I had done, let alone exploit it, by interpreting the transference, that is, by explaining the misunderstanding. At that time, any *ad hominem* reference alarmed him intolerably. For a long time after that, I was careful not to encourage him to take an interest in transference phenomena, though often I was aware of them. I feared that he would get his phantasy-life even more mixed up with the interpersonal and impersonal world he shared with the rest of us.

It also began to strike me that he suffered from two kinds of confusion. One seemed to have to do with the fact that thought-disordered self-absorbed people miss out on knowing obvious things, like that nobody wears a hat nowadays. William's father had worn a hat, so he wore a hat, never questioning it, though it was one of the things that made him look odd. He was isolated partly because he was ignorant of simple social conventions which his pre-occupations stopped him from learning about and which made other people avoid him or find him less than good company. The other had to do with disordered thought-processes and had led various assessors to suggest a diagnosis of schizophrenia. (In fact, his mental state improved rather too fast for that, as it turned out.)

It is interesting to speculate what is happening when people talk in what appears to be a confused random way. There is a doctrine that at those times a person is necessarily talking to and about the therapist, but I doubt it. Do we do these people a service or do we do them violence if we insist by the force of our authority that they are talking about us? My own conviction is that people sometimes talk at random—I do it myself, for instance while thinking at one level and having to talk at another. What I say has meaning, but whether it has to do with the person I am talking to is a matter of chance.

Rosenfeld's patient and "William" and many others did not have much sense of reality. I see them as representative of many who do not relate much to people and things in the world we share with them, but who do have feelings, and do have an idea, however vaguely, that these feelings are connected to events in the world, though not necessarily to the therapist, or not necessarily just to the therapist.

Illustrations of a single meaningful relationship into which all are recruited: no therapeutic alliance available

"Becky", a psychology graduate, wanted to train as a psychotherapist, but her wise G.P. had encouraged her "to get some experience of psychotherapy first". She had felt herself to have been ignored and exploited by her mother, not appreciated. It was to her like a running sore. She took the therapy almost at once into a grief-stricken transference, in which the therapist was the person uninterested in her distress. About this she was very brave and resigned. She behaved as though the therapist wanted her to be brave and resigned. On the surface their conversations were conducted in a pseudo matter-of-fact tone resembling a clinical consultation about other people and their motivation: the Prime Minister's motives, Anna Freud's, her neighbour's, the therapist's in using a particular technique she thought she discerned, etc. The therapist's occasional interpretations of the feelings he believed to be underlying her situation were experienced as intrusive, inept, negligible, wounding as she had experienced her mother to be wounding. From her point of view, she ignored them so as not to cause ructions between them. However, she came three times a week, and this gave them a lot of time to fill, and she did eventually begin to talk about other things, including more of what she was at the time experiencing as grievances, so that her own emotional reactions to what was happening in her life came at last to be mentioned. This enabled the therapist to talk more to the point about how she was experiencing her life and helped him to make her vulnerabilities more a focus of their attention. This in turn allowed her to let down her defences a bit further. She and her therapist at first talked mainly about her feelings in the course of events elsewhere or in the past, then also about what had happened between her and him in the past (initiated by the therapist); finally it became possible for her to permit connections to be made between what was happening between him and her here and now and what was experienced elsewhere, now and in the past. So they arrived at a point where transference interpretations might usefully be made.

"Arnold" was a very burdened man. His mother had told him that he was the outcome of her sole sexual encounter. He and his mother had always lived on their own. He described her as an unhappy woman, socially very isolated and apparently of very limited intellectual and emotional resources, easily upset, though fortunately her family was able to support her financially. Arnold had been able to leave her when he went to a university in another city, but they had been very close, and his mother had depended on him a great deal, I believe in a very conflicted way, often in spite of herself. Arnold was in a great deal of confusion about her.

A very distrustful transference (and countertransference) developed between Arnold and his therapist, which stood in the way of Arnold's ability to consider in a straightforward way anything the therapist put to him, either generally or as it appertained to the transference. He took everything the therapist said as quite possible but not proven, only provisional. But provisional possibilities cannot feel meaningful, and he had problems about feeling empty. Such mistrust was difficult to bring into the discussion in a way that Arnold could manage.

In my view Becky and Arnold suggest that people who have not had much experience of honest relationships in the past cannot easily have them later, for they remember being let down, losing face, and so on. That means they cannot use transference interpretations therapeutically for a long time.

In all the four illustrations so far, the transference phenomena may have been obvious to the therapist, but the patient's sense of self was unable to integrate an understanding of them so as to benefit. Rosenfeld's patient and William had a fragmented and very fragile sense of self; the bits were elusive even to themselves, as one could hear when they spoke of themselves. By contrast, Arnold and Becky were weakened by clinging to some parts of themselves and not integrating others. Becky's sense of her own identity was weakened in that some deeply painful life had been split off from the rest of her experience of herself, but the pain kept seeping through while the understanding did not. The ever-present pain poisoned her relationships continually and strengthened her defences. Arnold's mistrust similarly poisoned his relationships, thus strengthening his defences and keeping him from insight. Therapy that challenges defences against severe narcissistic pain is generally acknowledged to be a difficult task.

Illustrations of minimal recruiters

The next two illustrations, "Gerda" and "Velia", are of people only minimally engaged in recruiting. Both led economically and socially successful lives; their lack of inappropriate recruiting was obviously a help to them, whatever you may feel they lost out on.

Gerda had problems about attaching deeply to people, after a traumatic time in early infancy during which she suffered several separations from her family, she and her mother having each been hospitalized on several occasions, leaving her with one uninvolved care-taker after another. She had encapsulated her trauma successfully and was leading a well-adjusted full life, ever more so as the therapy proceeded along the lines she insisted on. The transference phenomena were obvious, but she could not be induced to explore them. The trouble was, they gave her too much gratification for her to want to give them up—this was part of what she was determined not to face. Neither the therapist nor the patient could get at the full dynamics in this case, but there are instances when the dynamics are better known, and yet the patient is reluctant to give up the gratification, and this can for a time create an insuperable resistance to understanding the transference. One way of overcoming it is to work satisfactorily at other issues, and this is what happened here.

In therapy, Gerda enjoyed the closeness of the relationship, which she could regulate, and she enjoyed reconstructing her life and making meaning out of it, and the therapist did quite a lot of non-transferential interpreting, which Gerda found interesting and useful and which she incorporated into her understanding of her life; transference interpretations she ignored. There were at times quite unmistakable negative transference phenomena, but in an underhand way that did not interfere with the reconstructions and working-through that she enjoyed so much. Her occasional defiances and sly digs at the therapist were inaccessible to her understanding until quite late in the therapy. Then, presumably, enough trust had finally been built up, and she was able to talk about the many subtle ways in which her hostility and destructiveness had operated in the therapy, often quite consciously though in a split-off sort of way. But in the interim a lot of important work on other aspects of her personality and behaviour had been achieved, including much on her destructiveness and covert hostility to people.

"Velia", another very successful career-woman, had had a depressed though functioning mother and a narcissistically preoccupied father. She dealt with her very unstimulating rather empty though unthreatening early years by premature ego-development and by displacing her need for object-relationships first onto transitional objects and later onto drawing, dress-making for dolls, story-writing, friendships outside the family, and, finally, an exciting career. The after-effects of a disfiguring accident in adolescence finally brought her to therapy in her mid-thirties. In her therapy much mourning was needed, and coming to terms with the recognition that life had denied her many good things. She cooperated well in most respects, but no complex transference ever developed, nor was it needed.

Velia, like Gerda, had a sound and stable personality, with perhaps rather underdeveloped emotional reactions, but she was rather rigid compared to Gerda. This rigidity had made it harder for her to integrate traumatic events such as those she encountered in her adolescence, but she too was now leading a happy well-adjusted full life, and had sublimated much into her career in a caring profession. She represents the kind of person who is reluctant to get very involved, either in the deep tangled emotions of early childhood or in the transference phenomena to which these lead—a style that characterizes people with a more feeling and less ordered start in life. The "Velias" are people who do not do much obvious recruiting and prefer to operate in an environment that is not purely and immediately overwhelmingly interpersonal. They do not often seek psychotherapy, and with the style at present preferred in this country, they may be discouraged if they do start, but with a different approach they can of course benefit.

The outcome of Arnold's and Becky's, Gerda's and Velia's therapy, like that of many others of whom they are representative, demonstrates to my satisfaction that in many circumstances the therapist may have to work at length to allow those ego-structures to be formed which are needed to enable the person to approach painful situations they have learnt to fear. Sometimes these changes can be brought about by interpreting the transference situation itself, but not by any means always, and it should be a matter of course that a therapist be allowed a choice of approaches.

Illustrating the ocnophil temptations of a therapist

Too ocnophil a therapist can do harm. One example of Joan Symington's has already been quoted. Here is another from her admirable practice. One of her patients "talked most of the time, using psychoanalytic jargon. The analyst interpreted this as a take-over of her mind and a simultaneous belittling of her, only to find this briefly acknowledged and then immediately fed back to her, as the patient repeated it as his own interpretive self-analytic work. There was no change in the patient's behaviour until the analyst reached out to interpret the desperate plight of the baby, clinging to the only way he knew of surviving, that is, by talking non-stop and doing it all himself" (Symington, 1985).

Both this example and her previous one show Joan Symington to be a sensitive and skilled analyst, easily able to recover lost ground, but it is easy to see that when patients' subjective experience of themselves is not taken seriously, but only their transferential experience with the therapist, the ego cannot grow. And people need an ego.

Words of caution to the ocnophil

People differ so much. There are some who can just about bear the strain of taking in new and disconcerting information about themselves, as long as they do not have to meet themselves directly. If they can do it in terms of other people rather than themselves here and now, they are alright. Others can bear the strain provided they can just stay inside themselves and not have to meet anyone else, not even the therapist, while they are doing it. Yet others can really only cope with here and now; for these, transference interpretations are the most natural comments you can make.

Some people almost force you to respond with a transference interpretation. They shove it at you, so to speak. But there is a range of others, about whom we may well ask ourselves whether transference is the first thing to concentrate on. There are many people who do not do much obvious projecting or recruiting, who are operating in an emotional environment that is not purely or immediately interpersonal. This is what many of those who write on these matters omit from their consideration—people can be doing a lot of other things than projecting their deeply archaic objects onto the next nearest person. The question is then—is it the most useful thing to induce a transference neurosis, or should therapists allow themselves to discover more about this person first?

Early in 1993 Donald Spence reported some work to the Research Group of the Institute of Psychoanalysis. There is in existence a complete transcript of an analysis, giving both the analyst's and the analysand's contribution in each session. Spence subjected some sessions to the complex computations made possible by advances in computer technology. He recorded the number of sentences in which the analyst made reference to the analysand's transference. These he correlated to the number of times the analysand said "You" (the analyst) and "I" (the analysand) in those sentences. He found that the analysand was regularly able to respond usefully to transference interventions when they were made at times when she was talking in terms of "you" (the analyst) as well as herself. When, however, he made transference remarks at times when the analysand was not referring to the analyst in terms of "you", this rarely produced anything positive.

We must be cautious about creating a transference neurosis. And even when it is a right thing to do, we must still be cautious not to create a transference neurosis that rests in the false self. The effect of that would be to have patients obediently going along with what the therapist has inadvertently taught them, while the original pathological personality-structures remain unaffected behind the façade.

Which patients are most vulnerable to letting themselves be guided into a false structure? To put it unkindly, what kind of people can be talked into buying a vacuum-cleaner from a door-to-door salesman? The docile—so much in need of a kind response from authority that they will quickly catch on to your way of doing things, and comply. The ambitious-to-do-it-right—patients in training and the well-read are good examples. A bit like them are the exotically inclined: those who feel that there must be some excitement in it over and above what comes from recognition and reflection. The cut-off—not easily engaged with you or with anyone or with their own sensations and convictions—they can play along with anything. I could extend this list, but this is enough. Lastly, I must agree that there are people buying a vacuum-cleaner at the door because they need one.

We therapists need to be particularly cautious when we are in an ocnophil mood, and more in need of recruiting someone onto our stage than able to hear what our patient is engaged with. We have to be careful not to intrude ourselves when people are reflecting, for instance, on a life-issue that they are working out for themselves, as they should: to leave a job or not, to marry or not. Perhaps afterwards they can talk about transference aspects if there are such. But for a time we have to listen in terms of what is involved for them in the issue. We have also to be particularly careful when people are in the middle of some grief or joy that must be lived through before it can be looked at. Our too early intrusion may indicate to the patient that they are feeling something they shouldn't. Remember Balint, the first to warn us not to interpret in the middle of a regression (Balint, 1968).

What kind of person can stand it if you take away from them what they are just then most conscious of experiencing? Is the ego strong enough to stand it? Transference interpretations are for people whose ego is strong enough to stand it. A hindrance otherwise.

If people do not have much sense of reality, it does seem a bad idea to tell them things about themselves that are remote from their experience of themselves. It might feel to them that you are telling them they should be feeling something different from what they are conscious of feeling.

Of course, therapists would agree that, in their profession, teaching is wrong. But mostly this process is not experienced by therapists as teaching. They have the idea that they are picking up some faint tremor of what the patient is feeling, and they believe in pointing it out to the patient. That is the theory. But sometimes, in seminars and in reading published papers, I get the feeling that something much cruder is going on. Now that is dangerous when one is interpreting anything at all. But how much more dangerous in the case of an interpersonal version of events. If a patient has trouble taking in the reality of other people's independent existence, is a transference interpretation the best way of getting them in touch with what is going on? If we insist on transference interpretations to people who are only intermittently in touch with our common realities, we get the paradoxical situation that our patients agree that what we say is going on is in fact going on, while not experiencing it for themselves. In this way, patients are cut off from the very thing they admit they are experiencing.

I think what is at stake here is how much importance we attach to letting our consulting-room and our listening be a space in which the patient can grow naturally, a space in which, whatever else we do in that room, patients feel free to develop in their own way. Constantly to bring that experience away from how the patient feels it to be, to what we believe it to be, may be very destructive of that person's growth. I know the counter-argument—that patients can be helped to bring only what represents their deepest worry of the moment. But I do not necessarily believe it, and where I can believe it, I do not approve of the procedure, crudely stated.

In Kernberg's view, only people with neurotic personality organizations can stand the full psychoanalytic rigour. (For those who are puzzled by this, non-neurotic people do not exist in his scheme—everyone is either neurotic or borderline or psychotic. Neurotic are the people who have the benefit of an integrated identity and ego-strength, as shown by their capacity for impulse-control, for sublimation, and for tolerating frustration, as well as by their ability to stay in touch with our common realities.)

People with a more borderline organization cannot always contain themselves, and in therapy they need more space, to express themselves and to talk, than neurotics do. Kernberg (1984) has a chapter on the management of the transference in their therapy, which he calls "expressive" therapy because of their great urge to be expressing themselves. Like Rosenfeld (and others), he notes that such patients may not be in a state to grasp "as if" ways of thinking, so that one may find oneself taken literally at unexpected moments, the patient believing, for instance, that you have just said you are his father (p. 115). But his conclusion is different from Rosenfeld's: less intense transference work. Kernberg also warns against interpreting what the patient is doing and saying to you as a direct repetition from early life. He sees this as a kind of condensation, characteristic of some Kleinian work, containing two errors: "It mistakes the primitive bizarre intrapsychic elaboration of psychic experience for actual developmental features", and "it telescopes complex slowly developing organizations of internalized object-relations into the first few months" (p. 116).

Words of caution about helping patients settle down to work

It seems to me that two things have brought psychoanalytically oriented psychotherapy into disrepute with the general public. On the one hand, people laugh at some of the incomprehensible

absurd-sounding interpretations that disillusioned patients
and their circle are unable to swallow. But, on the other hand,
disillusioned kin often wait for some change in their problem-
member while suspecting that the problem behaviour and
attitudes are kept being kept from the therapist.

Many people coming to therapy and meeting a stark-naked
transference interpretation, if not frightened off, think "Wow,
how amazing! I really am in therapy!" and start to work. Therapists who do not start off this way may have a problem helping
patients get to grips with the therapy because therapy does
not feel different enough from everyday life, not very exciting.
Often, in the first weeks, I may not be able to tell from the
conversation that there is anything much wrong. Of course, I
will be thinking about the problems that patients are bringing
at this time, but without any feeling that this is what brought
them into therapy. Perhaps we are building a situation of trust?
Almost certainly. But pretty soon someone is going to have to
do something more decisive, or else the pointlessness of the
situation is going to become obvious to the healthier kind of
person, and they will think that this is all that therapy has to
offer and they will leave. (Or of course they will healthily start
telling you about what the real trouble is.) The less healthy the
patient is, the more there may be relief that they are getting
away with being in therapy without having to change—and the
therapist is being recruited into this pointless fantasy! So then
it may be right for this to be the transference that is going to
have to be talked about—or it may not be right.

Let us take an imaginary twentieth session as an example.
Imagine a person coming three times a week, and paying good
money, worrying on for a couple of weeks about whether to
have their hair dyed. Do I say some version of "You are wondering if you are acceptable to me as you are or whether you have
to make changes"? Or do I say some version of "You are worried
about your looks and your acceptability to people as you are"?
Or do I say "Let us have a look at what we have been talking
about for the last couple of weeks. You have been trying to
decide whether your hair should be this colour or that, at
nearly a hundred pounds a week. Do you think this is because
you are having difficulty in tackling what you know you should

talk about"? Whichever I choose will, I hope, help the patient discern his problems more clearly.

Sometimes quite a struggle develops with patients denying that anything in their life is hidden. Only my suspicion that there is a split in their life of which they are not aware, or hardly aware, keeps me worrying away at the patient who is bringing bland material. Not a comfortable position for either of us.

I get here into the realms of countertransference analysis, which is not my brief. But it is not usually offensive to say to a patient that you are wondering why this or that is not being talked about.

Sometimes people are quite unaware of the behaviour, and the attitude behind it, that makes them unhappy, ineffectual, or unacceptable. Accordingly, they will be like that both in the consulting-room and outside it. What kind of intervention will help them? It depends. Would they find it less threatening to consider how it is between them and their boss or spouse directly, or would they find it easier to understand where they go wrong when they see it first between themselves and the therapist? The hair-dye patient may be trying to pretend that nothing serious is wrong or worrying him, in my room or elsewhere, and if I make this clear to him, this may be of direct help, especially if I can show that what keeps happening between us is something that he makes happen elsewhere as well. There are of course dangers to this, as the therapist's personal preferences, tastes, and values may intrude impertinently. I remember, years ago, a colleague "interpreting" a patient's attending the session in jeans; my colleague felt that this was symptomatic of her disrespect to parental figures: she should wear a skirt. Humility and self-knowledge are indicated, to which prolonged personal therapy should have contributed, and so should some knowledge of the various worlds we live in. This apart, I do very much believe that patients' behaviour and attitudes need to be discussed at the therapist's instigation if the patients have not themselves raised the problematic aspects. I do not believe that if you leave patients free they will invariably get there. Oh no. A repetition compulsion does not go away if allowed to repeat indefinitely and unchallenged. No compulsion does.

Some thoughts about control

Sometimes people indicate clearly from the very first session that they need to be freed from their compulsive recruiting if they are ever to lead less confused and more comfortable lives. They are easily recognized. Compulsive recruiters will, from the first encounter, recruit their therapists, who will, then or eventually, have to interpret this in order to keep some kind of control over the situation. Sometimes, however, one has to listen first to a good deal of narrative about other people— bosses, spouses, etc. Never mind, it allows one to point to where the person is repeating patterns of behaviour. Many people find this convincing. But if someone is constantly treating the therapist in what seems to the therapist an unrealistic way, then it can be very useful to interpret that that person is under a misapprehension, and that this misapprehension is one that often inconveniences that person. "You are afraid that I am going to talk about you to people I should not talk to. I won't, but I notice it worries you. Not surprisingly, because I remember you told me you felt betrayed both by your father and by your mother in that way", etc. etc. In this way the therapist is able to draw the attention of the patient to a habitual worry and its reasons, and at the same time help them free themselves so that they can attend to the therapy work from a more insightful perspective than just repeating "I can't and won't tell you".

In these ways, transference interpretation can control the course of the therapy. But it has its dangers, because anything to do with control puts almost irresistible temptations in our way. It can blind us to our unreasonableness in expecting people to be punctual ("caring about the therapy") when there has been a bomb scare on the underground, or in expecting people to come when the baby has chicken-pox ("not putting the therapy first, or the therapist or themselves"), or in expecting them not to complain when we take our holiday in June and charge them for not coming in August ("the patient is trying to control the therapist").

On the other hand, there are patients—psychology graduates, therapists in training, generally well-read people who know something about regression and transference—who believe that behaving badly in the consulting-room is their right: that they can scream and swear at you, fart, belch, interrupt, abuse you verbally, go on at length about lurid sexual phanta- sies, and that just doing this is part of the therapy and should not be interpreted because that implies that they shouldn't. I do encourage regressions actually, and I believe that they en- able people to hear themselves say things they did not know they had in them. But these are meant to be controlled regres- sions, not self-indulgent repetitions of infantile phantasies or deliberate recruitments of the therapist onto a person's private stage for the naive gratification of the very symptoms for the relief of which they have come to therapy. Repetition is not working through, either in the consulting-room or out of it. The insistence that they be allowed to do it is part of the patient's transference—often, I think, an enactment of a wished-for idealized parent who of course never existed, under the claim that this good mummy lets me.

Kernberg warns against believing too easily that patients are working through past conflicts when in fact they are just doing what comes naturally to them, or what some repetition compulsion dictates: "This cannot be considered working through, so long as the transference relationship provides the patient with instinctual gratification of pathological, and espe- cially aggressive, needs". Many of us have had patients who loved to storm at us, or involve us in horrid phantasies, while we were thinking that this had to be interpreted in terms of something more than or other than their pleasure at being unpleasant with impunity. Kernberg goes on to say that "some patients obtain much more gratification of their instinctual needs in the transference than would ever be possible in their extra-therapeutic interactions" (Kernberg, 1984, p. 116).

While I am on the subject of control and self-indulgence, it appears to me that at present there is also a lot of talk among some psychotherapists suggesting that walking about in some- one's unconscious fantasies is in itself a good thing, and that we therapists can always be discerned there. I belong to the more cautious Winnicott orientation, which respects the pri- vate core of the person as private and not to be entered without good reason, and in any case I do not believe that we are always to be discerned there. Sometimes walking about with someone in their unconscious world is a help to that person: it may give them more confidence in facing something they have feared to face in the past, allow them to become more familiar with their interior landscape and less frightened of the unacceptable bits, and more easily able to move between the conscious and the less conscious. Walking about with them, we represent for a while some accepting part of them. Rigidly superego-run people in particular benefit.

But some therapists, perhaps especially some claiming to be followers of Bion and Meltzer, go further and believe that, as we walk about other people's landscape, we can reorganize it to make it a better one according to a predetermined scheme. I think this is to assume more knowledge of human potential than we have, and I am almost sure that when people do this they do less than justice to their great exemplars' intentions.

Diagnosis: what can we tell, and how soon?

Are there people for whom transference work is definitely indicated from the start? Can we judge at that early moment the extent to which a person will compulsively re-enact episodes, relationships, reactions from the past, in a way that can only be understood in the transference? It would be handy to have some guidance on this, for the sake of accurate referrals, and also because it gives therapists and patients some space in those cases where transference work is not judged to be imperative from the start. Therapists could then more safely feel their way until they knew their patient better, and would not have to act on the dogmatic principle that transference work from the start is always best. The next question would be: for whom, later in the therapy, would transference work be right or wrong, as the work continues and the patient's personality becomes more understood? And, finally, what theory can be discerned to make sense of these questions?

How does one judge in a diagnostic interview whether or not a person can stand the full rigour of analysis, complete with transference work? We can use the kind of criteria Coltart or others use, and we can do what we always do anyway: judge empirically, make a transference interpretation, and see how the person responds. Kernberg has been doing this, in a more elaborate way, for some time, as part of building up a major diagnostic system. He distinguishes between people of three dispositions: neurotic, borderline, and psychotic. Both the latter kinds suffer from a malfunctioning ego-apparatus that makes it hard for them to contain their feelings, and so they tend to impulsivity, inability to endure anxiety, and inability to react constructively to frustration. The difference between borderline and psychotic lies in the extent to which common realities matter to the person.

It is Kernberg's practice, in the diagnostic interview, to make a comment at some point, which causes prospective patients to face a contradiction or omission or confusion in what they have just told Kernberg. If they are unduly upset by such a confrontation—quarrelsomely aggressive or weepily evasive—Kernberg ventures a transference interpretation about their upset, and he bases his diagnosis largely on their reaction to this interpretation (1984).

He believes that *neurotic* people are either not upset by his diagnostic confrontation, or they manage nevertheless to address themselves to the substance of Kernberg's observation. These people can stand *conventional psychoanalytic treatment*, with the analysis of the transference the main focus of the work.

Kernberg believes that people on the *borderline* are helped in their upset by his interpretation of the transference elements in the situation. He says it helps them to pull themselves together and seems, for the time being at least, to strengthen their realistic hold on the situation they are in. For these he recommends *expressive psychotherapy*, which focuses, without too much reference to the past, on their tendency to act too much on impulse, and on the conscious as well as the unconscious causes of their disturbed relationships with other people, including their therapist.

He believes that people with a *psychotic* personality organization are not helped out of their upset by a transference interpretation. They go to pieces even more—it undermines their already rather shaky hold on our common realities. For them he recommends *supportive psychotherapy*, using what opportunities there are for helping them adapt better in their everyday life.

I have found Kernberg helpful in organizing my thoughts, but, while respecting that he is overwhelmingly more experienced and more intellectually coherent than I, there is something about the way he writes about people that prevents me giving up my doubts for his certainties. I have also to confess that I could not do what he did, when I tried to follow his scheme.

So, without help from others as to diagnostics, what can I say about when transference work is indicated?

Transference work as the treatment of choice

First, there is Bollas' "unthought known". In the relationship that evolves between therapist and patient, experiences may be re-enacted which the patient has never yet conceptualized. They occurred so early in life that the conceptual apparatus was not yet in place, or not yet complex enough to incorporate the experience into meaningful patterns. Or it may be that the experience was so traumatic that the fragile, barely established framework disintegrated under the stress of it. Then the unbearable is somehow there in the mind—Bion might perhaps say that the beta-elements are there—but whatever it is has not been incorporated into the pattern of the personality. It is then the therapists' task to discern what is going on, conceptualizing it and communicating it back to the patient—sometimes at the time and sometimes much later, as seems appropriate. This may be the first occasion upon which the person has encountered the unthought event psychologically.

Secondly, transference interpretations have a kind of function, part educational, part (dare I say it) seductive, in developing therapy with very drive-driven people whose eye is firmly fixed on getting things, or getting things done, or getting somewhere, whose relationships are with objects in the Freudian sense: objects as targets to be aimed at for gratification and not objects as reciprocal in relationship. These are people who really fit Freud's paradigm. There comes a time in their therapy when reference to what is going on in the consulting-room between you and them begins to make sense to them, though it may be a considerable time before people generally become as interesting to them as straightforward object-cathexis is. Such people have needed to be introduced to a reality they had no grasp of—namely that people relate to one another, have feelings for one another, react to one another, care for one another, in a rich variety of ways, and are not just each other's instruments of gratification.

Moving still further from the sublime to the pedestrian, thirdly, transference interpretations do help to control the process of therapy.

Transference work is at times useful when people adopt certain stances or get into certain moods where they either get stuck with purely conscious material or find their material rigidly controlled by superego considerations. Some people are subject to this sort of thing habitually; for others it is a phase. I am thinking for instance of some people's tendency to be cerebral and abstract, or frustrating, or resistant, or flighty (as hysterics are thought to be). A person may habitually do any of these things on purpose in a schizoid sort of way, liking to defeat the therapist (itself a transference phenomenon), or it may be a half-conscious or unconscious thing.

People in a cerebral and abstract frame of mind will talk you to death about ideas that have nothing to do with anything much in their lives, and you eventually have to make a stand and help them reconsider the purpose of the therapy. Also, I remember the resistant/obstructive frame of mind of a woman I used to see—not very disturbed, but very difficult to help shift—always cheerful, polite, and positive, so that it did not strike me for some time that whenever I said anything about her self, however tentatively, she always started her response with NO. I mentioned this to her, and she became henceforth much more able to cooperate. The timing must have been just right. This woman was very defended against change, which she feared as a loss of identity and autonomy, and it was for this reason that she defended so against contact with people. Other people in a frustrating frame of mind, liable to dig their heels in against anything the therapist may offer, have an interest in getting the therapist to feel something, rather than in their own feelings directly. Then there are flighty people, doing a butterfly act, often displaying other hysteric traits. What the therapist talks about with them has to be at the personal level if they are ever to feel settled. The non-personal is no good to them.

When people have been stuck in any of these states of mind for a while, it is advisable to change the level of the discourse and to look at the process that therapist and patient are engaged in together there and then. "Isn't it odd", I might say, "what we are doing here, when we could be looking at what really bothers you. Is it that you are so irritated with me/so fearful of me/so disappointed in me/so glad to be here or whatever, that it is getting in the way?"

One has of course to be careful with the timing and with the nature of such insistences. One does not want to furnish one's patients with a compliant false self which agrees with one, but which is kept up by willpower and not by the natural springs of feeling and action.

It has also to be acknowledged that some people are just natural recruiters. Willy-nilly the therapist is recruited to play a part on their stage according to whatever character they have been cast for. Then, of course, the therapist uses this opportunity to work in the way that the patient has chosen—in the transference.

I have to say that I have by now seen a great variety of people, in therapy and in assessment interviews. I have seen, rather more than is the common experience, of people not strictly thought of as analysable and/or currently thought of as borderline. But I have also seen ordinarily neurotic people in quite a variety, and I have had some patients who were training to be therapists. My conclusion is that the severity of disturbance is not related in any obvious way to the need for transference work. No conventional diagnostic category has seemed helpful in this respect. But as I come to this conclusion, I ask "Is perhaps my purpose misconceived?" There may be no way of forecasting how a therapy will or should go. And, in fact, I now think that what we need is not a static forecasting system, but help in steering ourselves through uncharted seas: not a map, but a compass.

Ideas to end with: more than one dynamic and more than one mode of therapy

I have found Kenneth Wright's *Vision and Separation* (1991) helpful in thinking about different kinds of patient behaviour and the appropriate therapeutic intervention. He has re-arranged some familiar ideas in ways that illuminate whole areas of doubt and uncertainly. He identifies two ways of relating to the world, which I shall call "I seize" and "I see". The right mixture of "I seize" and "I see" allows for the good formation of a self and for good symbol formation. Things can go wrong in developing these. I may seize things without understanding myself or the world I am in. I may see things without ever acting on what I see, passively dependent on others. In either case something is wrong with my sense of myself, if it exists at all. This has implications for therapy. Briefly, should a patient get stuck in either of these ways, it is crucial that the therapist interpret what is going on in terms of the way the patient relates to the therapist—the therapist must make transference interpretations if the patient is to be rescued from deadlock.

Wright contrasts two ways the baby may relate to the mother. The baby may experience the mother primarily and urgently as a breast, an object of instinctual drives, that can be seized, used, replenished, and so on. This relationship to the breast is contrasted with something less urgent but no less profoundly affecting typified by the baby's experience of the mother when looking at her face, whose loving expression is desired but, however satisfying, not instinctually desired: it cannot be consumed; it is always at a distance. Sucking the breast is an immediate and sensory experience; seeing a face and experiencing love, an emotion, requires a distance, a separateness, a sense of me here and her there. This space is the precursor of other spaces that can be filled with symbols, of love and of other things.

This necessary gap is Winnicott's transitional space: it is not an absence but part of a relationship between two people. When one of them is not there for a time, the sense of relationship persists in the gap. Something remains in the mind about the absent one, a reminder of the relationship, of the other in the relationship, of oneself in the relationship. In favourable circumstances, this gap is something in which a greater sense can grow of self and other. Symbols and concepts can multiply there in ever more intricate ways—me, her, us, yum, love, yuck, hate, absence, presence, cuddle, joke, and so on.

Optimally, the developing personality needs a sufficiently facilitating environment, so that the absent object may be comfortably imagined (seen, symbolized, conceptualized, whatever) rather than urgently craved (seized). This means that there has to be a long enough absence every now and then for such crystallization to take place, but not so long an absence that the need to seize the missing object overwhelms all other experiences. Wright says that the person needs to "hold off" from the object to allow the symbol of it to form.

Wright's hypothesis is that, if mother and baby get along without too much stress, it is because the natural instincts or needs or drives have not been so urgent that getting to their satisfaction has been more important than anything else. But also, there has to have been no such overwhelming response to the first faint arousal of need at an instinctual sensory level (for sucking or whatever) that the distance between mother and baby got lost.

The next event of note comes with the introduction of a third figure, usually the father, to relate to the mother–infant dyad and to be seeing mother and baby looking at each other. When this happens, the baby gets a much more telling experience of distance and separateness, of objectivity almost. It gets a sense of a world that exists without it, a world in which there are onlookers who exist outside the dyad. Moreover, if father can look at mother-and-baby, baby can look at father-and-mother. Baby can be an onlooker, can look at important objects it cannot seize or own in the way the breast could be seized or owned. In this way, the advent of a third figure creates a space between the baby and the rest of the world, and between the baby and its cathexes, quite different from what it had previously experienced.

Also, the advent of a third person develops a new use of language. Words are the verbal clothes in which concepts and symbols are dressed; they are the "proper names" of concepts and symbols. In the primary maternal preoccupation of the

early mother–baby dyad, words were, at least at first, superflu-
ous. With the increasingly separate life of mother and baby,
words begin to help keep them together in new ways. Now that
father has appeared, communication by language becomes a
necessity for the child. Wright makes much of the associational
sequence: words–language–father–others–society–objectivity.

What with the experience of being an onlooker, and the
advent of communication in words as an important way of
relating, the young child has what Wright calls a decentring
experience: the child is able to be an onlooker at its own life, it
becomes an object to itself. The earlier lived-in structure also
becomes a looked-at structure (p. 213). There is a universe full
of planets, each of which can see itself as a centre and yet be
aware of others who see themselves as central. Objectivity.

Wright makes this shift in perspective analogous to what
Freud did for Breuer when he explained the process of transference to him. He explained that Anna O was not really in love
with Breuer, but that Breuer's care and interest had revived an
earlier relationship, which Anna had had with her father and
which she was now, as it were, reliving. Wright then looks at
the formal aspects of this shift from a more personal two-
person "seizing" to a more objective three-person "seeing"
frame of reference.

> Breuer had found himself in a two-person action frame
> with Anna O which was not the one he had intended. . . .
> Freud entered the scene as the third person with a differ-
> ent viewpoint. . . . By moving to Freud's position, seeing
> through his eyes, Breuer was able to see something about
> his interaction with Anna O that he had not been able to
> see before. He could get outside of his immediate experi-
> ence, because Freud had given him a place to stand and a
> view to see with. [Wright, 1991, p. 227]

On these foundations, Wright rests his belief that patients in
therapy, at one time or another, need two kinds of help, which
he calls the "Paternal Mode" and the "Maternal Mode". I regret
the nomenclature but for the moment will work with it.

Therapy in the Maternal Mode is reminiscent of the mother–
baby dyad when it is good. It allows patients to experience
themselves in safe happy communion with the therapist, and

all that that implies in the transference. If this goes well, there is a feeling, part well-being and part sense of self, which in Transactional Analysis is called "I'm OK, you're OK", rooted in the memories of the original contented baby with mother. Patients have an opportunity of getting in touch again with these feelings in the slow luxurious undirected exchanges and silences between them and the therapist.

> *The day that Gorbachev and Reagan*
> *met in Reykjavik,*
> *my grandson Matthew, one year old,*
> *grasping both my index fingers for support,*
> *led me into the garden;*
> *and there we sat,*
> *amid the fallen chestnut leaves,*
> *while he, engrossed,*
> *scrabbled the border tilth,*
> *discovering worlds in stones,*
> *and passing them to me*
> *for inspection, confirmation,*
> *and return.*

Peter Baynes, 1992 [unpublished]

In this process, elusive vaguely experienced pre-verbal and pre-conceptual fragments crystallize, clarify, and define themselves, and things feel right. It is out of this safe happy communion that new symbols, words, meanings, and understandings gradually emerge, of our life and of the life around us. This experience is essential to our well-being and can often be retrieved in therapy with an unhurried unworried therapist; it is of crucial benefit to people whose sense of self has been denied, crushed, or distorted. When later and clearer concepts and words get connected with this area of our experience, we are still in touch with this profound layer of our being, which Winnicott (1960, 1962) called the "True Self", and Balint (1968) the "Area of Creativity".

But this process may go wrong and the patient stay interminably in this mode. In the transference, such a patient feels fulfilled by the present relationship with the therapist and has no incentive to change, never wants anything more: seeing but never seizing. Stuck like this, a shift to the Paternal Mode is indicated.

Also stuck, though in a different way, are drive-driven patients unable to rest in any relationship, not really quite sure what relating is, and hence unable to use therapy to change. They are driven to seize. These babies want to nurse regardless of the mother. Patients in this mood do not get satisfaction from being with their therapist. Insisting on regarding therapy sessions as occasions for doing, for reassurance that they are in the right about a quarrel, or for explanations why they are not loved or rich or achieving or whatever, they feel constantly deprived. They want their cathexis.

> There is a refusal of symbols and symbol-making, because the need for some satisfaction with an actual object has become overwhelming. We could say that the mind, the space, in which the object is not, has become an empty space, not a space of (recollected) maternal presence. As a result there is an intolerance of symbolic objects, which are felt to be empty, hollow, and filled with nothingness, because they are not the thing to which they refer. [Wright, 1991, p. 288]

These patients, too, require therapy in the Paternal Mode. *Stuck patients need the Paternal Mode.* Whether they are stuck in an endless insistence on satisfaction or are basking stagnantly (not necessarily basking, actually—they could be entrenched in a hostile or nagging or scornful or any other passive relationship), Wright believes that the therapist then has, in Freud's phrase, "to struggle to keep in the psychic sphere all the impulses which the patient would like to direct into the motor sphere". In a deadlocked transference, therapists have to engage in a struggle with the patient, if necessary a confrontative one, allying themselves to that part of the patient that is willing to endure the treatment and able to "hold off": to see things rather than seize on them or insist on magic to bring about the desired result. The patient cannot at this point be left free to graze indefinitely among the free associations, but needs to be corralled and contained. The Paternal Mode is required, which involves using words and consciousness as the means to do this corralling and containing, whereby patients may eventually become onlookers at their own processes, sufficiently detached to conceptualize, verbalize, and evaluate what they are doing. However sympathetically we may enter the fray, it is with transference interpretations that we have to do so, when the time is right.

When the time is right. . . . Of course, if a person has not got a sense of self, or lacks the ego-processes to do this conceptualizing, verbalizing, evaluating, the time is not right.

> Freud is concerned with knowledge and representation—the primary aim of therapy is to know oneself, to make the unconscious conscious, to bring the word-presentation into connection with the thing-presentation . . . the aim is to see, to gain insight, to stand back and use the patterns of distanced paternal vision to organize and structure and make sense of previously disparate and unintegrated elements. It is to bring the isolated two-person elements, which are closer to live experience, into the organizing power of three-person vision. "Where id was, there ego shall be".
>
> Winnicott, on the other hand, is concerned with something more intuitive and gestational. He holds, contains, stays with, remains nearby. He tolerates those deeper movements that do their silent forming in the darkness. . . . He realizes that "light" and "seeing" and premature consciousness can be the enemy of this process: it is the *felt* joining together of things that has to precede their proclamation. . . . Insight, the seeing of forms from a distance, is here taking a second place to some more inchoate but tangible process of inner articulation, the articulation of forms the subject still inhabits. The paternal capacity to separate out patterns from the maternal matrix has to be used sparingly lest it interfere with this more spontaneous process of creation. [Wright, 1991, pp. 292–293]

With this, I am able to come to some conclusions about the proper use of transference interpretations. Their proper use helps to create and maintain particular relationships between different parts of the patient, between the patient and the therapist, and between the patient and the world "out there", a relationship called "space".

There are some dire experiences of space which a patient may want to abolish.

For instance, space may be experienced as an irrelevant nothing—it is just the frustrating thing that keeps the patient from the object in the Freudian sense (the object being "that towards which action or desire is directed", Rycroft, 1968). Space may be a delaying nuisance to object-cathexis, i.e. to getting the satisfaction you are aiming at. People experiencing space like this are like Kernberg's borderline or psychotic personalities, who have trouble containing their frustrations, anxieties, and reactions generally. In this case, the therapist has to keep pointing out that the patient is relating to the object-world (and to the therapist) in a bull-headed unthinking disorganized way, and suffering thereby from the disadvantage of being so much in a hurry that useful information and pleasant gratification are being lost as irrelevant in the rush towards satisfaction, which might explain why the patient feels thwarted and frustrated so often.

Or space may be experienced as a terrifying nothing that can take over when you are not in close contact with someone else. These experiences are very like those that Kernberg attributes particularly to the psychotic personality organization unable to maintain boundaries between self and other, so that the sense of identity and reality is easily lost. In this case, the therapist has to help the patient to endure and make sense of the pain of the terrifying nothing, both in the sessions in the transference, and in the object-world, e.g. after a loss. This the therapist does by being there, and by not being there.

On the other hand, space may be experienced as a good place where new things can happen, where people can discover the concepts and symbols that they need in order to grasp their identity and reality generally. To this end, therapists have to create an ambience where patients can discover a safe space for themselves, for their best and worst thoughts, their best and worst impulses and hopes and fears, and for the words to say it in (Cardinal, 1975). For some patients we may have to *create* a space, because they have as yet no identity and no sense of their identity—only in contact with the therapist can they gradually come to an awareness of their separate existence. For others, much the same process allows them to discover our existence (Fonagy, 1991).

Sometimes transference interpretations increase the space a patient needs for growth, sometimes they reduce it. It depends on that patient at that time. Wright comes to a very satisfactory conclusion about this.

> Therapy seems to offer the intimacy of a two-person relationship with the mother, a closeness that harks back to the first relationship with the mother, with the possibility of refinding or even improving on that earlier relationship. At the same time, it offers the constant perspective of the third person, the father, who disallows that which is longed for, and thereby creates a space for thought and for symbolizing and knowing what is lacked. [Wright, 1991, p. 298]

Patients need someone who will help them to understand themselves and to gain more control over their life, and they need someone close to them, in connection with whom they can create new forms, meanings, and understandings. They need the Paternal and Maternal Modes both, though some will lean more one way or another, at one time or another. Good therapists move flexibly in and out of whichever mode is required.

CHAPTER SEVEN

Using general concepts of structure to understand regression, transference, and the working alliance

P sychoanalytic theories have always tended towards anthropomorphic metaphors for psychic events, and towards phantasies in which parts of the mind or body are personalized to behave as you and I might behave:

The shadow of the object fell upon the ego. [Freud, 1920g]

The superego dips into the id. [(Fenichel, 1946]

The superego was to make it impossible for the child to rob her mother of the baby inside her, to injure or destroy her mother's body, as well as castrate the father. [Klein, quoted in Britton, 1989]

The infant splits off and projects its feeling of fear together with envy into the undisturbed breast. [Bion, quoted in Meltzer, 1978]

In psychic reality the vitality of an object can also be returned to it, as the body to the soul in theological terms.

Given for the Central School of Counselling and Therapy in April, 1994.

This can only be accomplished by the reparative capacity of the internal parents and their creative coitus. [Meltzer, 1973]

Some, a very few, patients talk spontaneously in this way. For myself, I have never been able to think spontaneously in such metaphors. Moreover, this kind of personalizing can be a hindrance to accurate and logical theory-building because we get misled by what we project onto the processes these metaphors are meant to represent, insofar as they derive from our ideas of human behaviour. I find it safer as well as more congenial to think less floridly, and in this chapter I experiment with ways of understanding at least some people better in terms of a conceptual framework that suits me. I am giving myself the freedom for once to describe people in my own terms, not Freud's or anyone else's, though it is clear that I am indebted to a range of writers, mainly those I relied on in *Our Need of Others.* I am also, incidentally, hoping to get away from some currently used diagnostic categories that I personally have found not to lead to useful clinical action in a reliable way. Especially the designation "borderline" seems to me not a diagnostic category. People who display "borderline" characteristics—impulsivity, intolerance of uncertainty, faulty sense of reality—do make life difficult for the therapist, but that is often all they have in common in treatment, in my experience at least. I have not found any of the current theories of borderline dynamics useful in practice, i.e. in indicating what I should do.

Psychic organization

My inclination is to think of the personality in terms of the organization of component parts or substructures. There are logical statements to be made about organization, whether it be an organization of carbon and hydrogen atoms as component substructures in the structure of a benzene molecule, or an organization of ice crystals as component substructures in the larger crystal structure of a snow flake, or an organization of people as component substructures in the structure of a barn

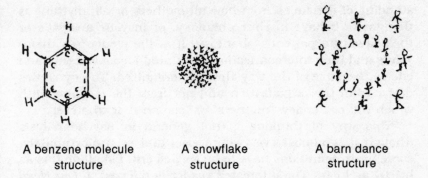

A benzene molecule
structure

A snowflake
structure

A barn dance
structure

dance. (Whether you call something a structure or a substructure depends purely on where you want to focus.)

What happens from one moment to the next in such organizations should be attributable to three factors: (1) what is the nature of the component substructures in question? (i.e. what is it in the nature of all carbon and hydrogen atoms, or all ice particles, or all dancing people to do? what are the rules they obey by virtue of what they are?); (2) what kind of structure are they in just now? (i.e. which component substructure is connected with which others?); and (3) what rules govern interconnections (i.e. what happens to component substructures as a result of their interconnections? what is transmitted through the connections?).

It is possible to think of the personality in terms of the organization of its structures and substructures, and in terms of how these structures function by affecting one another. Psychoanalytically derived theories give personalized names or intentions to these structures, but let us postpone doing this, and think for the present purely of structures following the rules that structures in general obey, by virtue of their structural characteristics: mainly that more information flows between elements in contact with each other. I have no great quarrel with you calling a particular structure "mother" or "penis" or "superego" or "claustrum", provided that my actual mother is not believed *a priori* to behave like your idea of her—in fact, provided that I am not asked to derive my understanding of dynamics from how all mothers or all anything is thought to behave in your phantasy, or in your analyst's or their favourite patient's phantasy. It is the structures them-selves and their interconnections that produce movements and effects, because of the way they are organized. The dynamics derive from the organization and not from the meaning with which you or I endow "mothers" or "claustra" or whatever.

This way of thinking is not general in psychoanalysis (though it is almost everywhere else) and so, unfortunately, some basic definitions have to be spelled out. I shall do this as briefly as I can. The interested reader is referred to *Our Need for Others* (Klein, 1987), part 1 and chapters 10 and 17, from which the present concepts are developed.

Structures

By structures or substructures of the personality I mean the organizations of memories of experiences, usually of significant events, with feelings involved and so on. These memories of experiences are the component substructures that make up the larger structures. We are of course concerned with subjec-tive memories here, of subjective experiences, which may at times bear little resemblance to what an observer with a video-camera might record. The word "phantasy" may be substituted throughout for such words as "experiences", "memories", "elements" or "structures", although the additional meaning derived from using structural concepts will be lost.

Whatever we call them, the structures connect with each other because they follow each other in temporal sequence, or because of some similarity like each involving Mr Jones or the planet Mars or whatever, or an emotional similarity like guilty pain or amorous delight. Some of these sorts of connections are more tenacious than others, perhaps on simple learning prin-ciples like frequency and recency, perhaps because of the nature or the intensity of the emotion, and also for reasons yet to be explicated.

The interconnected sets of memories of experiences serve as frameworks into which later experiences are sorted; they act as containers in which subsequent experiences are contained. They thereby provide the context in which the subsequent experiences find their meaning. This becomes important below, when regression and similar phenomena are considered.

Structures that are connected influence each other continually in a never-ending dynamic process. Through contact they adapt to each other, and they adapt each other.

Structures maintain their organization of connections to varying degrees. There are "weak" structures and "strong" ones. Some structures, "weak" ones, easily loosen their connections with the surrounding context and thus cease to be "contained" by them—a moment's lapse in attention will do it. For instance, I may decide to cut down on smoking, but in a stressful committee meeting I may have lit my tenth cigarette without remembering my decision to smoke only four a day. Other structures may be much more firmly held, such as the conviction that I must on no account break wind in public.

"Strong" structures are tightly organized ones, with many of its component substructures linked to many others, communicating with one another and capable of being used for contrast, and hence strongly able to affect how the next event is experienced. When the structures of the personality are fairly tightly organized in a strong way, we learn easily from experience because one experience evokes and affects other connected ones. Also, when the links associating our experiences are many, our sense of being an integrated personality is strong. When the structures of someone's personality are less in touch with one another, on the other hand, there is a corresponding weakness and lack of coherence, and with it a lack of the sense of being a coherent personality to whom things are

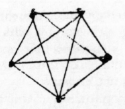

To the left:
A strong structure of five elements

Below:
a weak structure of five elements

happening here and now. The sense of being a unified person is weaker.

Ego-functioning

This, for me, is the general term that includes all the cognitive processes (as well as others, see below), both conscious and unconscious. Ego-functions enable people to register what is happening to them, now. People register information about "what is happening now" largely through their senses: *information* about heat, cold, sights, sounds, and so on. But the *meaning* that people give to "what is happening now" depends on what their previous experiences of similar situations have meant to them: "This smile means a nice surprise is coming!", "That smile means a sadistic surprise is being planned".

Classifying experiences as similar or different is an ego-function; remembering similar experiences or different ones, by comparison and contrast, is an ego-function. "Ego-functions" is the name for the processes by means of which structures are organized, i.e. given meaning: "This is how X used to smile when he . . ."; "This is how Y used to smile when he . . .". When there is a time-dimension to this, we get such processes as expecting, forecasting, anticipating, planning, steering a course (for the future), and (for the past), recalling, considering, reflecting upon, inventing, innovating, learning from.

Control by integration and/or splitting

The context into which events are organized gives them meaning and thus provides the monitoring process by which responses can be steered. In this way, structures not only contain but monitor: "When I see X smiling like *this*, I can relax"; "When I see X smiling like *that*, I must be wary."

Control and containment are in the very nature of organization. Present experiences provide a context and perspective from which a person can view past events. "I now realize that when X used to smile like this, it has always meant . . ." and, vice versa, past events provide a context in terms of which we experience the present. "I have learnt that when Y smiles like that, it always means . . .". In this way, past events have some control over how the present is experienced, and present events have some control over the past. This is how stable structures contain and monitor.

Awareness is not essential to this process, but of course in the case of conscious creatures, and self-conscious ones, our awareness of the context in which we have our moment-to-moment life is part of the monitoring by which we steer our present behaviour, and indeed our emotions and perceptions.

When one structure (of memories of experiences) cannot affect another much, we may say that there is a "split" between them, or a barrier—anyway, a something that prevents a greater degree of communication than there is. In terms of structure, splits and barriers are the means by which structures stay differentiated from one another. Of course, splits and barriers do not exist in themselves, except as absences and lacks of communication.

One way of looking at control or containment is to see it as exercised by the existence of barriers or splits between different structures, so that one set of experiences may not become, or may not stay, integrated with another, and thus not affect the other so much—less meaning will seep from the one to the other. "X and Y both smile, but I have to keep them separate in my mind because it means one thing when X does it and another when Y does it. . . ."

How would this come about? We have to remember that structures (of memories of experiences) provide the context in which we meet new experiences, come to conclusions, draw up plans. But sometimes an experience has been so painful that it holds great anxiety, which would become associated with other experiences if the impending integration with them were to take place. Then the potentially offending experience may be kept as an isolated structure and not integrated or connected with other structures. Indeed, people may fragment in order not to have to integrate something, or they may, for fear of having to do so, refuse to develop in any way whatever.

When structures are badly organized or poorly developed, they are necessarily also less differentiated. They may be childish or undiscriminating. Paranoid-like judgements may be made, as if the person had not learnt to distinguish one thing from another so that it feels as though "everyone outside the family is an enemy" or "educated people have a better understanding of life" or "children love Christmas" or "it is always better for them to be with their parents"—undifferentiated generalizations all. When structures are badly organized or poorly developed, the categories by means of which the person functions are grosser: less control is exercised by the understanding that is generated by the connections between experiences.

Faulty structures can be due to traumatic events during development, which may have distorted the normal development of a person's understanding of commonly shared realities, or they may be due to the slowing down of the normal course of increasingly refined structuring because of whatever causes low intellectual performance, or they may be due to such factors as illness, starvation, terror, or a singularly unstimulating environment.

Faulty structures can sometimes be corrected, in everyday life and/or in psychotherapy, if attention can be paid to them in a here-and-now context, and if there is enough stability in the less faulty parts of a person's psychic organization.

Clinical note

I propose now to look at some types and levels of faulty organization of structures. I shall present some faulty personality organizations as manifested by some patients I have known, directly or in supervision. Then I shall consider the working relationships and the regressions and/or the transference phenomena the therapist experienced with them. Further concepts will be adduced as they become necessary.

I shall not be sorting these patients into any generally used conceptual system; feeling intuitively that some patients shared some common factors of personality organization, and this being partly what I am trying to clarify for myself, I am presenting those who appeared to me to have something in common as possessing the same initial letter. So there are three As (Asterix, Anders, and Annie), and three Bs (Betty, Brenda, and Becky) rather less extreme in their unusual structural characteristics, and one Z, Zoe, as a contrast.

The three with the initial A are all from fairly early on in my career. I made more mistakes with them than with those who came later, mainly mistakes of impatience, but also because at times I could not bear to understand or be close to their state of mind—it is in connection with this that I admire Searles so. I knew at the time that my work was faulty—doesn't one always?—but I went on for reasons I believe worth advocating. For one thing, whatever stupidities of mine they had to suffer, at least they had a therapist, and one who was striving to do better. The As are typical of those categorized as unanalysable (or as uninteresting because the normal procedures of psychoanalytic psychotherapy could not be applied to them), and also, being really out of the ordinary and unemployable, they mostly had no money to pay a therapist. I do not think they were damaged by their experiences with me, and their successors benefited from my increasing understanding and ability to relate. These people are not so frequently seen by those who write up cases for publication, especially in connection with technique, and so the theory of technique is impoverished and falsified at certain points, because evidence from this quarter is sparse.

Confidentiality has presented more of a problem than usually. For a variety of reasons it has not been possible to ask each of these patients for permission to use my experience of them in public discussion. I have employed the usual devices to disguise them and guard their privacy. In addition, and this may be momentarily confusing to the reader, each person is described at a particular moment in the therapy, not as each is now, or as each was at the end of therapy.

Very faulty structures

"Asterix" is in early middle age and has been attending twice a week for some years. He has a wife and good friends and is intermittently employed as, let us say, a free-lance photographer and painter of phantasy-portraits that have a small but enthusiastic following. The structures of his personality are elaborate, but the links between them are often tenuous. It seems to me that they evolved to contain and manage the impact of deeply wounding threats to his safety and self-esteem at a very early age, at a narcissistic level, unfortunately in such a way that they never integrated to form a strongly organized personality with a clear unified sense of identity. He is, for instance, a well-read man, interesting to talk with, and he has sharp and intelligent reactions to what he reads. But what he reads—largely occult material and space-opera science fiction—is very much in the service of his need to both contain and yet isolate long-ago terrors and griefs, and perhaps guilts.

I doubt that he is very different outside his psychotherapy sessions from how he is within them. He does not relax in the sessions from a more organized to a less organized state—he normally lives in this fragmented way.

"Anders" is a tragic figure, more an asylum-seeker than an immigrant, still speaking English in a fashion that makes it difficult even to distinguish the words he is saying, let alone follow the sense. He has been attending once a week for some years and is now in early middle age. He would be in hospital or prison were it not for his affectionate family, which supports him emotionally and financially. Anders seems to me a Searles-type patient, behaving in a classically schizophrenic way. Though he can get about, catch the right bus, and so on, he does not really know what is happening to him: he lives a life of phantasy. Both in his therapy sessions and at other times, he is as little touched by shared reality as is possible and still stay out of major trouble. What he says to me is meaningful in that it can be understood as a weave of self-reassuring phantasies about the often distressing events of his current life, interspersed with scarcely disguised appeals for reassurance. I do not get the sense that he works *with* me.

I think Winnicott would describe Anders as characteristically unintegrated rather than disintegrated. It is less clear to me how Winnicott would describe Asterix. The difference, as I sense it, is that Anders is in many smaller bits (more structures and not many connecting links), while Asterix has rather fewer but larger structures not very much in touch with each other. I think some of Asterix's structures may never have been connected, so he is unintegrated in that sense, but he gives a more integrated impression because the chunks are larger. "Annie", the third of this trio, is rather more integrated than the other two, rather more like a typical very split personality.

"Annie" came once or twice a week for nearly three years, during her middle fifties. There were times, lasting perhaps ten minutes, when I felt we were working together, she with me, I with her, often when we discussed what another of her many previous analysts or therapists had said. She described herself as paranoid, and she certainly was touchy and quarrelsome. She was a much more strongly organized personality than Asterix and Anders, but there was nevertheless a good deal of weakness in the processes that should have linked what she was experiencing there and then with more established structures, breaks in the links that should have been giving her present experiences some containing context. To anticipate further definitions made below, her ego-structures could not contain her here-and-now life very well. But they did do so to some extent, much more than was the case for Asterix and Anders. She had a sense of herself. It was not always possible for her to see things in perspective, but it was possible quite often. And she could sometimes see herself in perspective. However, her monitoring processes often failed her, and she would then be completely absorbed in some more isolated fragment of her total personality; we might call it a regression. She would not be aware that this was happening, because of defects in ego-structure and functioning. In therapy sessions, as elsewhere, she would then suddenly (and, in my view, extravagantly) feel hurt, misunderstood, persecuted. That had always been her life. In therapy, these drifts into some isolated fragment were not predictably due to failures in tact or timing on my part. True, sometimes I precipitated a crisis by not understanding that she was not ready for what I said, or by not understanding a point she was making. But at least as often I could discern no trigger to the sudden uncontrollable deterioration.

The self as an integrative structure

There is a temptation to think of a structural approach as purely cognitive. Structures often are cognitive, but usually they are much more than that, because the elements of the structures in question are experiences, and experiences are usually not purely cognitive: sometimes they are hardly cognitive at all. There are sensations and emotions, and potentially all the contents of the id waiting to be meaningfully organized. They may be so non-cognitive as to be incapable of having words attached to them—Bollas' unthought known experiences. But usually they have at least some cognitive element to them, however little, whereby we may know them and think and talk about them.

Moreover, many if not all of our experiences include as a common element the fact that we ourselves were involved in the events (see also Stern, 1985; Klein, 1987). It is from this repeated coincidence that we derive our sense of self: "I was there . . .", "It was me . . .", "I did it . . .", "It happened to me . . .". The sense of self is a stable structure or set of sub-structures, though ever changing slightly as new information comes to us, and of course this sense of self is both cognitive and emotional, and indeed physical as well.

The more of the self is involved in a structure, the more we can call it an *ego-structure*. Because of overlappings and inter-connections, we can then speak not only of the ego-elements in various experiences, but of a set of ego-structures that together are a person's experience of himself or herself. One subset of such a set of structures would be a person's self-image, another might be an ideal self, yet another an idealized image of self. All these can exert control over people's understanding of their experiences, their life, their behaviour. Taking all the structures with an ego-element together, we have "the ego" or "the self", steering a person's responses to life.

Whereas past events in general form the context that contains and controls the experiences of the present, the ego-structures do so most particularly. They are very influential in determining when connections shall be made between past and current events, and where connections shall not be made.

The ego-structures contain, control, integrate, and *differentiate*. Just as the integrating context of past experiences provides a kind of control, so does the opposite process. Control can be achieved also by splitting or maintaining a split between structures. Splits make it possible for connections between events to be neglected and, in particular, for connections between events and the self to be neglected. Some people do not integrate what cannot be tolerated, what might damage their sense of themselves to an unbearable degree, or, for that matter, damage their preferred idea of the world they live in. "I don't believe it", they say, and they mean it literally. They have refused to integrate it. "I was not myself", "It was not me". *The Long Day's Journey into Night* is full of such disavowals.

For the sake of completeness, I should add that another way of making an unwanted event disappear is to so embed it in its context that it is no longer visible. The process is the same as that by which, in children's puzzles, at first you see only what you are supposed to see—for instance, Red Riding Hood walking through trees and bushes and flowers—but on closer inspection you can also see the outlines of a wolf, a hunter, a grandma, a gun, and so on. Other structures provided so much context as to make these things unnoticeable at first. In just the same way, some people rattle along in their thoughts or their conversations so as to conceal unacceptable items in a host of irrelevant detail. This is the process of embedding (see Klein, 1987, p. 132). Panics, some tantrums, and some "fits" serve the same function.

So the sense of self, and, even more, self-awareness, exerts an influence on the way current events are experienced. And they do so in more than one way. Control is exercised involuntarily and unconsciously by virtue of the particular interconnections between existing structures and the events currently being experienced. And it is also exercised voluntarily, intentionally, and sometimes even consciously in terms of the new experience's relative (in)compatibility with one's already existing sense of oneself.

In regression, a deterioration takes place, such that the control imposed by the way the structures relate to each other, whether by integration or differentiation, are relaxed. The self is a structure among structures. So is self-awareness. A regression occurs when awareness confines itself for the time being to one set of structures (of memories of experiences) and cuts itself off from others so completely that they are not part of people's sense of themselves. This is what Annie did. Unlike Asterix and Anders, Annie had a sufficiently "strong" personality organization for the process called regression to be perceptible to another person talking with her.

Working with Asterix, Anders, and Annie

Much as I liked them, for years I could only manage one or at most two sessions a week with people like these three. The concentration they call for is so intense, the knight's leaps of their thought often so frustrating (as well as beguiling), the agility they require if I am to stay in touch so demanding. The span of my attention has to cover their irrational processes and mine, and their way of thinking about things and mine, and this is hard. I never found a way of establishing a solid working alliance that is mutual and rational.

For instance, it is not difficult to talk with Asterix, but it is difficult to talk with him directly about himself. He loses concentration almost at once. Some of this is avoidance, of course. But I think it is also that he has left so many areas of experience out of his ego-organization (and hence out of consciousness) that almost nothing remains except abstractions. An extreme philobat, he has always avoided a coherent life, and he has no coherent image of himself, and no solid sense of identity. I have to hold on to my experience of him as a "whole object" when he has no such experience himself. I think he feels that to talk about "Asterix" is to talk about something very tenuous and, in Kohut's phrase, experience-distant (1971, p. xiv). It is much easier for him when he talks of himself in terms of what Spock does, or the Dune Messiah, or some other famous character in science fiction. When he feels threatened, which is quite often, his side of the conversation is explicitly about Spock, or whoever he has chosen as a vehicle, and he disregards whatever I am communicating when I say, "You, like

Spock, feel. . . ." I hope something reaches him where it matters when I do this, and I believe it sometimes does, but it is chancy.

I believe it is quite important not to allow him to deteriorate further—I must not behave in ways that make him fragment further or in other ways make him lose some of the controls he does have. (I think I may differ here from Little, 1981, e.g. chapter 5, and Kleinians generally.) In particular it seems to me important not to say anything that could be experienced traumatically as narcissistically wounding. My feeling is that this danger is always just under the surface. Humiliation was an extreme feature in his childhood, and probably largely accounts for his present personality-structure and processes. He tends to get defensively manic and/or drunk when, in his daily life, he encounters obstacles that undermine his sense of omnipotence. But he does not seek to damage himself, he is not self-destructive by intent. Rather, he creates situations in which he just possibly might be defeated but in which he scrapes through and triumphs. Most of his dreams are of this kind.

This sets me some tricky problems, as he often evades owning a feeling, projecting it onto a triffid or something like that instead, in order to avoid damage to his self-esteem; I fear that to press the point against these defences could make it too painful for him to stay in touch with me. Similarly, I feel that I have to be very very cautious in pressing a point which in other circumstances might help to integrate an experience (remembered but projected), if it means that he would have to recognize and accept himself in a humiliating position. I err on the soft side, since I believe that the therapy would not survive a serious blow to his self-esteem if it came from me. I am in the position of Kohut with a grandiose patient, or of a mother who admires her toddler's painting because not to do so might, at a crucial moment, destroy the nascent ability to develop further (1971, pp. 118–119).

Anders and Annie, quite as unwell as Asterix, do have some sense of identity, however illusory. I might not see them the way they see themselves, but at least we share an interest in the person under discussion.

Talking with Anders is hindered by his absolute and strongly defended lack of insight. He is highly intelligent and has read much philosophy, psychology, psychoanalysis. This enables him to couch his omnipotence in terms of "having thoroughly analysed himself"; and this he is able to use defensively to make it impossible for us to discuss what he is actually feeling. When I say, "That sounds as though I've annoyed you", he says, "No, I am not annoyed. I am beyond all that. I am never annoyed with any human being". Similarly he has said, "I do not ever miss you when you are away. I have encompassed you. I know myself so well that you are always in my mind." I am, as completely as can be imagined, purely an object in his inner life, and nothing else. Usually what I actually say has no impact. When this omnipotent organization is threatened, he does not come to the session. At first he used to cancel on the grounds of feeling too (physically) ill. Later, he would do so in terms of fearing that he might make me ill, or worried, or confused. Later again, he was sometimes able to say that he found these sessions too much of a strain.

The most I was able to do, at first, was to set boundaries that could remind him of our separate existence, and of the nature of our relationship as I saw it. He might call me his friend and, when appropriate, I might respond by saying that I was his friend, but that I was also his psychotherapist and that was why we met. But to the extent that such a message reached him at all, he would deny it, shaking his head in a sympathetic way and saying in essence, "Ah, you have to say that, but that is because you are so limited in your understanding. I know better, and soon you will know better too." In trying to get boundaries established between him and me, I was at least able always to end on time, even when it did not suit him, and indeed, this may have been the single most important factor in keeping our relationship on a reality level. It was not unusual for him to be walking out of the door still talking, while I in my chair was steadily saying, "I have to finish now, we have to finish now, our time is up now, we will have next session to look at that", and so on.

I was in charge of ending; he determined when to start. Sometimes he came quite late, at which I always expressed regret that it encroached on the time we had for working together. Sometimes he came very early; I had to change my entry-system on the days he was due, to keep this within bounds. Once he was over an hour early, knocking on the door in a quite desperate way, as though I would forever not be there, showing great relief when I let him in (fortunately I had no patient at that time), but also showing anger and hurt that I was not available to him when he thought I was. With that exception and a few similar ones, the other boundary I always kept was that I was always in my chair.

All this is very tricky to think out and manage: Do I adapt to his requirements so that I can ensure that he has his session each week, or do I stick to the allotted time, letting him forego his session when in his omnipotent confusion he comes at some other time? This is not in my view a question about how to manage the patient's manipulativeness in the transference— this state of mind does not admit of steady transference-work in my opinion. How can one attribute manipulation or motiva- tion to a person, when what is in front of one is more like a set of fragments, not under integrative control? I find myself hav- ing to choose whether to relate to this fragment or that. It therefore seems to me an urgent therapy-task to get some integration going so that there is a person to have an alliance with. I admit to a constant doubt that I am too soft, given the current climate of opinion.

Asterix was with me for many years, ever closer to living in a way that would eventually allow him to survive without support from psychotherapy. And I managed to hold on to Anders for four years—very little by Searles' standards— though there were periods of weeks at a time when he did not come because he felt he was too dangerous for me and might do me harm. I lost Annie because I treated her as more able to bear reality than she was, as events proved. I got impatient, or perhaps optimistic, several times making the mistake of destroying some phantasy that was important to her, and in this state of mind such invalidations are not forgiven. After a final false step of this kind, she was unable to contain her rage and hurt, and too fearful to believe I could cope with it, and left.

Relaxation, regression, transference, and the working alliance

A regressed state is one in which the forces that maintain the present personality organization (it will be remembered that this is the organization of structures of memories of experiences) are relaxed so that a previous personality-organization operates instead. (Why would this happen? It has to do with the strength of the ego-structures which hold the lot together—the sense of self, superego-processes, etc.) In regression, a person who at one time possessed more highly differentiated structures capable of more refined functioning, with an ego more in charge of understanding and of behaviour, finds all these in abeyance: the categories by means of which the ego functions are grosser, less control is exercised because the understanding which depends on the (now too tenuous) connections between things and the self has a less dominant influence on action and understanding.

Regressions happen, and show these characteristics, but there are also other states of mind that show these characteristics even though they are not reversions to a previous personality organization—they are just relaxations from what was a more organized structure.

In general, when the connections between structures relax, structures may come adrift. Then, some structures may be what they were years ago, before further experiences modified them—regression. Some of them may be very like the object-relationships of years ago—transference. Some may just be generally more primitive, less civilized, more extreme, less rational.

Structures may come adrift of one another for a variety of reasons ranging from misuse, through stress, to fear of knowing the connection. Bits that have come adrift will change their meaning because the context has changed, and meaning depends on context, or, to put it a different way, bits that have come adrift will change their meaning because the structures that control/contain a structure cannot operate when a structure is adrift. So a structure that is adrift is less controlled by reality or moral/social influences, because it is less controlled by influences of any kind.

Transference manifestations can be controllable, as can regression and similar phenomena, if the person is able to relax his or her hold at will and is able to recover control at will. Both regressions and transference phenomena can be therapeutic in the consulting-room, but it is clear that they must be controlled, either by the patient or by the patient with the help of the therapist.

This brings us to the central dilemma for therapists working with the people with certain kinds of faulty structures. We are trained to encourage patients to relax in therapy, at least to an extent that enables them to say aloud, in an uncritical spirit, whatever comes to mind. But we also speak with our patients at a more realistic rational level about what they have heard themselves saying. These two states of mind, relaxed and thoughtful, are by no means always compatible with each other. Only people with quite a bit of ego-control can switch levels at will or split the ego at will.

The working alliance is a complex interpersonal process which enables patient and therapist to talk reasonably with one another about what is happening at less rational levels. Talking like this requires controlled splitting of the ego, and controlled fusions of splits. One way of looking at some of the effects of differences in the organization of structures is to consider the different experiences they provide of transference, regression, and working relationship in therapy. Asterix, Anders, and Annie, for instance, were so fragmented that alliance with them was rarely possible, and, though it was possible and sometimes useful for the therapist to state what she believed to be just then the patient's feelings towards her, no more than that could be done by way of transference work. The patients discussed next were not nearly so fragmented, and it will be interesting to look at the faults in their personality structures, relating these to the working partnership the therapist was able to make with each, and how this affected transference work.

But, first, to stabilize our perspective, let us look at Zoe, who reminds us what it is to work with someone who does not present us with such problems.

Working with Zoe

Working with Zoe was relatively straightforward. She was enough in charge of herself to be able to cooperate with her therapist. In her twenties, she attended three or four times a week for some years. She was a well-organized personality, and her regressive moves were almost entirely under her control, so that she usually moved easily in and out of them. She had been very pleased to hear the therapist say, at the start of their work together, that while regressions antagonized people when indulged in the world of work or friendship, they do not do so in the consulting-room. At first deeply ashamed of her need to regress, within months she was usually able to contain it within the consulting-room and to be at whatever level her material required. Regressed or not, the therapist normally had the sense that they were working together.

She was afflicted with what Winnicott called premature ego-development (e.g. 1958, pp. 183, 281). She had had to grow up too fast, and had become very ambivalent about child-like behaviour. In therapy, she soon discovered the relief of regressing: raging, crying, thumping her fist. At first she felt it necessary to come momentarily out of these spells to tell the therapist not to be worried: she just needed to express herself this way. She hardly ever lost the therapeutic alliance entirely, although it was clear that there was a large transferential element to it. But she knew that she was intentionally letting some of her control go, and she made sure the therapist understood too. Her self—in Winnicott's sense of True Self—was at first mainly this regressed expressive uncontrolled child-like state, and her sense of self belonged largely to these experiences. Her reasonable adult way of being she experienced as alien and imposed on her. This split could heal to the extent that she could trust her therapist to be willing to be in touch with both sides. She eventually experienced herself as not rejected in her regressed states, which were, to her, her real self, but which she believed to be unacceptable to others.

Although she felt the child-like side to be wrong, she did not want to lose it or be taken from it prematurely. She had deep prejudices against adult ways of being. Whenever the therapy moved prematurely into the rational therapeutic-alliance mode to discuss what had been happening, i.e. before she felt ready for it, she was able to say "shut up" with much force but little lasting resentment. There came to be enough adult structure to give such episodes an air of playfulness and, sometimes, when resentment was stronger, of play-acting. On a later occasion, when she had had to govern herself in a very disciplined way at work, she came in and said "Today I am going to do analysis"— her word for the work done in these regressed states—and without a pause relaxed into loud sobs and rages. At the end of the session, she got up in quite a collected way and said she felt better. She was able to manage her regressions. The clinical problem she set the therapist was the much more usual one of when to permit the relaxations to continue unchecked, and when to analyse them.

Working with Betty, Becky, and Brenda

"Betty", in early middle age, had been attending three times a week for some years. She had been leading a busy and constructive life, more or less entirely out of touch with the roots of her feelings. Thus she was able to be angry and hurt when snubbed, for instance, or when deprived, but all she could do with it was to regard the other person as a horrible person. For the first two years of therapy, she seemed to have no cognitive access to more regressed states of being and seemed incapable of gaining insight into her feelings at any depth. She never acknowledged any connections between what was happening here-and-now and what had happened in the past or elsewhere, staying firmly at a matter-of-fact level. She could remember, and give an account of and discuss, past and present events, but she never gave me the sense that she was in touch with these events. She was unconscious of being unusual in this.

It was plain that her sense of self was only tenuously connected to her memories or to current experiences. It was a self that was capable of happiness and suffering, and of running the practicalities of life, but the connections with other structures were very selective, thin, and poor.

Betty considered we were working together, but in fact there was no working alliance. Often she did not even hear what I said. She would bring me stories of what she had done and what other people had done or said, and what she therefore had done, but that they . . . etc. etc. Sometimes she made statements about other people's motivation, but very rarely about her own. She would produce material: "My aunt brought the children chocolate again", but she ignored anything I said that was not directly about the actual aunt, the actual children, the actual chocolate. She knew too little about feelings to realize that what was between us was no more than what she felt for the ticket collector she showed her railcard to. I commented on feelings, experiences, projections, transferences, but the level at which she received my comments was shallow—I had little chance of reaching into those areas, persecutory and manipulative, from which they presumably often came. This is where I got stuck. At best, if something I said did touch her, she would react by resolving to alter her behaviour so as not to offend again—this was her barely unconscious idea of therapy.

It all felt very distancing and defensive, but as we had no foundation or context or relationship in which this distance and defensiveness could have a useful meaning, there was not much use in saying so. So it seemed to me that my first task was to establish a relationship in which she could trust herself and me to be more in touch with deeper layers of experience.

The way through came via a series of explosive quarrels. At last, it became possible to work usefully with the transference. Childhood feelings of not being attended to broke through into consciousness and changed her relationship to me. She began to have to cope with her awareness of her own vulnerability and her awareness that I knew about it now. So she had the choice of trusting me with her vulnerability or leaving therapy. She chose to stay. All this deepened the relationship and made it count for more. Her stately façade gradually crumbled, until one day the tears were not angry but unhappy ones. But it was to be another eighteen months before she was able to come to a session explicitly to talk about herself—her thoughts and feelings and motives—and to want to explore herself with me.

"Becky", already mentioned in the previous chapter, seems to me to be presenting similar difficulties. Rather like Zoe, she needed to regress and was deeply ashamed of the need. And like Betty, she was unaware of any strong need to do so. Very interestingly, she deduced from her reading that regression and transference are processes that happen in worth-while therapies, and naturally she wanted to experience them. But she could not get to the relaxed states of mind that she consciously intended. Her life had left her with many grievances, and much of the time she felt she would be a much better patient if the therapist would behave like her idea of a therapist. One of her grievances was that she had to tell the therapist where he was going wrong and what they had better do next. This was her idea of the therapeutic alliance, and it does overlap with the genuine article. Becky was not at that time able to recognize the transferential element in all this— a grief-stricken transference in which she was inadequately cared for. To put this a different way, she did not know that her relationship with the therapist was often regressed.

Nevertheless, I had the sense that she did try to work with the therapist at a level that counts.

"Brenda", middle-aged but very immature, had been coming twice a week for six months. Like Asterix, she had strong structures, with rather tenuous links associating the various clusters of experience. But whereas Asterix's structures were very much in the service of narcissistic security and were generally very much involved with id-impulses, Brenda's universe was one of object-relations. One might say too much so. She desperately needed her objects in order to feel secure—even, to feel she existed—an extreme ocnophil to match Asterix's extreme philobat. Neither of them was much affected by reality-considerations, in therapy or in everyday life. Similarly, the more important emotional relationships of both were generally at a fairly disorganized level. No alliance was possible with people who usually operate at these levels.

Like Becky, Brenda took the working alliance into the transference, but in a different way. She could distinguish between experiencing and talking about an experience—a distinction the working alliance requires. However, although she seemed to herself to be talking to me about her feelings because I was a psychotherapist who could help her sort them out, she secretly maintained another figure—Josephine Klein the magician— who remained unchanged and isolated as an indispensable figure in her inner life. She could discuss and understand and agree that she regarded me as a magician who could make her better today if I chose to do so, and she could talk with me about this quite sensibly. This might look like a working alliance, but her disappointment, and her anger that I had not made her better yet, was most of the time untouched by what might have looked like her insight into how she used me. In the same way, she could tell me that at times I was, as it were, her mother (bad, possessive, mad, but willing to make efforts for her welfare when Brenda had been a good girl), at times her pal (good to Brenda), at times her previous therapist (well-meaning but inept and eventually treacherous like her sister). She could talk about this in detail and with affect and insight, but not to much purpose as far as any abatement of her confusion and distress was concerned. Deep down I was still the recalcitrant magician. In sum, there appeared to be a therapeutic alliance, but her consciousness of her self and me in therapy was not linked with the unconscious structures in which I remained her magician. I thought at the time that she lacked the ego-strength to allow these structures to be integrated, and this was of course true. But I now think also that I did not sufficiently appreciate how much I-as-a-magician was directly rooted in very primitive experiences of infant with mother. Just my proper understanding and acceptance of this might have helped her feel sufficiently contained to carry on, held, as it were, by an inadequate but willing magician. In that case, her acceptance of my inadequacy might have facilitated the development of such ego-processes as would have enabled her finally to shift for herself.

Conclusions

What conclusions do I draw, or at least draw towards?

Since the early days of psychoanalysis, there has been an interest in techniques that enable people to regress, i.e. to relax the existing organization of their psychic structures. But, as Balint (1968) pointed out decades ago, it is not always safe to encourage this.

A person's present personality organization contains almost certainly some agonizing sub-structures, encapsulated or embedded at some previous time so as to avoid a feared catastrophe. If it is now decided to breach that protection, there has to be a change in the way the present structures relate to one another. The techniques of psychotherapy encourage such a relaxation of the structures' present interconnections. But the therapist has to be cautious. For the knowledge locked up in the hidden structure was, after all, hidden because it was unbearable at the time. Is the person strong enough now to confront it? Is there enough support, within and around? If not, such confrontations result not in proper integration but in greater anguish, fear and defensiveness, and, as the Gospel warns us in the matter of casting out devils, the latter state may be worse than the former. We should not meddle thoughtlessly, or "because it is there", lest worse befall. This is true of regressions, transference, and whatever other relaxations of structure there may be (as in uncontrolled encounter groups and other such).

What should therapists have to look for, then, in considering whether to encourage people to let go of their sense of reality and all the processes by which they hold their present structures in place? We have to look for the right kinds of differentiations, which allow for good ego-functioning, and for benign splits—i.e. we have to look for structural characteristics that by virtue of appropriate differentiation allow sub-structures to be connected for ease of comparison, contrast, and change of focus. We have to look for evidence that the person has a self and can differentiate between different kinds of reality. Specifically:

1. We have to be sure that the patient can move relatively easily between current commonly shared realities and the past, and between commonly shared realities and private phantasies.

2. Equally obviously, and related to the first point, we have to be sure that the patient can usually distinguish between self and others, and particularly between the self and the therapist as an independent object not simply a figment of

the patient's phantasy-life. Can the patient distinguish the therapist in the role of interpreter of the transference, as not quite the same as the therapist experienced in the transference?

3. Related to these two considerations, there has to be a standpoint from which patients can consider their experiences with some objectivity (Britton, 1989, Wright, 1991). Patients have to be both object and subject to themselves. They must be able not only to talk to themselves, but also to converse with someone else about themselves. Without this no working alliance is possible.

4. There has to be containment. Just as at first the parents hold the not-yet-organized vulnerable infant, so, in certain circumstances, in a parallel kind of benevolence, must the therapist hold the patient. And in just the same way, children and patients must be helped to evolve their own holding organization eventually. For this, they need:

5. ample experience of having been held,

6. sound self-esteem,

7. a sense that the object-world cannot be wholly controlled but is not wholly hostile, and

8. a proper use of ego-functioning: thought, reflection, memory, foresight, comparison, contrast, objectivity, logic even.

In my view, only Zoe fits into the category of someone who safely and usefully regressed almost from the start of therapy. Betty, Becky, and Brenda had ego-functioning, but it had developed rigidly in the service of defending a vulnerable infant-state, to protect it but not to integrate it. Their ego-functioning was limited in that though it enabled a working alliance to exist at times, there were too many areas inaccessible to it.

Betty and Becky were conscious of no problems about protecting their vulnerable selves, since they did not know they had them. Their sense of self resided mainly in their limited ego-structures and functions. Their therapists' dilemma was that these patients' main transferences kept them from accepting the kind of help they needed to build up the ego-strength they needed to understand their transference. For the therapy to work in a traditional way, ego-functioning selves were needed to help the patients hold and contain the vulnerable feelings which had been so anxiously isolated. The transferences were defensive and, in the short run, advantageous in that they kept up what ego-strength the patients had—they might have collapsed if they had let their defences go. But the transferences also prevented them from hearing much that their therapists were trying to say. The therapists could only trust to luck, and hope that the goodwill that was in them would get through eventually. And I think this did in fact happen with Becky and Betty. Real contact was eventually made, genuine trust established, not just some cerebral caricature of relationship, which was all they could manage to start with. Until this trust becomes available, no work could be done which involved deeper feelings.

Brenda, on the other hand—a war-time baby sent hither and thither, later an incest-victim—did know and fear her vulnerability. But she had had to show compliance to an extent that had interfered gravely with the development of good ego-organization and functioning, since she must never show what she called "defiance"—evidence of her own strength. Being helpless and doing what she was told had been her safest option. Unlike Betty and Becky, she was in touch with her infantile self and even, at times, from that position, expected me to take care of her, though usually only when she had been good and compliant with my demands. Unfortunately, she prematurely got hold of the idea that therapy would help her to take care of herself, and attributed that to me as my inexorable requirement, with extreme fear. To this figment she reacted: yes, she ought to take care of herself and ought not to depend on me—but she was also sure that she could not and should not. Neither my interpretations nor my explanations were able to reach her.

Brenda's regression was a malignant one from before she came to me. I did not encourage it; she came with it. But I was slow to recognize what was going on. She had a reasonably well-organized psychic organization, more than Annie, and much more than Anders or Asterix. I ought to have been able to hold her. I failed with her, as I did with Anders and Annie, who also left prematurely, because of the absence of those structures that could contain the notion of me as a safe person for them and as safe from them, and I was unable to get these notions across to them. I think Searles would have held them until the appropriate structures could operate. It takes a long time for this to happen, and it is taking me a long time to approximate to him.

CHAPTER EIGHT

Early attachments
and sources of later well-being

A utistic objects are small hard things—keys, pebbles, pencil stubs—which an autistic child might clutch in the hand to "shut out menaces which threaten bodily attack and ultimate annihilation" (Tustin, 1981, p. 100). The physical sensation of hardness in the hand somehow gives the child a sense of hardness interposing between itself and its fears of annihilation. On what I think must be the same principle, mothers-to-be used to be instructed to learn a piece of music and drum their fingers to its rhythms in order to interpose these sensations between their central awareness and the pains of labour. I know I use crossword puzzles to create a barrier between myself and unwelcome incursions from outside or inside. I wonder if people use Walkmans for the same purpose?

A version of a paper published in *Winnicott Studies, Volume 4* (1989), in honour of the Life and Work of Frances Tustin, under the title "The Vestiges of Our Early Attachments Become the Rudiments of Our Later Well-Being".

Looking for a topic in honour of Frances Tustin, I have taken these thoughts a bit further. What makes a person feel secure/safe/contented/integrated and generally all right? What resources do people have as an aid or refuge, talisman, or touchstone, when they feel their well-being threatened? When in danger of falling apart, people have recourse to something that will help re-integrate, re-establish or safely contain the bits which are about to lose their form and structure. What is it they use? Sometimes it is an actual hard object. What is it when it is not that? What good resources are we born with and continue with if things go well with us? And to what can we have recourse should we lack or lose some of our natural sources of well-being?

It is the purpose of this chapter to explore these questions, keeping in mind that the answers to them cannot be asserted but have to be discovered in each individual case, and to look tentatively at some individual cases.

I used to believe that the sense of well-being was rooted in an early merged or symbiotic state, that infants started with an experience of symbiosis with mother, and that there was a gradual separating-out in the baby's experience of what is baby and what is mother. Influenced by recent more empirical studies of infant development (Stern, Murray, Trevarthen), I have come to believe that though the infant may be confused about what-it-is-doing and what-mother-is-doing and where the boundaries are, a prolonged experience of being merged and unseparate is atypical of normal development. The problem with this belief is that it leaves unexplained the undeniable existence of such sources of well-being as the sense of mystical union, oceanic feeling, oneness with nature or in sex, and so on, reported by many and attributed either to the Goodness of an Outside Agency or to the original experience with a good mother. In a seminar with friends, debating this problem, we came to the hypothesis that there might be a moment, around birth, when the infant was physically so much part of the mother as still to be experiencing itself as a part of her, yet already separate enough to have a psyche of its own with which to do the experiencing and retain the (pre-conceptual) memory of that state. At the point of the physical separation of the mother and infant, at the latest, the sense of two-ness and individuation must have started. But, for a timeless moment, there may have been state in which one-ness and two-ness were experienced simultaneously or nearly so. This may be the clue to the sense of timelessness that many people have at exalted moments later in life. The experience of timelessness may also have misled some people, myself included, into believing the pre-individual period to be a prolonged one. In this prolonged period, the infant can then be assumed to be bobbing in and out of the merged state until complete individuation is achieved. I now believe this period is not lengthy. But of course "eternity" is not lengthy either: it is a state in which there is no time, no experience of the passage of time. Remembering this, it is possible to allow later experiences of one-ness to have that single moment as their forerunner.

Attachment and identity as sources of well-being

It is my belief that, in general, our continuing sense of well-being depends most on good experiences with our earliest attachments. Next in importance is how those experiences may be transformed by what happens in the early stages of individuation, and next in importance is what happens after that. In the most fortunate cases, the experience of attachment becomes the major source of well-being later. But developmental deficiencies or external disaster may impair what might otherwise have been happy memories of attachment, and then the sense of well-being has to derive from something other than those early events.

It is of cardinal significance that our first experiences, before the light of awareness illuminates our world, are experiences of attachment. The need for attachments evolved as something favouring the survival of the species. Read Bowlby. All our lives we make attachments and lose them, yearn for them, dread them, fight them or fight for them.

There is a great variety of physical attachments in early life, each presumably with an emotionally experienced counterpart:

in the womb umbilically, in arms, mouth-to-nipple, locked in loving eye-contact, and so on. There are also all kinds of separations: from the womb, from the warm familiar skin, from the exciting or lulling nipple, from borborygmae and lullabies, sights, sounds, sensations. Many writers on this topic, including Tustin at times, tend to see our experience of the nipple in the mouth as the prototype of all later attachments, and also as the prototype of the devastating absence of attachment: no nipple or bad nipple. I think it safer not to be so mono-causal. Our individual experiences of attachment have been unique, depending on what happened within our experiencing bodies, with mother, with hospital, with home and family. For some of us, attachment is essentially a mouth-to-nipple one, and thereafter for us the only meaningful metaphor to use for attachment experiences in the consulting-room. For others, however, attachment brings associations of being securely held like a warm parcel . . . or of being rocked and stroked . . . or of having our physical wants anticipated and satisfied . . . or of someone who processes life for us and protects us from the suddenness of what may happen . . . and so on.

This chapter will not pay much regard to the more painful experiences of attachment and separation, of being trapped or lost or tantalized in a relationship, helplessly dependent on a tormentor, or dropped like a stone. The focus will be on that positive aspect of our early attachment-experiences which left us with a sense of the goodness of things—which gave us a sense of well-being then and can do so now. In healthy development, a process of physical and psychic individuation separates the infant from the mother. When things go well, the pain of this loss is accompanied by the joy of the possibilities that have become available because of this loss: the joy that I am I, that you are you, and that we love each other. Of course, in psychotherapy we tend to be confronted mostly with the pain of separation, and with the pain of all that can go wrong between people. But for the present purpose the focus is on our sense that life is worthwhile and that we are worthwhile.

When things have gone well during the process of individuation, memories survive of the well-being experienced in those early days. According to the extent to which separation has gone wrong, those memories are tainted or even overwhelmed by shock and pain. In fortunate circumstances, the memory-traces of the good feelings from the earlier states remain available, and they colour one's later experiences of oneself and one's attachments. When things have gone well, the processes of individuation and separation have taken place gradually and tactfully: the gratifying experience of secure attachment has gradually differentiated and begun to show a particular structure with recognizable features: it has turned into an object-relationship with an "I", a "thou", and a potential space between the two. If all has gone well, my sense of well-being is coloured by all three of these features: my experience of myself is gratifying, so is my experience of the world of other people and things, and so is my experience of what is possible between us.

To the extent that good feelings from the attached state are now associated with my emerging sense of self, I can bear to be myself. I have an identity I care to know about and be in touch with. If my early attachments did not make me feel good, or the individuation went wrong, I may not like myself well enough to have a continuing sense of well-being just from being who I am.

Symmetrically, to the extent that the early good feelings also remained attached to my experience of the object-world, i.e. the world of other people and things, to that extent those good memories now keep me attached to that good world. Without a sufficiency of those good feelings, we emerge into a world where people and things are alien and terrible.

Summing up so far, then: after individuation each person is left with a pleasant or unpleasant but always unique sense of self, and a pleasant or unpleasant but always unique sense of the world of other people and things. How pleasant or unpleasant, and on what occasions, is determined by the early attachment experiences and by the experiences of separation/individuation. *The vestiges of our early attachments thus become the rudiments of our subsequent sense of well-being.* I think this is the point at which Tustin's button is almost visible to our eyes, buttoning the past to the present, our experience of self to our experience of people and things. If that button is defective, there can be the most dreadful hole, gap, or discontinuity. Something will be wrong with the sense of well-being that is potential within us. Our great source of well-being, if all goes well, is a sense that very little can go seriously wrong with us—based on the memory that very little did.

Sources of well-being come in great variety. A familiar one is the primitive narcissistic "I'm fine, loveable, don't have to earn love or understanding, don't have to prove anything, nothing disastrous can happen to me, and all just because I am me". The recognition of this kind of narcissism dates back at least 75 years to Freud's distinction between the narcissistic and the object-related (1914c). (The concept of a more defensive secondary narcissism goes back to 1927.) There is a great variety of object-related sources of well-being—some to do with whole objects, some to do with part-objects—a distinction that goes back at least to Abraham (1924). Some more phenomenal frequently used resources are:

- the mouth–nipple experience in smoking, drinking, kissing, eating
- masturbating
- getting oneself comforted by someone after distress
- getting oneself praised
- reminding oneself of good things done or had in the past
- reminding oneself of good things to come
- contemplating one's self-image accurate or idealized
- attaching oneself to another person or getting them attached to oneself
- getting someone who will listen well enough to recreate the early attachment experience

The list is endless and endlessly varied. More examples at the end of this chapter, in the context of other characteristics a person may possess.

Some related concepts in the existing literature

Finding new resources after separation has gone wrong

Winnicott (1960) conceived of a process by which a person gets cut off from the biologically based sources of satisfaction characteristic of what he called the "True Self". Such a person has to make do with the gratifications on which the False Self rests, which are crucially dependent on the good-will of other people; indeed, other people's good-will may afford more gratification than anything else does. He based his ideas on his observation of the mother and baby at the first stage of object-relations development (Winnicott, 1965, p. 145).

Balint (1959) also interested himself in that moment during the process of individuation/separation when much of a person's relation to the object-world is determined. After that moment, the person either prefers to hold on to the object from which separation must now be acknowledged—the ocnophil— or the person prefers not to be attached to the world of people—the philobat (see also Klein, 1987, chapter 7). After individuation, ocnophils derive their sense of well-being more from their attachments to other people and things, while philobats derive their sense of well-being more from the times when they are free of personal attachments. The former cling in times of distress; the latter go off on their own.

Balint, like Winnicott, saw that when people are cut off from their roots, they have to begin again. The way he put it is that an early trauma can create a land-slip in the mind, a "Basic Fault", where there is a break in those memories that connect us to our earliest attachments from which our first experiences of well-being derive. Once this discontinuity exists, we have to try and get our sense of well-being from other sources than those for which a beneficent early attachment is the prototype. We get it from later substitutes as a way of making the best of things. We have to make "a fresh start" (Balint, 1968).

Kohut (1977, p. 83 and *passim*) has somewhat the same process in mind when he writes of compensatory structures such as achievements, skills, and talents, which the child develops to make up for what would otherwise be a weak place in its self-esteem (see also Klein, 1987, pp. 218–227).

Hanging on to what remains
of early attachment resources

During the process of individuation, some experiences evolve which relate the self to the world of others, and which may hinder, maintain, or further the emerging individual's integration. Winnicott's concept of *the transitional object* refers to one such experience: the developing child clings to something that represents what were once non-symbolic experiences of attachment to whoever was the source of its well-being (1951). At much the same time, Balint was rather slyly pointing out that even the most determined philobats have to cling to something—the tight-rope walkers to their equilibrating poles, skiers to their ski-poles, and so on: *philobatic objects* (Balint, 1959). A little later, Frances Tustin came to understand the function of the small hard things that the autistic child clenches in its fist to give itself the sensation of hardness which it can imagine as surrounding and protecting it: *the autistic object* (1974). Recently Bollas (1987) has been writing of *the transformational object*, which provides an experience of being changed for the better, or of our situation being changed for the better, because the transformational object is there, enabling that good change to take place: initially of course this would have been the adult who understood and organized our as yet unintegrated processes.

Objects? Processes? Relationships?
Anyway, sources of well-being

The phenomena here being discussed are in my view more easily thought of as "processes" than in the sometimes inconvenient language of "objects". Bollas too has found this to be so. Within 400 words of the start of his chapter on transformational objects, he is warning us that this object is less an object than a process. The word "object" fits these very early phenomena so uneasily because the individuation has often not gone far enough to allow us to speak of subject- and object-world. At these stages, as those who work with very disturbed states of mind know, it is not always clear whether subject, object, or the relation between the two is under discussion. By the same token, it cannot always be determined whether the source of well-being is rooted in the subject or in the object-relationship.

To conclude, all these objects, relationships, or processes—transformational, transitional, autistic, philobat, ocnophilic, compensatory, or indeed masturbatory, delusional, bizarre, or whatever—all can be sources of well-being; they can all be resources to fall back on. The function of all of them is to allow us to turn to them when, in confusion, depression, or anxiety, we ask "Am I all right?" . . . "Where am I?" . . . "Can I survive?" . . . "What have I to live for?"

Some clinical implications

Sources of well-being
as manifested in the transference

Because of the way psychodynamic theory has developed, some kinds of attachments, and hence some sources of well-being, are more easily recognized than others. Oral dependence and greed, and the reaction against it, and the whole set of attachments whose prototype is mouth-round-nipple, have been thoroughly explored in psychodynamic literature. The terror of and the need for separateness has also had a good deal of attention. So has the need to control the other lest there be a wrong (feared) kind of attachment or a feared kind of separateness.

Patients who wish for an attachment whose prototype is being lulled and rocked were, at least until quite recently, regarded with disapproval in many case-discussions at which I have been present. They have tended to be regarded as showing resistance or a kind of laziness during which no therapeutic work can take place. Yet, as Balint (1968, chapter 24) pointed out 20 years ago, in the consulting-room it may be necessary to allow people to regress to a time before the trauma, when attachment was experienced as a happy and harmonious thing, now re-experienced in the transference. Similarly out of favour has been the type of attachment that manifests itself as a wish for recognition. The prototype for this kind of attachment is the memory of (not) having one's needs understood, of having to ask for it, work for it, or deserve it. This kind of positive attachment is one of the things we rely on in psychotherapy, to keep our patients coming when the material does not lend itself to any very discernible progress in the removal of the symptoms. Like the wish for attachment whose prototype is being lulled and rocked, it has not always been utilized as a transference phenomenon of a useful kind and has sometimes been seen as a wish to avoid working with unconscious material—for a therapist to go along with it has tended to be seen as a lapse into counselling, a falling-away from psychoanalytically based psychotherapy.

Non-personal transferential ways of relating to the therapist and others

Some interesting consequences follow from the assumption many of us make, I think rightly, that the best kinds of well-being depend on continuity of experience from our biological roots onwards without a break. However, I think that I, and perhaps others, have unwittingly devalued the resources used by those who have suffered major breaks in continuity; we have only to introspect on our associations to the term False Self to be in touch with this unconscious devaluation. Yet, to make a fresh start when one's emergent self has been wiped out by trauma is a creative act and deserves respect.

Such fresh starts may tend to the clinging ocnophil extreme or to the detached philobat extreme. Again I think that I, and perhaps others, have tended to undervalue especially the more philobat sources of well-being. I am thinking of people who go in for maths, jazz, long-distance running, and other more impersonal gratifications (viz. Sillitoe, 1959). I think also that people who incline to person-based fresh starts may have an easier time in the consulting-room than those who incline to the non-personal philobatic, whose transference has been less easily recognized as having positive aspects. In general, I think some of us may have been at fault, clinically, in trying to bring some people to a more intimate here-and-now situation than was in fact emotionally available to them just then, interpreting as evasive or as intellectualizing their efforts to use the resources that, under pressure, were in fact all they had to fall back on—art, philosophy, politics, or obsessive interests in the details of life. H. F. Searles had much to say on this in his *Nonhuman Environment in Normal Development and in Schizophrenia*, as early as 1960.

Can the sources of a person's sense of well-being be changed by psychotherapy?

I think the answer must be "in principle yes, in a sense". I do not think that one's deepest sources of well-being can change. Structures as basic as one's first experiences of well-being are unlikely to be shifted from their central place in the psyche. But I think that changes are possible in the extent to which a person is able to turn these sources into usable resources. I am supported in this belief by having seen people change, without benefit of psychotherapy, through chance events that changed their environment. A new environment can sometimes stimulate people to use what is now for the first time perceived as possible, and to elaborate it in directions that lead to a greater range of opportunities, these opportunities in turn lending themselves to further benign developments. I have seen people coming to reorganize their priorities in creative directions, or coming to recognize and seize opportunities for growth not previously visible or available to them: refugees, immigrants, army conscripts, even college students away from home. A major upheaval seems usually required.

However, if this is to happen in the course of psychotherapy, we would need to take a very long time-span into account. A systematic account of successes in this field remains to be written. Searles and Frieda Fromm-Reichmann, Balint and Little and Winnicott, among others, have things to contribute. Some patients may need to regress to very early states of mind for longish periods before they can stabilize in a fresh start. When therapists allow themselves to be used as the particular source of well-being (and of course of suffering) that such patients started with, that attachment, that state of mind

will be reproduced in the transference. Then, after a considerable amount of latitude has been given and after the patient is
out of the regression that accompanies these recapitulations, it
often seems possible to look at what happened and discuss the
ways in which the patient's capacity for getting the best out of
life was impaired by unexpressed split-off fear of grief, pain,
protest, rage, or spite.

If only there were more therapists available to do this ex-
pensive work, and if only it were available on the National
Health, moreover. I think society is the poorer for the loss
of talent buried in many a psyche. It has at times struck me
that some of the patients in question here, just because they
have been so long deprived of more bodily or socially based
gratifications, have developed other talents and skills, in the
performance-arts, in writing or painting or philosophy, which
are not properly utilized because of the depressions and anxieties that beset them.

Is work with patients in general illuminated by this way of thinking?

I took a cursory look at some of my patients from the point
of view explored in this chapter. Of the first six I thought of,
the stories of five were illuminating. The sixth was not, and,
on looking further, some others were not, but so what? Not
everyone is best perceived in the same light. It is, however,
interesting that the six I first thought of had more narcissistic
streaks in their personalities than the others seemed to me to
have, and that the five I describe in greater detail below were
people who—besides capitalizing on whatever direct simple
physical gratifications had been left undamaged by early distresses—tended to derive a good deal of their sense of
well-being and identity from more adult compensatory structures, mainly in work.

These five had all suffered severe narcissistic damage in the
early years. Of these, "Gerda" was exceptional in having had
loving and responsive parents. Of the remaining four, "Rose"
and "Frank" had very hostile mothers and no fathers, while
"Beth" and "Ken" had mothers who were emotionally distant or

absent, "Beth" with an inconsistent and impulsive very auto-
cratic father, "Ken" with a hostile and violent one.

Ken and Frank had in common very similar experiences in
their early years, of being neglected and crushed; this had kept
them from developing much awareness of feeling or thinking.
Both were timid adults: they tended to respond passively in
order to keep out of trouble. The ego was as little developed as
could be while still within the normal range. Both had one lively
living region—the penis—and this had always been their main
source of well-being. It makes me wonder whether the easy
availability of this source of well-being, so much more obviously available than the female equivalent, accounts for the
lesser frequency of depression in men. Both made ample use of
their penis, though neither could trust it to another person.
Neither smoked. Both liked being hugged. Both had split off
their anger and were unaware of it at the start of their therapy.
Progress, in the face of such deficient ego-functioning and self-
esteem, was slow but eventually rewarding.

Frank's mother had been floridly schizophrenic in behaviour all his life, with many bizarre ideas about Frank. He had
been in a number of residential homes, always a social isolate.
He over-ate and was somewhat overweight, and was a compulsive masturbator—the source of well-being of many a neglected
child. He frequently used minor obsessional rituals to contain
his anxieties and restore his equilibrium—one could not call it
well-being. He coped with threatening anxieties by thinking
about machines, mainly war-planes and tanks.

Frank was one of those to whom a major change came as a
blessing. Out of the blue, in his late twenties, while still living
with his peculiar mother, he had his first stroke of luck. He
made a loving relationship with a young woman, based on
mutual idealization and mutual need: her need to find someone
to love and care for, his need to give love to a caring woman,
although at first he did not know how to do that in a practical
way, such as by sharing thoughts or by doing little things for
her. She encouraged him to consider therapy. Therapy on a
once- or twice-a-week basis was difficult for him. The therapist
was at first experienced as an authoritarian giver-and-with-
holder who had to be placated, later as a nice well-intentioned
but rather boundariless woman like his girl-friend. He became

very trusting; he now had two nice people to relate to—perhaps the first two in his life—two auxiliary ego-functioners. With his girl-friend's (later his wife's) encouragement, he got into a technical college, where he did well and developed skills that gave him self-respect, and this he was able to maintain throughout a longish period of unemployment. His potency improved. Looking after his wife, when she did not feel too well emotionally, added to his sense of having a good self. He began to relate to other people as an equal and to size them up with a common sense that had hitherto been quite unavailable. Unique in my experience, all his resources, all his sources of well-being, seemed to be rooted in his current relationships—very fragile resources, but they enabled him to be surprisingly resilient.

Very few natural sources of well-being were available to Ken, with both parents in one way or another unable to allow him gratifications. When first in three-times-a week therapy, the only thing he could admit to finding comfort in was not being bothered, either by outer or inner demands. He experienced almost all stimulus as threatening to his peace of mind. Later he was able to tell the therapist about masturbation, which he had been trying to ration very strictly to once a week until then. In therapy, he began to discover his existence in more interpersonal terms, and some pleasure in his right to exist, though it took several years during which he was aware of the therapist rather more than he was aware of himself. He experienced the therapist gratefully as a provider of a good atmosphere and interesting insights, and was only barely aware of himself being there as a grateful beneficiary. At that time the therapist was his resource, the source of his well-being, with very little negative feeling in the relationship, without extravagant anger or sorrow at her inevitable occasional failures. But in the course of this very prolonged therapy, he was able to lose "not being bothered" as his major source of well-being, masturbated more spontaneously, began to play tennis, went sailing, and took up dancing as a major source of pleasure. He also took pride in steady promotion at work. He finished therapy secure in his potency as a human being, though still needing to confirm that his penis could be a source of pleasure to others.

Therapy with the two men was very slow. Both fell very soon into an idealizing positive transference which actually was a climate favourable to experimentation in thinking, and in thinking more positively of themselves as well. Neither ever developed much of a negative transference, perhaps partly because they had no great objection to feeling negative towards their unkind tormenting mothers once they felt the therapist had given them permission to feel so. They were very different in many respects, but both progressed steadily if slowly towards awareness of their feelings in relation to other people.

Therapy with "Rose" and "Beth" was also very slow, in their case because their sense of self (and both of them had a much more distinct self than the men) was carefully defended against torment and assault. Both became very hostile whenever they sensed any rapprochement with the therapist; any comment on this would aggravate their hostility and cause distress. Nevertheless, the repeated re-experiencing of these violently negative and painful feelings, and their analysis, was one of the factors that enabled some self-love and some love of others to develop.

Rose had a hostile self-absorbed mother, and had been deserted by her unsteady father at 18 months, but he seems to have been fond of the little toddler and had kept in intermittent though fond contact with her. She had this one crumb of early comfort, and it may have been what enabled her to derive something like well-being from friendships with others of her age from school-days on. There had also been some support from a kind neighbour. It was a great source of self-esteem to her that she went to work, however dreadful she felt. She was often in great mental anguish, but she kept on working and, after the early years of therapy, climbed steadily up her professional ladder. Although work was always hard for her, for reasons she recognized as often neurotic, she did also derive self-esteem and satisfaction from her good performance. This in turn enabled her to use her therapy more to her advantage, and to be less often destructive of it.

"Beth" was the oldest of several children, rather close in age. Her mother appears to have been on the verge of breaking down for the first ten years of Beth's life, finding her domestic responsibilities hardly manageable (being also rather obsessional), and easily upset by changes in routine. Not very loving and certainly not demonstrative, she used Beth as the container of her fears and phantasies—as her own source of well-being, one might say. Reciprocally, Beth seems to have adopted, as her own source of well-being and her major resource, an image of herself as competent and able to cope with whatever life might throw at her—just what her mother needed.

Rose and Beth were both consciously proud of their toughness, stoicism in adversity, endurance, and capacity to survive, and I think they did use this sense of themselves as one might use an autistic object. Is it too much to speculate that it derived from very primitive moments when their survival may indeed have depended on some physical will to live, to not fail to thrive, to go on being? (Symington, 1993). At more familiar levels, both used oral satisfactions as sources of well-being. And oblivion: both of them drank—rather more than I thought good, but not immoderately by current standards—and both smoked pot, not by any means addictively, to keep themselves in equilibrium. Rose had a remarkable ability to sleep, as a form of comfort. Both had developed normal ego-functioning. Rose was almost as crushed as the men when I first knew her, but there was a lot of hostility in her, and bringing this out helped her develop in the therapy rather faster than they did. Beth was fiercely counter-dependent and used her sense of competence as a source of well-being from before I knew her. Rose began to do the same after some years of therapy.

"Gerda", the patient with good-enough parents, was, like the other four, very apt to feel narcissistically wounded, and, even more than Rose and Beth, she derived great compensation and satisfaction from being the best, in the right, competent, on top, etc. But she was different in that she was able to take normal undistorted pleasure in less delinquent and less achievement-oriented sources of well-being: people, friends, children, husband, food and drink, health. Her personality had a very different feel to it, more in the normal range.

To sum up: While some patients with severe narcissistic damage have very few resources to help them survive life's strains and stresses, the sources of a person's well-being can, at least sometimes, be made more available by psychotherapy. But there are reservations to be kept in mind. First of all, it takes a long time. In the second place, for long periods the therapist has to be tolerant of conversation about the practical aspects of living, or the trivial aspects of living such as the weather, or the intellectual aspects of living such as the relative merits of two novels. Such topics are normally used to interpret states of mind in depth, but in these cases their real merit may lie exactly in the therapist's tolerance of the chatty (because lonely) patient. It is as though the patient uses this as a means of reassurance that his or her concerns take first place, not the therapist's agenda. Thirdly, what goes on between patient and therapist is for long periods not an acceptable topic for discussion, not even when the whole success of the therapy depends on understanding that the patient's unhappiness with the therapist, or the patient's much-resented lack of progress, or whatever, is rooted exactly in that relationship. Presumably patience, brilliant intuition, impeccable tact in timing and phrasing, perfect acceptance and recognition and understanding are among the characteristics that would help the therapist to contain and eventually help such patients.

PART THREE

CONCERNING THE
DEVELOPMENT OF IDEAS

CHAPTER NINE

Fathers:
changes in psychoanalytic ideas
on men's relationship
with their children

The history of ideas is a salutary subject for study because, whatever else we learn, we learn that ideas do not usually become accepted or disseminated purely for reasons of logic or evidence. Style of presentation, personal and political influences, the thirst for new and tasty experiences, chance factors, all play their part. Also to be taken into account are the personal limitations of the would-be historian. Thus, in the present chapter we meet again the problem encountered in chapter two—how to write with decent humility about a subject for which the writer is in important respects unqualified. I am not much of a man, absolutely not a father, and hence I lack an element of intuitive understanding based on experience, which seems to me irreplaceable for the time being. True, I know many men who also do not have this intuitive understanding. Nevertheless, if anything I say sounds dogmatic, definitive, or even very plausible, remember that I ought only to be edging it

---

A version of a lecture given in March 1992, for the Guildford Centre for Psychotherapy.

towards you cautiously for your consideration and interested examination.

His own understanding of himself was all Freud had when he began the introspective examination that led to his theories about fathers and sons. It was a tremendous task to undertake, in an intellectual and emotional climate that was hostile to many of the psychoanalytic ideas we now take for granted. I would not wish to be thought contemptuous of him, or of the shortcomings to which his ideas are inevitably subject. But it can be no surprise to us that, being male, he made the little boy in himself the centre of his theoretical world. For many years, psychoanalysts thought more about little boys than about little girls, and so did the informed general public that read about children.

Moreover, Freud found it easier to explore the relationship between himself and his father than the relationship he had with his mother. A recent paper by a respected Freud Research Group (Barron et al., 1991) suggests some interesting reasons why Freud's mother was less easily accessible to his introspective free-associational methods. Whatever the reasons, the beginnings of psychoanalytic thought concerned fathers and sons, with mothers as the more or less unaware temptresses responsible for trouble between a man and his father. This was of course the climate of the times. The dominant cultures of the time tended to think of women as "dear things, God bless them, but don't get near them or they'll captivate you and mess up your pure manliness". Mothers were thought likely to unfit a boy for the world of men, the world of the army, of business, of the church, whatever. A good Edwardian viewpoint, variations of which are to be found in the late Victorian and Edwardian literature of our country, and no doubt on the continent too. Certainly it reflected the emotional climate of pre–First-World-War Britain. Of course, the sexual link was popularly denied, but the connection between women and the fear of being castrated, or unmanned or unmanly, is often evident to us. Thanks to Sigmund Freud.

In the inter-war years 1919–1939, there was a revulsion of feeling, a revolt against the old men who had helped so many hundreds of thousands of young men off to the war to be killed, while the old men stayed at home and profited from their sacrifice. The social climate made Uranus more credible—the father who ate his children, the jealous castrating father. (In another milder version, in *Everyman's Classical Dictionary*, Uranus is described as "sometimes the son, sometimes the husband, of Ge, the Earth, by whom he had children". In this account, he did not eat them, but immediately after their birth confined them in Tartarus, the underworld. However, as a consequence he was unmanned—by his son Chronos, as it happens.)

Freud started with the little boy and his father, who was first rival, then threat, and finally an ideal to be internalized. The little boy's relation to the mother was first that she was sexually desirable, then that she would endanger him, and finally that she was an unattainable ideal, but able to inspire in him a passion that would survive to give the little boy an interest in females when he grew up.

The little girl was vaguely thought to be some sort of symmetrical counterpart. She was supposed to be sexually longing towards the father, and angry with the mother for being in the way, and also angry with the mother for not having supplied her with a penis. Many male psychoanalysts and some female ones are even now convinced that a penis is so desirable to all women that everyone of them must want one. Little girls were either supposed to have been born knowing they ought to have a penis, or else it was supposed that they would see one—father's, brother's, or whoever's—and this would make them immediately wish for one. And this seems to fit some women, but by no means all (Breen, 1993).

All this takes us too far afield to explore here, and I move to a development in psychoanalytic theory that began to take place in the inter-war years, through Melanie Klein's work, and after the Second World War also through the work of others to whom I refer below. The effect was to increase the importance of the mother-and-baby pair both in theory and in psychoanalytic practice. In general, Freud did not go back much beyond what happened to the boy at the Oedipal stage, which involves three people: father, mother, and baby boy. And to Freud, the father was the important parent. For Freud, the Oedipal situation developed at age 3, 4, 5, when the boy can talk. But when one considers, it is quite a mature achievement to be able to cope with two other people as well as oneself—three people are needed for the Oedipal triangle. We are more aware now than Freud was in his day that, before the classic relationships between father, mother, and boy, there was a mother–baby pair in which other happenings may have been important. But in Edwardian time, i.e. in Freud's times, what went on with babies at an earlier age, and what went on between mothers and babies, was very much something from which men tended to be excluded and from which they were supposed to be excluded. The norm appears to have been "Hush, child, don't disturb your father".

By the inter-war years, at least three other forces were more strongly at work: (1) Melanie Klein's ideas on the infant's experience of the mother. From what I understand of Melanie Klein as a person, she seems not to have been a woman to overestimate the importance of a man in any sphere, and so of course she does not figure largely in this chapter, which is to do with fathers. The role of the actual father (any actual person really) is minimized by her and her followers. Donald Meltzer, who was analysed by her and deeply influenced by Bion who had also been analysed by her, appears to me to have reduced the role of the father to phantasied small penis-like appendages which somehow keep order inside the phantasied body of the mother (1973, pp. 68–69). But enough of that. (2) A second factor was the interest, during the Second World War and soon after, in infant mortality, morbidity, and health: mothers were understood to have a major responsibility for their children's health, and so mothers were perceived as more actively involved in their children's well-being. It is interesting to note that, in the United States, interest in the mother–infant relationship developed later than it did in Britain. In the United States, recruitment into the armed forces was on different lines, so that class-differences in fitness, due to differences in diet and hygiene and other cultural factors, became obvious rather later. There was also no wholesale movement of children such as came with their evacuation from places vulnerable to hostile bombs. So public interest in how babies were affected by their socio-economic background in general, and by their mothers in particular, came later in the United States. (3) A third force increasing the importance of the mother came from analysts who had been deeply influenced by their medical and hospital experiences. Among these, I would single out Donald Winnicott.

Winnicott was working in general paediatrics for decades, and so his experience of children and their parents was wide and realistic; his understanding was less affected by theories derived from the consulting-rooms, but based rather on hospital out-patient work and home-visits. His attention was therefore attracted in the first place not by the Oedipal three-person relationship, since fathers did not often attend the consultations, but by the two-person mother-and-baby relationship, and even before then, when the baby was not yet clearly aware of the mother as a separate out-there person. (Balint, 1968, formalized an interesting and still usable conceptualization of what happens at these three-, two- and one-person levels of experience.) So thoughts about fathers, as people who matter a whole lot at these earlier levels of child development, got rather squeezed out.

Winnicott, with his capacity for identifying with so many kinds of people, did make room for fathers in his scheme of things, though I cannot help suspecting that his thoughts are based rather more on hopes than on what he saw. Winnicott believed that the husband-role became more of a father-role in the later stages of pregnancy, as the mother became more preoccupied with the coming baby. (The passage that follows is an abridgement of some pages from Davis and Wallbridge— I just cannot do it better.) The father becomes "the protecting agent who frees the mother to devote herself to the baby . . . saving her from having to turn outwards to deal with her surroundings at the time she is wanting so much to turn inwards" (published as a paper in 1949, and in a book in 1964). In due course, when the baby is born, the father provides protection so that the mother can properly provide "the stability of the home" while father gives something of "the liveliness of the street; of impulse and experiment" (1969, as yet unpublished). The father opens up the world of work and outside interests for the children, he takes them out, lets them see things through a new pair of eyes. He acts as authority and hence can be kicked against and tested; the child's destructiveness, in the sense in which Winnicott means it, can be directed against the father who won't yield, and thus the child has further opportunities to learn to contain itself. In Winnicott's description of the father's part in the child's life, the idea of the child's "use of the object" can be clearly seen to recur. Winnicott also saw the father as playing an important role in weaning children from the mother by allowing them to discover a human being about whose separateness there had never been a confusion and whom they could therefore not easily merge into, a being who had always been "out there", an object, and different. To this aspect of the role of the father I return later when looking briefly at the contribution made by French writers like Lacan and Chasseguet-Smirgel.

Winnicott, that humane man, was rather apt to look on the bright side, for instance when he said in 1966 (as yet unpublished) that "there had been a change in orientation in this country in the last 50 years so that fathers have become real to their infants more in the role of duplicate mothers than they did a few decades ago". The struggle to allow mothers to be in receipt of child benefit and/or income allowances went on throughout the 1960s and 1970s in Britain. The debate is not over. There are those who say that if allowances are given to the father (the breadwinner, the natural financial expert, etc.), the family will benefit as a matter of course. On the other hand there are those who say, would that it were so. Once the mother has no control over the money, it can too easily be regarded as the father's income (and in some cases regarded as his reward for being virile enough to have children). Some fathers will, and some fathers will not, use it for the family's benefit. "Give it to the mother", it was said: "she *will* use it for the child". It is interesting by the way that the idea that there may be bad *mothers* is still very unacceptable to our culture. All honour to Estella Welldon and others who endeavour to bring this possibility out of our unconscious, where it rests with witches, step-mothers, and mothers-in-law, into the light of day, but that topic is not for this chapter. Nor is it for this chapter to do more than point to the drive towards splitting that is endemic in our culture. We have to have goodies and baddies. If all fathers aren't all goodies, they must all be baddies. If all fathers are baddies, mothers must all be goodies. And the thing to do with baddies is to Keep Them Out.

Winnicott's concept of the father who protects the mother/baby unit did well enough in liberal circles until, say, the 1950s. But from the 1960s onwards, three mutually encouraging trends started to produce an interesting result: the movement towards a New Man. The three mutually encouraging trends were (1) that another period of labour shortage meant that, for a while, women at many levels had again had better access to work till then traditionally done by men; (2) that more women at many levels did become more questioning about their traditional roles and more assertive about the right to choose between a mainly domestic life and an economically independent life outside the home; and (3) that, with better contraception, women gained more control over conception and hence over their destiny. I saw all this happen and I can assure you, it cheered a lot of women up a lot. Concurrent with this there was a sometimes cheerful, sometimes vengeful, move to put the old man in his place, the Old Man, the MCP, the male chauvinist pig.

Of course, they still exist, the MCPs, but more of them are, you might say, left-overs, if not as yet dinosaurs. But when I was young, even the nicest men were MCPs. It was in the culture, in everyone's superego. That is no longer so. Not in everyone's. We now have New Men in a whole range of stages of development.

The change to consider here is that which appertains to the New Man's fatherhood. Some aspects of that change are so pervasive that we now no longer think of them as new or, in the main, controversial. Many more men have started to bath their babies, feed them bottles, spoon goo into them, change their nappies, pot them, and so on. And not only that, they often enjoy it, at least occasionally. And not only that, some of them are so liberated that they feel free to moan about it just as women do at times. Of course, these are pioneers. The majority of men, I guess, go on just as before, but the climate has changed, the climate of opinion.

And goes on changing. It is no longer enough for many men to be a protective presence surrounding the woman who actually relates with the baby. Not only do some now take a hand in some of the baby-care roles traditionally allotted to women—feeding, cleaning, etc. Even this no longer satisfies all the aspirations of all New-Men fathers. The change in women's consciousness of themselves has brought about, for some men at least, a corresponding change in men's consciousness. In 1991, I went to a very moving and interesting day put on by Andrew Samuels at the London Centre for Psychotherapy, in which he claimed that the father was more than an ancillary to the mother's functioning even in the earliest days of infancy. Samuels claimed a unique place for the father from the hour of birth: a father-role and a father-relationship that is as real to the infant as the mother's but different. (Incidentally, Juliet Hopkins, 1990, noted that a most important finding has emerged from attachment research, as regards fathers: "Contrary to psychoanalytic expectation, the infant's relationship to his father cannot be predicted from the nature of his relationship to his mother. It is independent of it and reflects the qualities which the father himself had brought to the relationship".) I was interested to see how difficult we found it, in the seminar at the LCP, men and women alike, to grasp and work with this idea of a unique father-role in infancy. Over and over, in the discussions, Samuels had to point out that we were again depleting and diminishing the man's significance to the infant, making it a pale copy of what the woman was doing, giving the baby a bottle just as ably as the mother gave the breast, for instance. No, he cried, the father is not just a mother-substitute and a second-best mother to the infant. There is a valuable unique relationship between father and infant, even neonate. I was vividly reminded of the time when I was learning to be more conscious of my unconscious racism, when over and over again I had to have it pointed out to me that I was making an assumption that somehow put a black person at the diminished or secondary end of some dimension or other. In the Samuels workshop, once I caught on, I was amazed how unselfconsciously offensive we were all being to men and to what they could be to their infant: how hard it was to imagine a relationship of a father to an infant that was not modelled on what the mother does. Samuels himself was struggling with this. He knew it had been there between him and his babies, and he knew it was there sometimes in the consulting-room between the infant in the patient and himself, the same unique thing. But that was as far as we could get on that occasion.

I still wonder about this, and which direction things will take from here. I suppose it must have something to do with the nature of loving. There may be something different about the way you love if you are a man in this culture, different from how you would experience yourself as loving and are experienced as loving if you are a woman in this culture. This is perhaps not directly about what you *do* with the baby—the handling of it, as it were—but about what is conveyed in the handling, analogous to how the embrace of one person is experienced as different from the embrace of another. Samuels, being a Jungian, would, I speculate, say that the loving of a person where a father-archetype is manifesting itself is different from the loving of a person where the archetypal mother is. I wonder if that is part of what he was trying to get at in that workshop.

Some Freudians, particularly in France, might point more to the parents' unconscious phantasies about the nature of maleness and femaleness as expressed by the genitals (Breen, 1993). Such phantasies would certainly affect the parents' handling of the baby and hence the baby's experience of itself as a sexual/genital person.

In a couple of very interesting articles, Samuels speculates that the sexual relation of the father and the child are forces for growth, just as the sexual relation of mother and child have been seen as forces for growth since Freud's day. He picks up Jung's phrase "metaphoric incest", by which he certainly does not mean overt genital behaviour, but the mutual attraction and fascination that fathers and daughters, and fathers and sons, have for each other. Samuels asks "How do we grow?" and answers:

Getting really close to somebody who is more developed than you psychologically leads to some kind of enhancement or enrichment of the personality by virtue of the extreme closeness. The idea that a person actually grows *inside* by relating in a very close way with people *outside* who has qualities he or she has not yet manifested is at the heart of psychodynamics and object-relations. [Samuels, 1988, p. 417]

Samuels points out in passing how this also happens in the consulting-room, in the intimacies of transference and counter-transference. He concludes:

> The psychological function of (metaphoric) incestuous sexuality is to facilitate the closeness of love. Desire in a relationship guarantees the closeness of that relationship. It can go tragically wrong; it can get acted out; it can possess generation after generation of a family. But incestuous desire has the function of providing the fuel for the means by which we get close to other people and hence grow: love.

These forces for growth, as Samuels sees them, though I cannot do justice to all the interesting and useful things he says, have to do with the father as "other". The father represents "other" in the sense that he represents gender-differentiation, though what different cultures make of that gender-differentiation depends on a lot of factors. It is thought that generally in the West, at present, a good father in relation to his daughter makes her feel more feminine and loving and sexual, and makes his son feel more masculine and aggressive and sexual.

Let us look at some more theories to help our imagination along. In what seems to me an acceptable development of orthodox Freudian theory, Peter Blos (1984, quoted by Breen, 1993) speaks of the father having for the small boy "a charismatic quality which is different in its constitutional disposition and bodily responses from that of the mother", and considers that the different ways mothers and fathers hold their babies demonstrate this difference. This is a pre-Oedipal relationship, and he quotes Freud's view (1925j) that before the appearance of Oedipal rivalry, there is a period which "includes an identification of an affectionate sort with the boy's father". Blos comments that "this early experience of being protected by the father and caringly loved by him becomes internalized as a lifelong sense of safety. When the sense of this strong loving bond revives in adolescence, it can act as a defence against the fear of being forever tied to the mother."

Kohut, from the 1970s on, makes a distinction between a mirroring relationship and an idealizing one. By a mirroring relationship he means one in which one person reflects back to another, in this case the baby, just what the baby needs to see: wholehearted acceptance and recognition of its worth, and love of just what the baby is and does. This is not quite what Winnicott means by mirroring, or Lacan; this is Kohut. Kohut sees mirroring as a typical maternal function, not usually a paternal one. By contrast, the father's function has to do with an idealizing relationship, in Kohut's view of things. In Kohut's idealizing relationship, one person is willing to be adored and admired and copied by another, usually the small child. Where mirroring fails, so that tiny children do not develop the solid core of self-assurance and worth that good mirroring (of the Kohut kind) should give, Kohut sees a second chance for their development to come right, if the somewhat older toddlers have, as role-models, fathers who are willing to be loved in an idealizing way, so that these somewhat deprived toddlers, too, can develop the notion that it is possible to be wonderful, and that in father they possess access to this possibility. The thing is to become like wonderful father, and then they, the toddlers, will be wonderful too. Yes, some of you will have seen the snag. A little girl who is not mirrored benevolently by mother may perhaps also adore the idealized father, but if she internalizes him, uses him as a model, she is going to have some developmental difficulties of her own to tackle.

Never mind where that leads us; the relevant bit is that we have here two ways of relating that, as far as I can see, do not seem essentially tied to maleness and femaleness. Mirroring in a rather adoring way, and allowing oneself to be idealized and adored, seem two useful parental roles to play in helping the child towards a rounded development. There seems to me something in the socialization of men, and something rather different in the socialization of women, which finds being adored very pleasant. If we could cleanse this gratification of guilt on the one hand, and exploitativeness on the other, good.

I am being careful to avoid the controversy about whether there are inborn masculine and feminine psychological traits that reappear in the parental roles. I think we do not know. Whatever we think we know, we think we know from "first principles", because we are Freudians, or Jungians, or whatever.

Next, a look at some less egalitarian more phallo-centric approaches. There is a pleasantly amusing account of the Oedipal father as he is experienced in the clinical practice of a modern sometimes rather idiosyncratic Independent-minded Freud-oriented psychoanalyst, Christopher Bollas, in a chapter called "Don't Worry Your Father" in *Forces of Destiny* (1989). Bollas, presumably partly summing up the phantasies of his patients but, it must be said, like almost everyone, imagines a world in which the father gets up early in the morning, gets his breakfast, and goes out to earn the money that is so important for the survival of the family, in contrast to the more leisurely world of the mother with her children (none of whom seem to have to be got ready for school or for the child-minder before she rushes out), and he envies the mother her more intimate contact with the child's (only one child's) emotional needs and events. It is clear he is writing from a man's perspective. Anyway, he sees the man's life as clearly cut into two kinds of time: one—the tense hard-working bread-winning rule-governed kind of time from which the rest of the family is excluded; the other—the more relaxed domestic time, which is his only at second-hand. The man must not be told too abruptly about the domestic life when he comes home, because he needs time to adjust from one sphere to the other: "Don't worry your father".

Bollas does not write explicitly as though he feels this is the natural order. He is just writing of what his patients suggest to him. In one example, a patient saw his father as an Odysseus who ventured forth in the morning but might not come back, wandering about the world driven by the (sexual though sublimated) curiosity that the patient, as a boy, had had about the grown-up world of work and sex. But the lack of irony makes me uncomfortable. At the end of the chapter, Bollas contrasts two universes of experience, which he calls "Maternal Time" and "Paternal Time", without any irony I can detect.

Maternal Time	Paternal Time
intimate	impersonal
eternal (cannot imagine life without mother)	mortal (some day he won't come back)
timeless (or governed by intervals of sleep, hunger, etc.)	timeful (get up, go to work, etc.)
instinctual and gratifying	social (but I think Bollas means economic, and he refers to the father machine that makes money)

This takes what Winnicott said about the functions of the father a bit further. It is another variant of what is currently said about the father in the Oedipal situation. And if we take this development only one step further, the grain of truth that is in it seems to me to get lost in a great cartload of nonsense. I am sorry to say this nonsense comes mainly from France: from Lacan and Chasseguet-Smirgel. Its starting-point is that the father is regarded as an incest barrier (? the father? the father as incest barrier against the mother's incest? Yes, you heard aright, and there is a grain of truth in it if you think of a sort of emotional incest. But is this a wise way of thinking? Don't fathers commit actual real genital incest more often than do mothers? Never mind, get on with the story.)

The argument starts with a seductive mother who makes much of her little son and tells him that in all that matters he is as good as his father. She obliterates realistic considerations. Age does not matter, experience does not matter, size does not matter—there are no important differences between father and the toddler, who thus comes to believe that his penis is as good as his father's. Only the presence of the father can stop this mother/son couple from remaining coupled for ever, can help restrain these unrealistic distortions which, in Chasseguet-Smirgel's view, are characteristic of all perversions. I think this theory can be useful in the analysis of some perversions—it is of course much more elaborate than I have needed to present here. But it is just worth noting that incest has here become the woman's offence, that little girls (i.e. one half of all children born) are once again left out of consideration, and that men have been elevated to the status of incest-preventers. Somewhat more sensibly, we can accept that the father may be regarded, *in some situations*, as the representative of shared reality, who says, of the wish to be forever cosily enclosed in a delusional mother/baby dream-world: this cannot be. But it is not useful to romanticize it with capital letters. It is a useful idea, but it cannot be central to a good general theory: it embodies a bogglingly unrealistic idea of what most mothers do.

Some pages back, we noted Winnicott's contribution to our understanding of the father's unique role in protecting the mother/baby couple, and we noted also his recognition that the father is separate and because of this is able to present to the baby a human being about whom there was never any phantasy of being merged, who can therefore represent the Forever Other in human experience. It is this strand of experience that has become more important in recent thinking. But with Lacan and Chasseguet-Smirgel we find this useful perspective detached from any particular situation, and generalized: the Father as the Male Principle *is* Reality: he is seen as the one who insists on reality over against the mother. I cannot but feel that this is a generalization evolved in the consulting-rooms of alienated analysts and upheld by other alienated people: conceited fathers, conceited husbands—strange people, none of them acquainted with any women running a household with two or three or more children on a limited income. Who is more in touch with life's realities and limitations—a woman in such circumstances, or a man who goes off to work every morning? So I think in general this idea will not wash (or cook or shop). But I do find it useful to keep in mind that there needs to be a person beside the mother, a person who breaks into the mother/child experience, a person who was never part of the child in the sense in which the mother has been.

I prefer another theory, which interests itself in the child's encounter with reality and in the loss of the illusion of omnipotence that goes so easily with the illusion of being merged with the mother. This theory brings into relief the importance, for the child's development, of love between parents. This theory is part of recent re-evaluations and clarifications of Melanie Klein's original ideas (Britton, Feldman, & O'Shaughnessy, 1989—see particularly the paper by Britton).

In this version of the Oedipal situation and its implications, one of the things that matter is what is called the Oedipal disappointment. The child is disappointed that father and mother have a genital and procreative and loving relationship that is important to them, and from which the child is excluded. The child, whatever its sex, does not have this relationship with the parent, whatever the sex of the parent. This is a deprivation the child has to accept, and it helps the child to understand that its place in the world is not at the world's centre, that other people really exist in themselves and not just in relation to itself, and that other people have relationships. Of course, if things go well, the child also understands that one day it too can have relationships from which the parent is excluded.

Britton also looks at the consequences of the child's inability to accept a place outside the marital couple. This seems to him to depend on the absence of a secure base—a securely internalized good mother, to use his language. The sense of deprivation, if the child has not been able to come to terms with it, becomes a source of continual blame, of self or of other people, and a constant wish to push in, to get in there, and so on. This seems an important thing to look out for in clinical practice.

Where does all this leave us? With a lot of as yet unsolved questions, I'm afraid, and I do beg you not to answer from your own deeply felt convictions too soon, but to wait for more varied less culture-bound evidence.

There are still, it seems to me, major difficulties in the way of finding much that is unique about fathers and the fathering role, and also about mothers and the mothering role, other than what is specifically anatomical. Leaving the anatomical aside for a space, let us play with some ideas, even if it involves us in tiresome jargon. Let us speculate. Let us keep in mind the rich variety of cultures around the globe. Does there have to be in every family a father who had the procreative role and who is a non-mothering parent? Does there have to be someone in each family who was the procreator? Does the non-mothering parent have to be a man? Can two women do good parenting? Does there have to be someone with a grown-up penis in every family? And should there never be more than one grown-up penis in the family? Can there be more than two? Can a man be a mothering parent? Can two men living together be parents together? We do not know the answers to such questions, but let us not prevent ourselves from thinking further about them.

I certainly want, next, to say something about the usefulness, to a child, of having a variety of personalities to relate to, of having more than one loving and loveable adult to identify with and/or incorporate bits of and/or fight with and so on, during the time of development, of self-discovery, of self-creation. It is bound to make a difference to an infant to be loved by more than one person from early on. And it must make a difference to an infant to be loved by two people as different as a father and a mother. But I am allowed to ask—why two? why not three? four? Could we try to think about this? And while we are about it, could we try to think what may be the advantages to a child when the original parents split up and a new adult has to be taken in? The disadvantages have often been explored—can we now think about how advantage may be taken of the new situation?

We do know some of the things children need, and need a plentiful supply of: devoted love from someone who is able, for love, to put someone else—the child—first; and devoted love from someone who is able, for love, to draw the line and refuse someone else—the child—when it wants what is not good for it just then, or not good for the family just then; and stability; and predictability so that a sound ego may form; and respect given and received; and the sight of its grown-ups giving and receiving respect mutually and in relationship with others outside the immediate family, and so on, and so on. These relationships are by no means often to be found between parents as we have them now, or between parents as we have them now and their children. There is a lot to be done in improving the quality of traditional relationships, and in exploring the possibilities of less traditional ones.

CHAPTER TEN

The contrasting histories
of psychoanalytic thought
in the United States
and the United Kingdom

When we look at the contrasting traditions of psycho-analytic thought in North America and in Britain, we have cause to celebrate, both having made major contributions to the development of modern thought. Also worth celebrating is an epoch in British and American history of which both may surely be proud, when hospitality and humane concern combined to give a welcome to many talented people who would otherwise have been murdered. These themes deserve a serious historian, but I hope this brief outline may serve a purpose nonetheless.

My purpose is mainly epistemological and moral: it is to show how an accumulation of social and often accidental events in two countries developed two very different understandings of what is appropriately psychoanalytic. These developments had little to do with the effects that rational debate or empirical evidence might have on existing theories or practices; they depended largely on events that had nothing to do with psy-choanalysis at all: successive waves of analysts arrived from the Continent of Europe, rescued and supported by native-born British and American people and by former colleagues who had recently reached safer shores. Having arrived, they began to disagree with one another.

In the United States, where the Frontier Mentality could still operate, the disputants then split and went elsewhere in that great country, separately developing their unique interests and thereby contributing to a great flowering of ideas in philosophy, psychology, and other moral and social sciences, relatively undistracted by disagreements with colleagues elsewhere. What psychoanalysts actually did, in the privacy of their consulting-rooms, was left relatively unaffected by these benign explosions, with the results that, until recently, psychoanalytic practice in the United States seemed like a fly in amber to British analysts, so closely did it adhere to what had been orthodox in the 1920s.

In Britain, on the other hand, there was nowhere to go but London. Fairbairn, out in Edinburgh, was under-rated and snubbed. The history of psychoanalytic thought in the Britain of the inter-war years 1919–1939 had the two dominant figures of Ernest Jones (almost an avatar of Freud in Vienna, though of course he and the redoubtable Anna were welcomed in Britain just before the outbreak of war) and Melanie Klein. In this era, the main tenants of Klein's innovatory doctrines were formulated. It is an impressive list of ideas:

- that the infant from birth has a phantasy life in which internal objects hold the stage;
- that the infant's death instinct operates from birth and involves it in storms of hate;
- that, from birth, fear of retaliation makes the infant's phantasy life a time of terror;
- that from this position the infant may progress to a more depressive sort of anxiety as a consequence of worrying lest the object on which it depends be damaged by its hate;
- that, as well as phantasy-objects who represent people, the phantasy-life generates part-objects usually representing parts of the body such as breasts, bellies, and genitalia;
- that from birth the infant engages in a complex process of projecting its phantasies onto its objects, then introjecting them in modified form, then out again, then in, and so on;

- that, clinically, the only useful therapeutic procedure is the explication of the phantasied object-relations as they are discerned in interaction with the analyst (this at a time when it was thought that only the undoing of repression and the analysis of defences against knowledge made people better).

These new ideas were regarded with doubt and antagonism by other British analysts, but there was no getting away from them in London, and so, there, opinionated and exigent people of all persuasions had to fight things out at close quarters. Rancour was aggravated because, London being the only place to be, there were economic problems. London was where one got patients, students to train, status, respect. However, eventually better sense prevailed, and a kind of solution was worked out. From 1942, when Melanie Klein came back to London after an absence, there were meetings between the factions to discuss the concepts at issue and to plot demarcation lines. The main disputations became known as the Controversial Discussions (King & Steiner, 1991).

The controversies were at times very acrimonious. Much damage must have been inflicted on the more timid creative minds daunted by the fierceness of the disputants. We shall never know how much deep but tentative quiet understanding was blighted in the bud. And yet, on the other hand, one cannot but recognize how, eventually, theory and practice benefited from this all-in-wrestling. Analysts of all persuasions, including Jungian, and many psychoanalytically oriented psychotherapists, now use the fought-over concepts when they judge them to be clinically appropriate. Ideas that originated with Klein are now in common use. And Kleinians have become less fierce with time, less monopolistic.

From all this strife have come many useful concepts and practices, over whose provenance it would in my view be invidious to quarrel: countertransference analysis, the use of regression, psychoanalytic work with "unanalysable" borderline and psychotic phenomena—these came to be increasingly a matter of course in London from perhaps the 1960s on, and were widespread by the end of the 1970s. A nice spread of talent survived, or appeared: Bowlby for both attachment theory and separation anxiety, Paula Heimann, Susan Isaacs, the Balints,

Fairbairn, Winnicott, Guntrip, R. D. Laing, Rosenfeld, Bion, and, more recently, Britton, Steiner, Meltzer, Casement, Bollas, Symington—major and minor figures, but all interesting and original and contributing to the theory and practice of psychoanalysis and psychotherapy, contributing directly to these, not—as in the United States—around them.

All the important writings on education and work with troubled and distressed people, especially the young, which came about as a result of psychoanalytic ideas are regretfully omitted from this account. In Britain we should honour the many directly influenced by August Aichhorn (of the Vienna Circle), Anna Freud, and Dorothy Burlingham, and such a diverse crew as Susan Isaacs, A. S. Neill, David Wills, Bunny Barron, Marie Paneth, Mr Lyward. In the United States, Bruno Bettelheim, Fritz Redl, and many others.

In the United States, interested and well-to-do Americans had, like interested and well-to-do British people, been going to visit Freud in Vienna, from the beginning of the century. Sometimes Freud "analysed" them, for periods lasting from a fortnight to six months or even longer, six times a week. That is how it was done in those days, and it was how knowledge of his ideas spread among the intelligentsia internationally.

I write "Americans" because that was what people from the United States were called at the beginning of this century, and sometimes even now, South Americans not counting for much internationally at that time. To keep things simple, I will keep to this nomenclature, with an apology to those around and below the equator, and to Canada.

Freud himself had visited the United States and lectured there, and had been hospitably received, among others by Morton Prince (of "Sybil" fame) and James Putnam of Harvard Medical School. The Americans who took an interest in Freud were mainly from the medical profession, and from the beginning this medical bias was characteristic of the American psychoanalytic scene. It was a thing Freud particularly disliked, and he said so on many occasions, e.g. "The Question of Lay Analysis" (1926e), but that was how it was in the United States, and he argued and scolded in vain.

This is a very interesting and currently relevant issue just now in Britain, where people are trying to get psychotherapy recognized as a profession that can keep out the quacks and the inadequately trained, and trying to do it on a European rather than a purely British basis. In several European countries the practice of psychotherapy has been confined to members of the medical profession, and in most others people have first had to belong to what has come to be called a core profession—social work, teaching, academic psychology, clinical psychology, or whatever. Psychotherapy on its own is not thought to be rich enough fare for study—odd, because when you think about it, it should be as possible to construct academically acceptable foundations for the practice of psychotherapy as it has been for teaching, social work, and other vocations that have long had a place among post-graduate university courses. It has to be remembered, also, that all those core professions have been criticized—often rightly, in my view—for not turning out professionals who are sufficiently competent practically to do their work with common sense, humanity, and depth of skill. That is the really difficult truth to face. Making people be imperfect social workers or incompetent psychologists or whatever first, before allowing them to train as psychotherapists, is not a way of facing the truth but of avoiding it. In my view, insisting that people should have seen and understood something about the problems of living in a variety of settings seems nearer the mark. But it is not economically possible, as things are, for an institution to insist that people go away for a few years to do some more growing up or rounding out before training, if the institution only gets paid for the students it actually enrols. Meanwhile, there is a medical predominance in psychoanalysis in the United States—less than there was, but still formidable.

In 1911, the New York Psychoanalytic Association was founded. The moving spirit and leader was Abraham Brill, who had been translating many of Freud's papers. For the next ten years or so, the Association was an open society—anyone interested could join—provided they were medically qualified, of course. It was not till 1922 that a personal analysis was required of its members. Incidentally, Ernest Jones was on a visit to Canada in 1911; he had quarrelled with Brill and disapproved of him, and he set up a rival association from Toronto in the same year: the American Psychoanalytic Association, for

238 CONCERNING THE DEVELOPMENT OF IDEAS

those outside New York (Roazen, 1975, p. 380). There was great
mistrust between these two bodies, and I understand there still
is to some extent, but the main thesis of this chapter is that
quarrels did not matter so much in that huge continent—there
was room for everyone, in a way that the hegemony of London
did not permit.

In the late 1920s, the New York Association wished to
become a training organization. Typically of many new organizations, they did not invite any of their own distinguished men
to direct it, but an outsider: Sandor Rado, from the Berlin
Institute. Paul Roazen, a great source for the history of this
period, writes of him that he came to be seen as a psychoanalytic "traitor", his contributions being known mainly within
medicine (Roazen, 1975, p. 494). Rado is described as having
drifted away from Freudian psychoanalysis almost from the
start, though his ideas are much more generally acceptable
now. He had been analysed by Karl Abraham, and in turn had
analysed Otto Fenichel, Heinz Hartmann, and Wilhelm Reich—
three top-rankers with very different relationships to orthodoxy.

Sandor Rado came to New York in 1930—an interesting
date. From this time on, with the rise of European fascism,
Hitler, Nazism, anti-communism, and anti-Semitism, an increasing number of psychoanalysts emigrated to the United
States, some afraid for their lives, but many others to breathe a
freer air. Free spirits of all kinds, few of them were likely to be
meek conformists to the rules and regulations either of the
countries they had left or of their new host country. Some went
to Britain, Freud and Anna Freud and Melanie Klein famously
among them; many other equally marvellously original and
stroppy characters went to the United States.

Waves and currents around the Statue of Liberty

The first wave of refugees from the continent of Europe was
perhaps the most remarkable. They are called Dissenters by
Paul Roazen, while their particular chronicler, J. A. C. Brown,
calls them Post-Freudians. The name that seems to have stuck

best is Neo-Freudians: Erik Erikson, Karen Horney, Erich Fromm, Abram Kardiner, all came over in the 1930s. Next to be considered in this chapter is the Chestnut Lodge School, of whom H. F. Searles is the most eminent exponent but which started with Harry Stack Sullivan and, soon, Frieda Fromm-Reichmann. After the Second World War, building on the work of another immigrant, Heinz Hartmann, who developed important theories on the functions of the ego, we get Otto Kernberg, who calls himself an ego-psychologist like Hartmann, and the self-psychologists, of whom Heinz Kohut is the most eminent. Finally, there is the splendid American empirical tradition of child-development studies with Spitz, Margaret Mahler and her co-workers, and Daniel Stern.

But first, two extremes: major figures defining the limits of psychoanalytic study at either end.

Otto Fenichel and Wilhelm Reich

In the 1930s both Otto Fenichel and Wilhelm Reich came to the United States from the Berlin Society. They were political refugees, neither of them Jewish, but very left-wing politically. What a contrast, though!

On the one hand, we owe what is still the best general handbook on classical psychoanalysis, *The Psychoanalytic Theory of the Neuroses* (1946)—sane, balanced, and careful—to Otto Fenichel, who settled in California.

On the other hand, we have Wilhelm Reich, a drop-out beatnik before his time, who used to attend Freud's seminars in Lederhosen, camping in a field by the Danube and walking into Vienna for meetings. Finding the Vienna Circle stifling, he went to Berlin, where he, with others, was instrumental in starting a psychoanalytic clinic that helped people without requiring payment. He was thrown out of the Communist Party because he would not conform. Soon the International Psychoanalytic Association also expelled him for non-conformity. He left Berlin and wandered through the Scandinavian countries for a while. In 1939 he came to the United States. Alas, he was as unwelcome there as he had been in Europe, hospitable as the United States had been to many others. Reich's ideas seemed to drive people to frenzies of violent antagonism, in ways his own books predicted and explained. In 1954 he was arraigned under the Federal Food and Drugs Act for claiming that his orgone box was therapeutic. He refused to appear in court, as he did not think scientific research should be subject to a court of law. He was jailed for two years for contempt of court and died in a penitentiary.

All who knew him recognized his genius although, alas, he was mad, lacking those ego-adaptations even then being conceptualized by Heinz Hartmann, which enable most of us to survive in uncongenial conditions. Ironically, he understood the functions of the ego and its relation to the whole character of a person better than most people did at that time. It was he who tried to divert attention away from defence-analysis to character-analysis. It was also he who, in Vienna, decades before his time, started a seminar for analysts to discuss the cases they had failed with.

Reich sought to ameliorate human suffering not only through psychoanalysis but through social changes, politically, and also in family structure. He advocated the prevention of Oedipal problems, rather than just their identification and cure after the fact. Simply by the dissolution of the middle-class family of the time, he argued, could the Oedipus complex be vanquished. Roazen comments that the experience of the Israeli kibbutzim would later prove him right in this; he also comments that most Freudians felt that he had betrayed the purity of the psychoanalytic mission by such ideas (p. 493).

Reich was among the earliest psychoanalysts to consider the interrelation between individual and society, to take up the notion of character, and to single out the development of the authoritarian character as a socially important issue. The outstanding book from all these points of view is *Character Analysis* (1933), but see also *The Mass Psychology of Fascism* (1943) and his delightful little illustrated paperback, *Listen, Little Man* (1948). He was also one of the earliest analysts to be interested in psychosomatics—see *The Functions of the Orgasm* (1942)—but his ideas in this field are generally thought doubtful and full of crankiness. In Britain, at least, however, there is quite an important Reichian following (John Kellner, 1975; Alexander Lowen, 1971).

Waves and currents around the Statue of Liberty: the Neo-Freudians—individuals in their society

Eric Erikson

On the face of it, Eric Erikson had a lot in common with Reich, and it is sad to contrast their careers. Erikson encountered the Vienna Circle in 1927, when he was tramping through Europe, sketching as he went. Roazen's account of what happened is touching to read: how Erikson came to be recruited into child analysis, Anna Freud's goodness to him, and her father's too, his own modesty and at-the-time unfashionable liking for working with children. He worked with Peter Blos and August Aichhorn as well as with Dorothy Burlingham and Anna Freud (Roazen, 1975, pp. 500–501). He became a full member of the Vienna Institute in 1933. But he also may have found the atmosphere stifling, for he soon went to the United States, where his rise was again meteoric. He was by all accounts a peaceable and pleasant man, loyal to Freud, to whom perhaps he attributed some of his own ideas so as not to feel too divergent. He became associated with both Harvard and with Yale, never needing to move from the East coast to avoid acrimony. He had the friendship of the famous anthropologists of the day: Gregory Bateson of double-bind fame, Ruth Benedict, Alfred Kroeber (Ursula Le Guin's father), Margaret Mead. His major book, *Childhood and Society* (1951), explores the links between childhood experiences and adult living, in two American-Indian tribes and in "America"; it contains his famous eight developmental dilemmas, the solution of each of which contributes further to a person's sense of identity:

- trust vs. basic mistrust
- autonomy vs. shame and doubt
- initiative vs. guilt
- industry vs. inferiority
- identity vs. role diffusion
- intimacy vs. isolation
- generativity vs. stagnation
- ego-integrity vs. despair

The elaboration of the sense of individual identity was Erikson's lifelong interest (1968); Roazen names him as influential in the development of ego-psychology.

Erich Fromm

Before he was a psychoanalyst, Erich Fromm was an important student of sociology, first at Heidelberg and later at the important Frankfurt Institute of Social Research. Immensely creative, he made important contributions in a wide field of social and ethical thought:

1946: *The Fear of Freedom*

1948: *Man for Himself: an Enquiry into the Psychology of Ethics*

1950: *Psychoanalysis and Religion*

1952: *The Forgotten Language: An Introduction to the Understanding of Dreams and Myths*

1955: *The Sane Society*

1957: *The Art of Loving*

1959: *Sigmund Freud's Mission: An Analysis of his Personality and Influences*

1961: *May Man Prevail? An Enquiry into the Facts and Fictions of Foreign Policy*

1967: *Marx's Concept of Man*

1967: *You Shall Be as Gods, a Radical Interpretation of the Old Testament*

1969: *The Nature of Man*

1971: *The Anatomy of Human Destructiveness*

Fromm came to the United States in the 1930s, an alumnus of the Berlin Institute, where he had had high status. He is interesting not just because of his own work, but also because his first wife was Frieda Fromm-Reichmann, who was to become an important member of the Chestnut Lodge group.

It is worth even now recalling two of his major concepts: the internalization of external necessity, and the fear of freedom.

His interest in the cultural determinants of character shows
him to be a typical member of the Neo-Freudians, and so, very
noticeable in his analysis of the anxious personality, does the
lack of reference to either libidinal development or the mother–
child nexus:

> There is a "social character" which is . . . the essential
> nucleus of the character structure of most members of a
> group, which has developed as the result of the basic expe-
> riences and mode of life of that group. [Fromm, 1946,
> Appendix]

Fromm concludes that the subjective function of character
is to lead a person to act according to what is necessary for him
from a practical point of view:

> If we look at social character from the standpoint of its
> function in the social process, we have to start with the
> statement that by adapting himself to social conditions,
> man develops those traits that make him desire to act as
> he has to act. [ibid.]

This is the internalization of external necessity. Fromm
gives the work-ethic as an example, as poignant a one in the
1990s as it was in the 1930s, with their lack of employment
opportunities. As he saw it, ever since the Reformation and the
beginnings of modern industrial and banking technology,
punctual and regular work has become necessary to keep
things going, and work—punctual and steady work—has become internalized as something you must have not just for the
income but for self-respect. Unemployed through no fault of
your own, you feel nevertheless down-graded. In times of major
social change, the conditions that validated previously acquired internalized values no longer obtain, and many people
come to grief and break down.

Like the other Neo-Freudians who had lived through the
rise of Nazism, Fascism, and Communism, Fromm tried to
understand what was responsible for the spread of an authoritarian type of personality in a nation. In *The Fear of Freedom* he
maps out his ideas, deriving many of them from a contemporary controversy about whether the breakdown of feudal
society led to its transformation into a capitalist one, or vice

versa, a controversy starting from Max Weber's *The Protestant Ethic and the Spirit of Capitalism* (1926) and R. H. Tawney's rejoinder *Religion and the Rise of Capitalism* (1930). It struck Fromm that when people were released from the traditional social pressures-of feudalism backed by the Catholic Church, they did not feel free, as one might naively expect. On the contrary, feeling lost, many took refuge in other authoritarian ideas and practices. Particularly, they tried to prove that they were saved (in the Protestant sense) by saving money, which they saw as evidence of God's goodwill to them.

> The new religious doctrines were an answer to psychic needs which themselves were brought about by the collapse of the mediaeval social system and the beginnings of capitalism . . . freedom from the traditional bonds of mediaeval society, though giving the individual a new feeling of independence, at the same time made him feel alone and isolated, filled him with doubt and anxiety, and drove him into a new submission and into compulsive and irrational activity. [Fromm, 1946, chapter 4]

The distinction between a state of mind in which people feel *free from* a compulsion, and a state of mind in which people feel *free to* do what they want has passed into general usage—"freedom from" *versus* "freedom to".

Karen Horney

Better than any of them, Karen Horney represents the spirit of those days:

> The two main movements in the history of psychoanalysis have been a response to Freud's biological assumptions which stimulated on the right wing an ever deeper penetration into infantile experience (as in the Kleinian school) and on the left wing an opening-out into the individual's social and cultural back-ground (as with Horney, Fromm, and Sullivan). The right-wing approach was of course implicit in Freud's own work, since it was in large measure a filling-in of gaps along lines he himself in part foresaw. . . .

But the left-wing socially orientated movements aroused considerably more hostility amongst the orthodox because, in their desire to emphasize the modifiability of human nature which is usually implicit in a socially oriented theory, it was found necessary in the long run to attack the very foundations of orthodoxy. The inevitability of anatomy in determining the psychological differences between the sexes, the inevitability of the stages of libido development and the Oedipus complex, were rejected and the importance of interpersonal relations and the cultural background emphasized. . . . When this left-wing tendency first became apparent is difficult to say, because those who came later to be regarded as its supporters do not seem initially to have been at all clear where their thoughts were leading. [Brown, 1961, pp. 129–130]

After acknowledging Alfred Adler's influence on Horney, Brown continues:

The beginnings of interpersonal theory in analysis appear with Ferenczi, but in its modern form interpersonal theory derives from Horney, Fromm and Reich, who were associated in Germany prior to assuming American nationality, and of course from a long line of American social psychologists.

Horney came from Norway, where she had trained as a doctor, to study at the Berlin Institute for Psychoanalysis, and she taught there for fifteen years, so she was obviously orthodox enough at that time. Like Fromm, she went to the United States in the 1930s, and soon became Director of the Chicago Institute of Psychoanalysis and lecturer at the New School for Social Research. From there she wrote a challenging series of books, which were still very fresh when I was an undergraduate in the 1940s:

1937: *The Neurotic Personality of Our Times*
1939: *New Ways in Psychoanalysis*
1942: *Self Analysis*
1945: *Our Inner Conflicts*
1950: *Neurosis and Human Growth*

Much in these books she had in common with the more orthodox psychoanalysts of the time. Remarkably, much of that is now no longer regarded as so central to the faith, while many of her heterodox ideas have come to be accepted in some form or other: on women, on differences due to social factors, on the place of instincts and defences. Her ideas on what makes a personality grandiose ("anspruchsvoll"—1950) are very like Kohut's and others'. She also has a theory of narcissistic injury very like theories developed later—again, rather like Kohut's.

Like all Neo-Freudians, she was very far from postulating a universal destructive instinct. Like them, she believed rather that the baby is full of potential for good, which will develop if it is given warmth, security and the right guidance. When these conditions do not sufficiently obtain, there develops instead a profound lack of rootedness and a vague apprehension, which Horney called "basic anxiety"—a feeling of isolation and help-lessness in a hostile world. Neuroses are strategies to cope with basic anxiety. People will move neurotically either *towards* other people in a compulsive quest for affection, or compul-sively *against* them, or else *away from* them.

Her interest in the non-instinctual environmental and social factors affecting behaviour caused her to drift away from the orthodoxy of the time, which believed so absolutely in inherent biological determinants. Particularly she had her doubts about the inferiority girls were supposed to feel or to have because of their lack of a penis. Like most of those splendid early women-psychoanalysts, she appears to have had no problems about self-esteem.

Abram Kardiner

Like Sullivan and Searles, Abram Kardiner was not a refugee from Europe, but American-born. He was analysed first by one of the few analysts in the United States of whom Freud approved, H. A. Frinck, and later by Freud himself. In 1930, he was one of those instrumental in founding the first psychoana-lytic training institute in the United States—the New York Institute (Roazen, 1975, pp. 381–382). His provenance could not be purer. Nevertheless, it is as a founder of the important Cultural School of Anthropology, which later included such people as Margaret Mead and Ruth Benedict, that he has his major claim to fame—viz. his two great books: *The Individual and His Society*, subtitled *The Psychodynamics of Primitive Social Organisations* (1939), and *The Psychological Frontiers of Society* (1945). He is also held to be the grandfather of James West's *Plainsville, USA* (1945), the first anthropological study of a modern town.

Crucial to Cultural Anthropology is the concept of the basic personality-type. Ralph Linton, first Kardiner's pupil, then for fifteen years his collaborator, and finally his successor, summarizes the postulates on which this concept rests in his foreword to *The Psychological Frontiers*:

> The concept of basic personality types as developed by Kardiner and myself rests upon the following postulates:
>
> 1. that the individual's early experiences exert a lasting effect upon his personality, especially on the development of his projective systems (i.e. his religion, philosophy, sociology, psychology, his general way of explaining the world and himself),
> 2. that similar experiences in childhood will tend to produce similar personality configurations in the individuals who are subjected to them,
> 3. that the techniques which members of any society employ in the care and rearing of children are culturally patterned and will tend to be similar,
> 4. that the culturally patterned techniques for the care and rearing of children differ from one society to another. [Kardiner, 1945]

Linton goes on to say that if these postulates are correct it follows that

> a. members of any given society will have many elements of childhood experience in common,
> b. as a result they will have many elements of personality in common,
> c. which are different from the norms of other societies.
>
> [ibid.]

So off they went and studied ten primitive societies, as they were then called, and ceased to be called partly as a result of such studies. They looked at such things as maternal care (constancy of attention, feeding regularity, help in walking and talking, weaning, sphincter control, etc.), at the induction of affectivity (encouragement to respond—through handling, fondling, playing, etc.), and at the nature of early discipline (slapping, removing the offending child or the offending object, etc.), right up to intellectual systems like religion and folklore. This work was very influential in the study of child-rearing practices both in the United States and here (see, for an excellent example, R. R. Sears, E. F. Maccoby, & H. Levin, *Patterns of Child Rearing*, 1957).

Waves and currents around the Statue of Liberty: Chestnut Lodge—working with schizophrenia and extreme anxiety

Important contributions to our understanding of schizophrenic phenomena were made by a group of people who at various overlapping times worked at a mental hospital in Maryland called Chestnut Lodge. Harry Stack Sullivan, Frieda Fromm-Reichmann, and H. F. Searles are the most celebrated of them. They share with Neo-Freudians the conviction that classical drive-theory was wrong about human motivation, about the nature of human experience, and about the difficulties of living. They took the culture's contribution to personality-formation as seriously as everyone did in the United States at the time, and it is this, Greenberg and Mitchell (1983) comment, that sets the Interpersonal Psychoanalysts apart from the other major non-drive school of thought at the time—the British Kleinians.

    Not everyone has an affinity for schizophrenic phenomena. The people at Chestnut Lodge had. Freud did not, according to Roazen, who quotes a letter in which he writes: "I do not like these people. . . . I am annoyed by them. . . . I feel them to be so far distant from me and from everything human. A curious sort of intolerance, which surely makes me unfit to be a psychiatrist." Roazen goes on to say that Freud seems to have thought that in the future such patients might be accessible to psychoanalytic technique, but that he did not want to participate in this work himself. "Freud was not flexible enough to adapt his technique to the treatment of psychotics. His stand-offishness to them now looks defensive, a reaction to some inner threat. One has to be, at least superficially, more warm and less distant to be concerned with psychosis" (Roazen, 1975, p. 157).

Reading Sullivan or Frieda Fromm-Reichmann or Searles, it is indeed their humanity that strikes one first, and I think this is because they go for whole-person experiences and for people in their context. They do not go for their drives or their instincts, as was the normal way in the 1920s and 1930s, or for other part-objects, as is often the way now. They do not imply that very confused people will get better if you interpret their motives or other bits of them. They imply that you have to relate to the whole person, with some overall sense of who is there before you. It can be a desolating experience to be talked to by someone who sees you as a target for a therapeutic technique, in terms of your archaic processes only, like seeing your own skeleton in an X-ray. I think that even today, theories and concepts can get in the way of helping very disturbed people.

Harry Stack Sullivan

American-born, Harry Stack Sullivan seems to have been at Chestnut Lodge before the others, in the 1920s and the 1930s. A psychiatrist who had had a Freudian training analysis, he gradually relaxed from the doctrines of his day, like his friends Fromm, Horney, Kardiner, and others. He never published much himself; his colleagues did so after his death, from lecture notes and other material he had left:

• *The Psychiatric Interview*, edited by Helen Perry and Mary Gawel (1954), really takes one into the consulting-room:

structuring the situation, early stages, the detailed enquiry, patients' expectations, the psychiatrist's contributions, and so on.

- *Clinical Studies in Psychiatry*, edited by Helen Perry, Mary Gawel, and Martha Gibbon (1956), benefits from an easy humane yet precise and detailed way of writing about his experience with patients, covering hypochondria, paranoia, dissociative processes, hysteria and obsessions, manic-depression, with useful case-illustrations.

- *Psycho-Analysis and Interpersonal Psychiatry: The Contribution of Harry Stack Sullivan*, by Patrick Mullahy (1970), gives a systematic analysis of all his ideas.

Sullivan's colleague Mullahy makes clear his primary interest in what we would now call object-relations:

> According to Sullivan, two people acting together, reciprocally, make the situation. Pre-existing fixed drives do not explain an interpersonal situation, because they are not observed. . . . It is, then, a person-integrated-in-a-situation-with-another-person, an interpersonal situation, which one studies. [Mullahy, 1955, pp. 245–247]

Sullivan is quite oddly misrepresented by Brown. Equally oddly, Guntrip finds him boring, perhaps because he does not agree with Sullivan's way of looking at the self. He seems to me to write in a very accessible plain style, very experience-near, with many telling illustrations.

Under Sullivan's influence and his co-workers', some very innovative and humane work was done with people diagnosed as chronically schizophrenic or generally psychotic. The tone they used in addressing themselves to people's problems seems to me strikingly different from the manner then prevailing. Their rapport and respect for people's anxieties is noticeable. More than Horney, more than Erikson, they were interested not only in general cultural influences, but also in minutely specific bits of parental behaviour that might generate or alleviate a child's anxieties. And when they write about techniques in psychiatry, it is obvious that they know how easy it is to increase anxieties in the course of professional procedures, to the detriment of the patient.

Neo-Freudian and Chestnut Lodge theories

Both the Neo-Freudians and Chestnut Lodge tend to be thought of as relatively less preoccupied with the more deeply unconscious layers of personality, and this is so. However, to my mind, this does not mean that their patients were handicapped in that respect. Having theories about those depths is one thing, being in touch with the pain and anxiety that spring from there is another and is quite as needful.

Guntrip (1971) attributes such lack of depth to Sullivan, and I think this was based on just this confusion of those two desirables. People behaving in schizophrenic ways are often very disturbed indeed, often underperforming intellectually, nowadays often uneducated, often from a culture that does not encourage introspection. Hospital doctors, such as those at Chestnut Lodge, have constantly to keep in mind what is called the management of the patient. "Management" is a term for what one does for patients, especially masses of patients as in a hospital, when one is not doing pure analysis with them, when one is not helping them to make some unconscious process conscious by means of a verbal comment called an interpretation. One cannot always contain people's feelings by pointing out the unconscious elements in what they are saying or doing, especially when group processes are also at work. Some patients need management if you are to talk with them at all, and in the era we are now considering, there was no such medication as we now have.

Frieda Fromm-Reichmann

Frieda Fromm-Reichmann had worked for years in Dresden as a psychiatrist and was a member of the Berlin Institute. Before emigrating, she was already a leading authority on the treatment of psychotics. Roazen adds that when she first came to work at Chestnut Lodge, an emissary from the American Psychoanalytic Association came to at least one of her seminars to find out whether she was teaching unorthodox ideas (Roazen, 1975, pp. 498–499). Sullivan is one of the four to whom she dedicated her *Principles of Intensive Psychotherapy* (1953), the others being Sigmund Freud, Kurt Goldstein, and Georg Groddeck—collectively: "My Teachers".

More, much more than Sullivan, she skirts round the assumption of the 1930s' version of orthodox psychoanalysis, that the intellectual aspects of analysis do much for the patient. Making the unconscious conscious, and pointing out to people where they are defensive, was the main therapeutic procedure of that time. She seems vague in her book about what does get people better (possibly because the concept of therapeutic regression had not yet properly evolved in the United States, or travelled there, and that was what she was partly after), but she used her own emotionally intelligent personality to understand what the patient wanted to tell her "from the core of his or her self, not from the defensive symbolizing structures". Because she focused on what the patient wanted to communicate and related directly to that, she needed to use much less interpretation. She did not interrupt the patients' attempts to be in touch with themselves or with her by pointing out their defensive manoeuvres. Just understanding got her to the core. Concepts like self and core are very typical of her and of all the Chestnut Lodge people, as, incidentally, they were at that time to R. D. Laing in Britain, another psychiatrist interested in schizophrenic phenomena.

It appears to me that the main concept she operated with was reaction to psychic pain. This has much to commend it, it being easier for us to see pain than to see some structural process such as an inner object. It is not difficult to see people defending themselves against pain, by being passive, or noisy, or blaming, or whatever. She does not even feel the need to distinguish between painful anxiety and painful depression. She stays with the world that is more easily known to the patient, writing in a way that suggests that what she saw going on between her and her patient was governed by her perception of what they were feeling. She was careful to go at the patient's pace, to give respect. In this connection it is also warming that the first 45 pages of *Principles* are about the psychiatrist's needs, feelings, and experiences.

Principles of Intensive Psychotherapy (1950) is still a helpful book for students to buy, though supervisors are wary of it because it sometimes appears to assume that you help your patients through kindness and sympathy rather than through accurately feeding back to them explanations about the anxieties from which they suffer, which is what students have to learn to do. Frieda Fromm-Reichmann does indeed give that impression, but I think we need to understand that she takes all the rest for granted. Without kindness and common sense, no technique will work. And we know how she did in fact work, because one of her ex-patients, writing under the pseudonym Hannah Green, wrote a moving novel about her work under the title *I Never Promised You a Rose-Garden* (1964).

H. F. Searles

The first of the post–World-War-Two generation to be looked at in this chapter, Searles, is in my view the greatest of the Chestnut Lodge group, and perhaps the greatest and most original psychoanalytic writer to have emerged in the United States. His work is convincingly based on clinical experience and written in acceptable prose. Searles moved from medicine to psychiatry in reaction to his war-time experiences, and thence to psychoanalysis, as many others must have been doing at much the same time, including Sutherland and Bion in Britain. For fifteen years he worked full-time at Chestnut Lodge with chronic sufferers from schizophrenia, with some of them for all of those fifteen years, some even longer.

Searles' originality shows first in *The Non-Human Environment in Normal Development and in Schizophrenia* (1960), whose main point is to confirm the validity of what we can feel for the non-human world: a landscape, a fine building, a symphony, "kinship with one's non-human environment generally" (1960, preface). We relate to the non-human not only by a displacement of feeling from some interpersonal or intrapsychic relationship (an existing inner object-relation, in British terms) but also because we are capable of a direct response, to a cat *as being a cat*, to a tree *as being a tree* (Searles' italics).

One of his acknowledgements in 1960 is to Frieda Fromm-Reichmann. And in his next book, *Collected Papers on Schizophrenia and Related Subjects* (1965), he again acknowledges his debt to her in the preface:

I especially value her insight into the schizophrenic patient's own experience of his world; her steady focus upon the flowingly dynamic process of the therapeutic relationship rather than one's focusing too much upon, and becoming lost in, the context of the patient's words; and her personal example of the essential place which not only intuitive tenderness but also unflinching toughness have in the treatment of schizophrenic individuals.

Robert Young (1994) discerns three themes, very much, I think, in order of their importance.

1. the particular kind of closeness between patient and therapist which Searles calls symbiosis;

2. the ways in which patients function as therapists to their therapist;

3. the pleasure some patients take in tormenting their therapist, and the harm done if the therapist ignores it.

Reading Searles in the 1980s and 1990s, in London, it is striking how much and how early Searles was writing about transference and countertransference, as well as processes very like projection and projective identification, usually without using these words. In this connection, Young points out that Searles was already interested in these phenomena in 1949, before object-relations theory had got properly off the ground and even in Britain people were still analysing in terms of drive-derivatives and defences. According to Young, Searles tried to publish his first paper on countertransference in 1949 and was repeatedly advised by the orthodox journals of the day to stick to the mainstream of psychoanalysis. His important 1961 paper on the therapy of schizophrenia was first published in a British journal of psychological medicine (Searles, 1961, chapter 18).

One of Searles' favourite concepts is what he calls "therapeutic symbiosis". He means a particular phase of therapy to which he became sensitive in his work with people beset by schizophrenic ways of thinking and feeling. He became aware that he did not always experience a clear and firm boundary between himself and a patient (1979, p. 32). He does not have recourse to the concept of projective identification: for him that sense of the slopping-over of the patient's mental contents into the therapist is not a patient's way of intentionally if unconsciously communicating with him. But he writes of a way in which therapists can allow themselves to be open to largely non-verbal cues as to a patient's state of mind—a state the patient is often by no means aware of and by no means wishing to do anything with, rather in the way in which we can be open to a landscape and feel for it without attributing intentionality to the landscape. It is possible to catch cues from people's body-language, from the way they say things, and from the gaps in what they say. Much is achieved when therapists let their inferences, based on their own experiences, come into consciousness (1979, chapter 22: "Transitional Phenomena and Therapeutic Symbiosis"). Where therapists repress these inferences, they cannot operate at this level. For instance, if therapists are afraid of and have repressed their own violence and hate, then they cannot receive these accurately.

As Searles sees it, it is possible for therapists to be open and undefended in allowing into consciousness their own violence, erotism, panic, chaos, or whatever. When these things are not disowned but recognized and accepted in ourselves, we can be sensitively in touch with them in other people, and we need not distort or disown their ebb and flow in the patient.

We need to be both flexible and secure in our own identity for this. Searles writes of experiencing, at the beginning of his career as a psychiatrist, "the well-known problem of how best to cope with the massive amounts of data which need to be assimilated quickly—what criterion, what points of orientation to employ in order to find coherence in what transpires".

I have found that the most reliable data are gained from my noticing . . . the vicissitudes of my own sense of identity during the session.

As a therapist, I have to stay aware of my own love or fear or boredom or whatever, and to be accepting of the knowledge that this is the sort of person I am being. Then eventually, and after a good deal of process, the patient can see that I, the therapist, am accepting and acknowledging my feelings and "object-identifications", without any harm ensuing: I am living with them in a relatively anxiety-free way. The patient can see

me containing myself—and this is what the patient internalizes.

Waves and currents around the Statue of Liberty: ego-psychology and self-psychology— from Hartmann to both Kernberg and Kohut

Heinz Hartmann

Heinz Hartmann's contribution to psychoanalytic theory is the
notion of the ego as a "conflict-free sphere". Because of its
original interest in pathology, psychoanalysis had tended to
view ego-development simply in terms of the conflict between
instincts and what thwarted their expression. The interest
Alfred Adler took in such notions as the ego and the will to
power had been part of Freud's quarrel with him. At that time
the ego was thought of as just a thin skin between the demands
of "reality" and the demands of the instincts. But by the 1930s,
ego-psychology began to be more important, and some writers
diverted their attention from the vicissitudes of the instincts to
consider the mechanisms by means of which the ego optimizes
the outcome of conflicts between demands. Anna Freud was
one of these, but she was mainly interested in the defensive
functions of the ego. Heinz Hartmann, however, endowed the
ego with more adaptive functions as well: he lists perception,
object-comprehension, recall, and the acquisition of language
skills, as well as motor skills like crawling and walking. He
proposed the term "conflict-free sphere" for that assembly of
functions which at any particular time is not affected by the
eternal battle of id versus ego and superego. This was a far-
reaching innovation, though Hartmann had not wanted it to be
seen as this. He felt himself to be a loyal follower of Freud.
Nevertheless, he left Vienna in the 1930s, though he did not
need to do so for political or religious reasons; eventually he
became President of the American Psychoanalytic Society.

Hartmann's revolutionary contribution was to give a much
more important role to what he and Freud agreed to be the
functions of the ego. For Freud, the ego had three tyrannical

masters: the external world, the superego, and the id. The ego had the practically impossible task of manoeuvring with instinctual energies "as a rider does with his horse". Hartmann, instead of continuing to see the ego as a purely dependent psychological variable, purely a desperate rider clinging on, wrote of ego-processes that were free of intrapsychic conflict— he saw the ego-functions as steering people through life's problems. In the then psychoanalytic climate, people did not steer themselves: what they did was the more or less helpless outcome of instinctual and reality pressures. For Freud, conflict was the central notion. For Hartmann, it was adaptation.

Hartmann never went so far as to hypothesize an independent ego, an identity. Guntrip voiced his disappointment at this: "The person is taken for granted, and all the emphasis is on the systems-ego, true to the id-plus-ego-control-apparatus of Freud's theory. It is a structural theory, not a personal one" (Guntrip, 1971, pp. 29–30).

Heinz Kohut and Otto Kernberg

Often presented as contrasting, both Kohut and Kernberg took that decisive step to a "personal" theory of the ego. With them, we move definitely from considering the generation of immigrants who came before the Second World War to look at those who came after.

Kohut became President of the American Psychoanalytic Association after Hartmann, and nothing can surely be more establishment. But in 1971 he published *The Analysis of the Self*, and in 1977, *The Restoration of the Self*, unacceptable to the strictly orthodox of that time. He had become increasingly interested in the self as the core of a person's consciousness of identity and continuity, a self that is much more than a badgered interface keeping inner and outer reality in some kind of balance. This took him to a reconsideration of Freudian theories of narcissism. In his view, when things go wrong with the sense of self, narcissistic disorders ensue. When Kohut was training, narcissistic disorders were thought of as inaccessible to the psychoanalytic method—the ego could not be strong enough or free enough to cooperate with the analyst. Kohut evolved a fairly complete working theory from his experience in the consulting-room, of working with narcissistic phenomena. He starts from the sense of self, particularly of self-esteem, and the consequences of wounded self-esteem. Narcissistically hurt people repeat, in their relationship with the analyst, all the hope, fear, grief, and rage that come from not having been recognized properly in their early days as people in their own right. This is the mirroring transference. As well as this, or instead, the narcissistically wounded person will develop an idealizing transference, which ensures that there is at least some feeling in the room that someone is wonderful, whether it be patient or analyst. These ideas are very interesting in themselves. But they are made the more interesting by Kohut's emphasis on rapport, intuition, and empathy as therapeutic agents, and also as ways of knowing what the other feels. It was this emphasis, perhaps above all, which offended his orthodox colleagues: that Kohut should derive his theory from what he believed he was intuitively understanding about his patients, instead of validating what he experienced in terms of the tried and tested concepts of established theory.

* * *

Kernberg has been important in bringing under the aegis of psychoanalytic psychotherapy both psychiatrists and many patients who had hitherto been refused as unanalysable. Representative of his wide interests are *Borderline Conditions and Pathological Narcissism* (1975), *Object Relations and Clinical Psychoanalysis* (1976), *Internal World and External Reality* (1980) (both the latter include chapters on falling in love, on group phenomena, and on hospital treatment), *Severe Personality Disorders* (1984) (which presents a highly structured framework for the diagnosis of mental disturbance and recommendations as to treatment in each category).

I have given credit to several of Kernberg's interesting ideas throughout this volume, but not yet to the contribution made by his *Object Relations and Clinical Psychoanalysis*, which spells out his reconciliation of what had been thought two incompatible theoretical ideas: that motivation arises from object-relations, and that motivation derives from instinctive drives. He proposes, as the reconciling link, the Affect that accompanies the Subject's instinctive drive towards the Object. This Affect makes the Object valuable to the Subject. So here we have people (Subjects) in affective relation to their Objects (other people), and lo! a true O–R theory, which nevertheless respects the motivational force of the instincts. Kernberg generously—perhaps over-generously—acknowledges his indebtedness to Edith Jacobs, Margaret Mahler, and, unusually for any analyst, Fairbairn. It is also interesting, from the British point of view, that Kernberg was for long the closest anyone in the United States had come to seeing the psychic world in a Kleinian way.

In Britain until recently Kernberg was mainly known for his views on aggression, which teachers loved to contrast with Kohut's. Kernberg postulates a death instinct inborn and therefore very much to be reckoned with in the treatment of every patient, while Kohut sees aggression mainly as the outcome of severe narcissistic wounding and therefore not necessarily of paramount importance in the treatment of every patient. Setting the two by the ears in this way does both great theorists an injustice; they have much more to offer than that. Both give firm (albeit not identical) directions on the treatment of narcissistic disorders, particularly as regards the handling of transferences.

They also have a less felicitous trait in common. It is a curious fact that continentals who came to Britain have tended to fall in love with the English language and write it with exquisite polish and care, whereas those who went to the United States appear to have cloth ears. Both Kohut and Kernberg write unacceptably turgid prose.

I have singled out Kohut and Kernberg from the post–World-War-Two developments of psychoanalytic thought in the United States. There are other interesting and important figures, among them Roy Schafer, Robert Langs, and Thomas Ogden, and, from the 1970s, well outside psychoanalytic boundaries though originating within, there has been another outburst of creative therapeutic ideas: Encounter, Gestalt, Bio-energetics, Transactional Analysis, and other such. Reconciliation with these is hard to imagine as yet. But there have been important

developments in another field of study which had psychoanalysis as its source and which is now feeding back into the mainstream.

Waves and currents around the Statue of Liberty: respect for empirical research into childhood— Spitz, Mahler and co., Ainsworth and co., and Stern and co.

Outside psychoanalytic circles, empirical research is understood to be a procedure by which hypotheses are clearly stated,
first in their abstract and theoretical form, and then in opera-
tional terms—that is, in terms of what the facts would have to
be either to confirm or to invalidate the hypotheses, after a
statistically acceptable number of instances have been exam-
ined. Strict rules have to be obeyed as to what counts as
evidence: other researchers have to be able to replicate the
procedure and the results, and so on. This idea of research
needs to be stated explicitly for psychoanalytic readers as it is
very different from what many of them think.

Nowhere is the difference more clearly visible than in theories about the life of children, and this is the final thread
weaving through the rich tapestry of the American traditions of
psychoanalytic thought. It is spun by R. A. Spitz, by Margaret
Mahler and her co-workers, and more recently by Mary
Ainsworth and others, and Daniel Stern and the many research-workers he draws on. Until recently, the only British
representative was John Bowlby, from whom Mary Ainsworth
drew her inspiration; now there are Colwyn Trevarthen and his
co-workers, and Lynne Murray and hers, and others.

At much the same time as Bowlby was looking up the
statistics on "forty-four juvenile thieves, their character and
home-life" (published in the *International Journal of Psychoanalysis* for 1944), Spitz's papers on what he called hospitalism
were being published in the first two volumes of *The Psychoanalytic Study of the Child* (1945–1946). Thus was started a
new kind of study—of the actual behaviour of the little white
English-speaking baby and of the relation of this to later per-

sonality-configurations. The English philosophical tradition of empiricism and pragmatism had run down by then, and Bowlby's interest earned him the cold shoulder from the then pillars of the British psychoanalytic establishment, though he is admired and loved in other traditions of psychological study, and respected by Eric Rayner, whose book, significantly, is called *The Independent Mind in British Psychoanalysis* (1991; see also the warm obituary of Bowlby in the *International Journal of Psychoanalysis*, by King & Rayner, 1993). Bowlby took a great interest in Spitz's work and often referred to it; he also criticized Spitz for explaining his empirical findings by psychoanalytic theories that did not fit those findings very well. Margaret Mahler, in somewhat the same tradition, was to have the same problems of fitting empirical to theoretical notions, and recently Daniel Stern, the latest and most noted exponent of the empirical study of the child, initially encountered similar non-comprehension on visits to London from the Kleinians here, who kept pointing out that what he said did not fit their theories of child-development. In 1992 something like the "Controversial Discussions" took place, seeking rapprochement—to what effect, is as yet unclear. What, in my view, empirical research has to recommend it is that if Stern is wrong, facts will appear that will prove it to him. But in the first encounter it seemed as though his challengers could never be unhorsed by any research. I believe that a respectable theory can only be built on the basis of a verifiable and falsifiable kind of research.

Spitz

Spitz made a comparison between two sets of infants, one from a nursing home where mothers from a corrective institution had their babies and waited with them for them to be adopted, the other set from a foundling hospital. In the former, the mothers were around their babies a good deal, and the babies had plenty to watch throughout the day, from their cribs in the mother-and-baby ward. In the latter were seven nurses for 45 babies, and only a few mothers visited even intermittently. Each baby lay in a cot screened from the other by sheets hung as curtains. Striking differences began to show after four months, in morbidity, mortality, and a syndrome Spitz called "hospitalism"—a pitiable state of torpor and unresponsiveness such as we have recently seen in the tragic films of orphanages in Rumania and other temporarily benighted Balkan states, with marked retardation of speech and of intellectual and physical development generally. In the second year, of the 26 foundling children then under observation, only two were able to walk, and only these two spoke at all, and only just a few words, while the development of the "nursing-home" babies went normally.

From this research onward, other studies produced similar results. A climate began to be created that made it possible to try to understand what children actually did, in contrast to the still generally prevailing psychoanalytic interest in reconstructing the child's experience from the adult patient's behaviour in the consulting-room.

To those accustomed to attributing motivational force to infantile phantasy, empirical research may appear lacking in emotional and motivational interest. I have to concede that what you can gain by watching a baby's behaviour from the perspective of empirical research is more likely to be cognitive/social/emotional, because that is technically easier to set up: the current kind of empirical research is less likely to cast much light on a baby's unconscious phantasy-life in any way on which impartial observers would agree. But it does seem to me to have considerable explanatory power. The issue needs a great deal more thought as well as experimental work.

Margaret Mahler

Margaret Mahler, like Spitz, went to the United States just before the Second World War, he from the Berlin Institute, she from Vienna, where she had been a paediatrician, as Winnicott was to be in Britain before long. Being a child specialist makes a lot of difference to the way you theorize, even if you are an analyst. You have seen a lot of children in the flesh; you are not making deductions about them from what you intuitively feel to be the child part of the adult patient on your couch.

Like Sullivan, Mahler seems not to have liked writing much herself, but to have relied on her co-workers (Mahler & Furer, 1968, Mahler, Pine, & Bergman, 1975). She watched children in her nursery at various ages, and concluded that there were distinct stages in the development of their individuality and in the way they related to their mothers and to other people. Bowlby, and others, consider that she had a lot of difficulty reconciling development as she saw it, with the then mandatory sequence of oral, anal, and genital libidinal interests in which the child was thought to engage. But Kernberg, that pillar of orthodoxy, took her up again in the 1970s—perhaps in a form she might have difficulty in recognizing as hers (Kernberg, 1975, 1976, and especially 1980). Her interest, like Sullivan's, was not only in the child, but quite as much in the behaviour and attitude of the mother as a determinant of the child's personality—a view abhorrent at that time to Freudians as well as Kleinians. She conceived of the child as empathizing with the mother's anxieties, as making efforts to elicit tenderness from the mother and other care-takers, as trying to mould itself to the expectations of its parents. This consciousness of the importance of parental attitudes in moulding the child is very different from the drive-oriented theories of motivation that held the field in the United States in Mahler's day.

Mary Ainsworth

Mary Ainsworth, from Canada, worked with Bowlby in the 1960s, inspired by his and the Robertsons' work on separation anxiety. Where the Robertsons (Robertson, 1952) mainly filmed what was happening to parents and children (just as Spitz observed) in an uncontrived way, Ainsworth, like Mahler, set up laboratory-like situations that could be (and often have been) replicated by other research-workers. Her cardinal contribution is the invention of the "Strange Situation" set-up, filmed many times now with many variations, but basically: mother is with baby, stranger enters, mother leaves, mother returns. Three main categories were identified straight away, predicted by Bowlby's monumental collating work. The children's responses proved to be markedly determined by the

mother's habitual ways of being with the baby: (1) the secure
baby, who cries when mother leaves and is pacified when she
returns; (2) the anxious clinging baby, who cries a lot anyway
and is hard to pacify; and (3) the anxious avoidant baby, who
acts out a see-if-I-care mode. Many interesting refinements
have followed (see Main, Kaplan, & Cassidy, 1985; Main &
Solomon, 1987; Main & Weston, 1981).

Daniel Stern

Daniel Stern's distinction lies in his respect for the masses of
empirical work on child development being contributed by
other research-work, and in his genius for putting the results
together in what is actually a blurry outline of an empirically
based general theory. Some of the evidence may be a bit shaky,
some will be disproved or modified by later work, or, perhaps,
with a shake of the kaleidoscope, the whole picture will change
as new ways of looking at things emerge, but whatever eventu-
ates, it will be on the basis he and his like propose, directly or
in reaction to it.

Stern, like Searles though probably young enough to be his
son, is American-born, of the post–World-War-Two generation,
and a psychiatrist. He acknowledges indebtedness to an array
of people which makes him unique among psychoanalysts: to
the ethologists, who study animals in their natural habitat, to
Margaret Mahler, to his predecessor and model Robert Emde,
and, finally, to the experimental methods of developmental
psychology. By gathering all these into his acknowledgements,
he takes practical steps to diminish the great gap between what
psychoanalysts think they know—ignorant as they are outside
their own field, and what experimental psychologist think they
know—repelled as they are by psychoanalytic ways of thought.
(A very telling British version of this mutual aversion is manifested in Bion's views on the nature of thinking, which show no
awareness that more than a hundred years of experimental
work has been published on this topic elsewhere.) Characteristic of the post-Freudian tradition, Stern is interested in the
development of the self and of the sense of self. Unusually, he
writes of the infant as if it were an independent individual from

birth. He finds no evidence of anything like an original merged or symbiotic state followed by a slow process of separation/individuation from the mother. Nor does the infant need to project or introject—all that kind of theorizing is bypassed.

Stern, a kind of self-psychologist, sees the infant as, at the start, the locus of processes that it has not yet the full equipment to perceive or conceive of—he calls this the stage of the emergent self. From the second month onward, this stage is accompanied by another, during which there is a growing sense of what Stern calls a core-self, and the baby gets a sense of the connectedness of itself to its arms and legs and such, of the flow of time, of recurrent visual and other shapes. All these experiences have the effect of creating a sense that there is a world of others, of not-my-arms, not-my-legs, of others who come and go, and so on. By the second half of the first year this leads to something like a discovery that there are not only other things, but that some of these have minds not unlike the baby's own, and that interchange and communication is possible. Of course, the infant has been communicating before this, but it did not know it. Now there is more of a sense that there are two persons. I, the infant, can say to you, the other, "Milk", meaning essentially, "Would you please hand me a mug of milk", whereas previously my cry of "Milk" had meant essentially, "I have milk on my mind". The mother is not now a self-object, in Kohut's sense. Sharing becomes possible. Stern calls this phase the development of a subjective self. By fifteen months a sense of a verbal self develops, and so, with this, a sense of privacy, and there is less dependence on rapport (which Stern calls "affect attunement"). All this is interesting, but the really important point is that many of these bits of theory are based on bits of empirical research, much of it brilliant in its ingenuity.

* * *

We cannot see into the future. It may be that, with the astonishing recent developments in the ease with which ideas can be instantly communicated by fax and computer network, there will be an increasing consensus of theory world-wide. That such consensus has a desirable side is obvious, but what this chapter has illustrated is that the space to diverge can also have very creative consequences, in breadth if not in depth.

That there is need both for conformity and for space to differ, contributes to a belief I would dearly like to maintain: that if sufficient people are sufficiently serious about their views, and more interested in their views than possessive of them, but more possessive than complacently obliging—in short, if they have humility, courage, and balance—the outcome of enquiry cannot fail to be creative in the longer run.

> *We must be humble. We are so easily baffled by appearances*
> *And do not realize that these stones are one with the stars.*
> *It makes no difference to them whether they are high or low,*
> *Mountain peak or ocean floor, palace or pigsty.*
> *There are plenty of ruined buildings in the world but no ruined*
>   *stones.*

Hugh MacDiarmid, *Stones*

REFERENCES

Abraham, K. (1924). A short study in the development of the libido, viewed in the light of mental disorders. In *Selected Papers on Psychoanalysis*. London: Hogarth Press. [Reprinted London: Karnac Books, 1979.]

Ainsworth, M. D. S. (1982). Attachment: Retrospect and prospect. In: C. M. Parkes & J. Stevenson-Hinde (Eds.), *The Place of Attachment in Human Behaviour*. New York: Basic Books; London: Tavistock.

Ainsworth, M. D. S. (1985). I. Patterns of infant–mother attachment antecedents and effects on development. II. Attachments across the lifespan. *Bulletin of New York Academy of Medicine*, *61*: 771–791, 791–812.

Ainsworth, M. D. S., Bell, S. M., & Stayton, D. J. (1971). Individual differences in strange situation behaviour of one-year-olds. In: H. R. Schaffer (Ed.), *The Origins of Human Social Relations*. London: Academic Press.

Ainsworth, M. D. S., Blehar, S. M., Waters, E., & Walls, S. (1978). *Patterns of Attachment: Assessed in the Strange Situation and at Home*. Hillsdale, NJ: Lawrence Erlbaum.

Anzieu, D. (1987). Some alterations of the ego which make analysis interminable. *International Journal of Psycho-Analysis, 68*: 9–20.

Badaracco, J. E. G. (1992). Psychic change and its clinical evaluation. *International Journal of Psycho-Analysis, 73*: 209–220.

Balint, M. (1959). *Thrills and Regressions.* London: Hogarth Press. [Reprinted London: Karnac Books, 1987.]

Balint, M. (1968). *The Basic Fault.* London: Tavistock.

Bernstein, B. (1971–1977). *Class, Codes and Control* (Series). London: Routledge & Kegan Paul.

Bianchedi, E. T. di (1991). Psychic change: The "becoming" of an inquiry. *International Journal of Psycho-Analysis, 72*: 6–15.

Bick, E. (1968). The experience of the skin in early object-relations. *International Journal of Psycho-Analysis, 49*: 484–486.

Bion, W. R. (1962a). *Learning from Experience.* London: Heinemann. [Reprinted London: Karnac Books, 1984.]

Bion, W. R. (1962b). The psycho-analytic study of thinking. *International Journal of Psycho-Analysis, 43*: 484–486. [Also in: *Second Thoughts,* London: Heinemann Medical, 1967; reprinted London: Karnac Books, 1984.]

Bion, W. R. (1967). *Second Thoughts.* London: Heinemann. [Reprinted London: Karnac Books, 1984.]

Bion, W. R. (1970). *Attention and Interpretation.* London: Tavistock. [Reprinted London: Karnac Books, 1984.]

Blatt, S. J., & Behrends, R. S. (1987). Internalisation, separation-individuation, and the nature of therapeutic action. *International Journal of Psycho-Analysis, 68*: 279–298.

Blos, P. (1984). Son and father, before and beyond the Oedipus Complex. *Journal of the American Psycho-Analytic Association. 32*: 301–24. [Also in D. B. Breen, *The Gender Conundrum.* London: Routledge, 1993.]

Blum, H. P. (1992). Psychic change: The analytic relationship and agents of change. *International Journal of Psycho-Analysis, 73*: 255–266.

Bollas, C. (1987). *The Shadow of the Object.* London: Free Association Press.

Bollas, C. (1989). *Forces of Destiny.* London: Free Association Press.

Bowlby, J. (1944). Forty-four juvenile thieves, their character and home life. *International Journal of Psycho-Analysis, 25*: 19–52,

107–127. [Also London: Baillère, Tindall and Cox, 1946.]

Bowlby, J. (1969). *Attachment and Loss, Vol. 1: Attachment*. London: Hogarth Press; New York: Basic Books.

Bowlby, J. (1973). *Attachment and Loss, Vol. 2: Separation: Anxiety and Anger*. London: Hogarth Press; New York, Basic Books.

Bowlby, J. (1980). *Attachment and Loss, Vol. 3: Loss: Sadness and Depression*. London: Hogarth Press; New York: Basic Books.

Bowlby, J. (1988). *A Secure Base*. London: Routledge.

Breen, D. B. (1993). *The Gender Conundrum*. London: Routledge.

Brenton, H. (1982). *The Romans in Britain*. London: Methuen.

Britton, R. (1989). The missing link: Parental sexuality and the Oedipus Complex. In: R. Britton, M. Feldman, & E. O'Shaughnessy (Eds.), *The Oedipus Complex Today*. London: Karnac Books.

Brown, J. A. C. (1964). *Freud and the Post-Freudians*. Harmondsworth: Penguin.

Cardinal, M. (1975). *The Words to Say It* (tr. from the French). London: Picador, 1983.

Casement, P. (1985). *On Learning from the Patient*. London: Tavistock.

Casement, P. (1990). *Further Learning from the Patient*. London: Tavistock.

Chasseguet-Smirgel, J. (1984). *Creativity and Perversion*. London: Free Association Books.

Coltart, I., Covington, C., & Sherman, A. (1988). The lost ones. *British Journal of Psychotherapy. 4*: 380–392.

Coltart, N. (1988). Diagnosis and assessment for suitability for psychoanalytic psychotherapy. *British Journal of Psychotherapy. 4*: 127–134.

Cooper, A. M. (1992). Psychic change: Development in the theory of psychoanalytic technique. *International Journal of Psycho-Analysis, 73*: 245–250.

Davis, M., & Wallbridge, D. (1981). *Boundary and Space: An Introduction to the Work of D. W. Winnicott*. London: Penguin. [Reprinted London: Karnac Books, 1981.]

Emde, R. N. (1988). Development terminable and interminable, I: Innate and motivational factors from infancy; II: Recent psycho-analytic theory and therapeutic considerations. *International Journal of Psycho-Analysis, 69*: 23–37, 283–296.

Erikson, E. (1951). *Childhood and Society*. New York: W. W. Norton.

Erikson, E. (1968). *Identity, Youth, and Crisis*. London: Faber & Faber.

Fé d'Ostiani, E. (1980). An individual approach to psychotherapy with psychotic patients. *Child Psychotherapy*. 6: 57–79.

Fenichel, O. (1946). *The Psycho-Analytic Theory of Neurosis*. London: Routledge & Kegan Paul.

Fonagy, P. (1991). Thinking about thinking: Some clinical and theoretical considerations in the treatment of a borderline patient. *International Journal of Psycho-Analysis*, 72: 639–656.

Fonagy, P., & Moran, G. (1991). Understanding psychic change in child analysis. *International Journal of Psycho-Analysis*, 72: 15–22.

Freud Research Group (J. Barron et al.) (1991). Sigmund Freud: The secrets of nature and the nature of secrets. *International Review of Psycho-Analysis, 18*: 143–165.

Freud, S. (1895d) (with Breuer, J.). *Studies in Hysteria. S.E. 21*.

Freud, S. (1912b). The dynamics of the transference. *S.E. 12*.

Freud, S. (1914c). On narcissism: An introduction. *S.E. 16*.

Freud, S. (1914g). Remembering, repeating and working-through. *S.E. 16*.

Freud, S. (1920g). *Beyond the Pleasure Principle. S.E. 18*.

Freud, S. (1923b). *The Ego and the Id. S.E. 19*.

Freud, S. (1925j). Some psychical consequences of the anatomical distinction between the sexes. *S.E. 19*.

Freud, S. (1926e). *The Question of Lay Analysis. S. E. 20*.

Fromm, E. (1946). *The Fear of Freedom*. London: Routledge & Kegan Paul.

Fromm-Reichmann, F. (1950). *Principles of Intensive Psychotherapy*. Chicago, IL: University of Chicago Press. [Also London: Allen & Unwin, 1953.]

Fromm-Reichmann, F. (1965). *Collected Papers on Schizophrenia and Related Subjects*. Chicago, IL: University of Chicago Press.

Giradoux, J. (1953). The Tiger at the Gates [from *La Guerre de Troie N'Aura Pas Lieu*]. London: Methuen.

Green, H. (1964). *I Never Promised You a Rose-Garden*. London: Gollancz. [Also London: Pan Books 1967.]

Greenberg, J. R., & Mitchell, S. A. (1983). *Object Relations in Psycho-Analytic Theory*. Boston, MA: Harvard University Press.

Greenson, R. (1967). *The Technique and Practice of Psycho-Analysis*. New York: International Universities Press.

Guntrip, H. (1961). *Personality Structure and Human Interaction*. London: Hogarth Press.

Guntrip, H. (1971). *Psychoanalytic Theory, Therapy and the Self*. London: Basic Books. [Reprinted London: Karnac Books, 1985.]

Haessler, L. (1991). Relationships between extra-transference and transference interpretations: A clinical study. *International Journal of Psycho-Analysis, 72*: 463–478.

Hartmann, H. (1939). *Ego Psychology and the Problem of Adaptation*. New York: International Universities Press.

Hescott, B. (1983). *The Feast of Fools*. London: Gulbenkian Foundation.

Hoffer, W. (1956). Transference and transference neurosis. *International Journal of Psycho-Analysis, 37*: 377–379.

Hoggart, R. (1958). *The Uses of Literacy*. London: Chatto & Windus.

Hopkins, G. M. (1977). Spring. In: *Selected Poems*. London. Heinemann, Pelican.

Hopkins, J. (1990). The observed infant of attachment theory. *British Journal of Psychotherapy. 6*: 460–470.

Joseph, B. (1992). Psychic change: Some perspectives. *International Journal of Psycho-Analysis, 73*: 237–244.

Kellner, J. (1975). *The Betrayal of the Body*. London. Tavistock.

Kernberg, O. (1972). Psychotherapy and psychoanalysis. The final report of the Menninger Foundation's psychotherapy research project. *Bulletin of the Menninger Clinic. 36*: 1–275.

Kernberg, O. (1975). *Borderline Conditions and Pathological Narcissism*. New York: Jason Aronson.

Kernberg, O. (1976). *Object Relations and Clinical Psychoanalysis*. New York: Jason Aronson.

Kernberg, O. (1980). *Internal World and External Reality*. New York: Jason Aronson.

Kernberg, O. (1984). *Severe Personality Disorders*. Yale University Press.

Killingmo, B. (1989). Conflict and deficit: Implications for technique. *International Journal of Psycho-Analysis, 70*: 65–80.

King, P., & Rayner, E. (1993). John Bowlby's obituary. *International Journal of Psycho-Analysis, 74*: 823–828.

King, P., & Steiner, J. (Eds.) (1991). *The Freud–Klein Controversies.* London: Tavistock/Routledge.

Klein, J. (1987). *Our Need for Others and Its Roots in Infancy.* London: Tavistock/Routledge.

Kohut, H. (1971). *The Analysis of the Self.* New York: International Universities Press.

Kohut, H. (1977). *The Restoration of the Self.* New York: International Universities Press.

Lacan, J. (1988). *The Seminar, Book I: Freud's Papers on Technique 1953–1954* (edited by J. Forrester). Cambridge: Cambridge University Press.

Laing, R. D. (1960). *The Divided Self.* London: Tavistock.

Laplanche, J., & Pontalis, J. B. (1973). *The Language of Psychoanalysis.* London: Hogarth Press. [Reprinted London: Karnac Books, 1988.]

Little, M. (1981). *Transference Neurosis and Transference Psychosis.* New York: Jason Aronson. [Reprinted London: Free Association Books, and London: Karnac Books, 1986.]

Lowen, A. (1971). *The Language of the Body.* London: Collier.

Macauley, R. (1956). *The Towers of Trebizond.* London: Collins.

MacDiarmid, H. (1992). *Selected Poetry.* (edited by A. Riach & M. Grieve). Manchester: Carcanet Press.

MacNeice, L. (1972). Entirely. In: *Collected Poems.* London: Faber & Faber.

Mahler, M. S., & Furer, M. (1968). *On Human Symbiosis and the Vicissitudes of Individuation.* New York: International Universities Press.

Mahler, M. S., Pine, F., & Bergman, A. (1975). *The Psychological Birth of the Human Infant.* New York: Basic Books. [Reprinted London: Karnac Books, 1985.]

Main, M., Kaplan, N., & Cassidy, J. (1985). Security in infancy, childhood and adulthood: A move to a level of representation. In: I. Bretherton & E. Waters (Eds.), *Growing Points in Attachment: Theory and Research.* Monographs of the Society for Research in Child Development, Serial 209 (pp. 66–104). Chicago, IL: University of Chicago Press.

Main, M., & Solomon, J. (1987). Procedure for identifying infants as disorganised/disoriented during the Ainsworth Strange Situation. In: M. Greenberg, D. Cicchetti, & M. Cummmings

(Eds.), *Attachment in the Pre-School Years*. Chicago: University of Chicago Press.

Main, M., & Weston, D. (1981). The quality of the toddler's relationship to mother and father. *Child Development, 52*: 932–940.

Meltzer, D. (1973). *Sexual States of Mind*. London: Clunie Press.

Meltzer, D. (1978). *The Kleinian Development, III: Bion*. London: Clunie Press.

Meltzer, D. (1983). *Dream Life*. London: Clunie Press.

Mullahy, P. (1955). *Conceptions of Modern Psychiatry*. New York: Hemisphere.

Mullahy, P. (1970). *Psychoanalysis and Interpersonal Psychiatry: The Contributions of H. S. Sullivan*. New York: Science House.

Murray, L. (1988). Effects of postnatal depression on infant development: Direct studies of early mother–infant interactions. In: R. Kumar & I. Brockington (Eds.), *Motherhood and Mental Illness, Vol. 2*. London: Butterworth.

Murray, L. (1991). Intersubjectivity, object relations and empirical evidence from mother–infant interactions. *Infant Mental Health Journal, 13*: 218–231.

Murray, L., & Trevarthen C. B. (1986). Environmental regulations of interactions between 2-month-olds and their mothers. In: T. M. Field & N. A. Fox (Eds.), *Social Perception of Infants*. New Jersey: Ablex.

Namnum, R. (1968). The problem of analysing and the autonomous ego. *International Journal of Psycho-Analysis, 49*: 72–82.

Ogden, T. H. (1991). Analysing the matrix of transference. *International Journal of Psycho-Analysis, 72*: 593–606.

Parkin, A. (1991). The two classes of objects and the two classes of transference. *International Journal of Psycho-Analysis, 68*: 185–196.

Pine, F. (1992). From technique to a theory of change. *International Journal of Psycho-Analysis, 73*: 251–254.

Pulver, S. E. (1992). Psychic change: Insight or relationship. *International Journal of Psycho-Analysis, 73*: 199–208.

Rapaport, D. (1967). *Collected Papers*. New York: Basic Books.

Rayner, E. (1991). *The Independent Mind in British Psycho-Analysis*. London: Free Association Press.

Rayner, E., & King, P. (1993). John Bowlby's obituary. *International Journal of Psycho-Analysis, 74*: 823–828.

Reed, G. A. (1990). A reconsideration of the concept of transference neurosis. *International Journal of Psycho-Analysis, 71*: 205–218.

Reich, W. (1933). *Character Analysis.* New York: Orgone Institute Press, 1945.

Reich, W. (1942). *The Functions of the Orgasm.* New York: Noonday Press.

Reich, W. (1943). *The Mass Psychology of Fascism.* London: Faber & Faber.

Reich, W. (1948). *Listen, Little Man.* London: Pelican, 1975.

Renik, O. (1990). The concept of transference neurosis and psycho-analytic methodology. *International Journal of Psycho-Analysis, 71*: 197–204.

Rickman, J. (1951). Methodology and research in psychopathology. *British Journal of Medical Psychology. 24*: 14–21.

Rickman, J. (1957). Number and the human sciences. In: C. Scott (Ed.), *Selected Contributions on Psychoanalysis.* London: Hogarth Press.

Rizzuto, A.-M. (1991). Shame in psycho-analysis: The function of unconscious phantasies. *International Journal of Psycho-Analysis, 72*: 297–313.

Roazen, P. (1975). *Freud and His Followers.* New York: Knopf.

Robertson, J. (1952). *A Two-Year-Old Goes to Hospital* (film). Ipswich: Concord Films Council. [Also New York: New York University Film Library.]

Robertson, J. (1970). *Young Children in Hospital* (2nd edition). London: Tavistock.

Rosenfeld, H. (1952). *Psychotic States: A Psychoanalytic Approach.* New York: International Universities Press. [Reprinted London: Karnac Books, 1982.]

Rosenfeld, H. (1987). *Impasse and Interpretation.* London: Routledge & Kegan Paul.

Rycroft, C. (1968). *A Critical Dictionary of Psychoanalysis.* London: Nelson.

Samuels, A. (1988). A relation called father. *British Journal of Psychotherapy, 4*: 416–426; *5*: 66–76.

Sandler, J. (1992). Reflections on developments in the theory of psychoanalytic technique. *International Journal of Psycho-Analysis*, *73*: 189–198.

Schwaber, E. A. (1990). Interpretation and the therapeutic action of psycho-analysis. *International Journal of Psycho-Analysis*, *71*: 229–240.

Searles, H. F. (1960). *The Non-Human Environment in Normal Development and in Schizophrenia*. New York: International Universities Press.

Searles, H. F. (1961). *Collected Papers on Schizophrenia and Other Subjects*. New York: International Universities Press. [Reprinted London: Karnac Books, 1986.]

Searles, H. F. (1979). *Countertransference and Related Subjects*. New York: International Universities Press.

Searles, H. F. (1986). *My Work with Borderline Patients*. New Jersey: Jason Aronson.

Sears, R. R., Maccoby, E. F., & Levin, H. (1957). *Patterns of Child-Rearing*. Evanstown, IL/White Plains, NY: Row, Peterson & Co.

Sillitoe, A. (1959). *The Loneliness of the Long-Distance Runner*. London: W. H. Allen.

Slochower, J. (1991). Variations in the analytic holding environment. *International Journal of Psycho-Analysis*, *72*: 709–717.

Smith, D. (1991). *Hidden Conversations*. London: Tavistock.

Smith, H. F. (1990). Cues: The perceptual edge of the transference *International Journal of Psycho-Analysis*, *71*: 219–240.

Sodre, I. (1990). *Treatment Alliances: Therapeutic and Anti-Therapeutic*. Paper given at the weekend conference for English-speaking members of the European Societies of Psycho-Analysis.

Spence, D. P., Dahl, H., & Jones, E. E. (1993). Impact of interpretation upon associative freedom. *Journal of Clinical Consultative Psychology*, *61*: 395–402.

Spence, D. P., Mayers, L., & Dahl, H. (1994). Monitoring the analytic surface. *Journal of the American Psychoanalytic Association*. *42*: 43–65.

Spitz, R. A. (1945/1946). Hospitalism: An enquiry into the genesis of psychiatric variations in early childhood; and follow-up. In: R. S. Eisler et al. (Eds.), *Psycho-Analytic Study of the Child*. New York: International Universities Press.

Spitz, R. A. (1965). *The First Year of Life*. New York: International Universities Press.

Spitz, R. A. (1983). *Dialogues for Infancy. Collected Papers* (edited by R. N. Emde). New York: International Universities Press.

Stern, D. (1985). *The Interpersonal World of the Infant*. Boston: Basic Books.

Stewart, H. (1987). Varieties of transference interpretations: An Object-Relations View. *International Journal of Psycho-Analysis, 68*: 197–206.

Stewart, H. (1988). Review of Harold Searles' "My Work with Borderline Patients". *International Journal of Psycho-Analysis, 69*: 569–572.

Strachey, J. (1934). The nature of the therapeutic action of psycho-analysis. *International Journal of Psycho-Analysis, 50*: 275–292.

Sullivan, H. S. (1954). *The Psychiatric Interview* (edited by Helen Perry & Mary Gawel). New York: W. W. Norton.

Sullivan, H. S. (1956). *Clinical Studies in Psychiatry* (edited by Helen Perry, Mary Gawel, & Martha Gibbon). New York: W. W. Norton.

Sutherland, S. (1987). *Breakdown*. London: Weidenfeld & Nicholson.

Symington, J. (1985). The survival function of primitive omnipotence. *International Journal of Psycho-Analysis, 66*: 481–488.

Symington, N. (1993). *Narcissism, a New Theory*. London: Karnac Books.

Tawney, R. H. (1930). *Religion and the Rise of Capitalism*. London: Murray.

Trevarthen, C. (1984). Emotions in infancy: Regulations of contact and relationships with persons. In: K. Scherer & P. Eckman (Eds.), *Approaches to Emotion*. Hillsdale, NJ: Lawrence Erlbaum.

Trevarthen, C., & Hubley, P. (1978). Secondary inter-subjectivity: confidence, confiding and acts of meaning in the first year. In: A. Lock (Ed.), *Action, Gesture and Symbol: The Emergence of Language*. London: Academic Press.

Trevarthen, C., & Logotheti, K. (1989). Child and culture, the genesis of cooperative knowing. In: P. Gelatly, D. Rogers, & J. A. Slobads (Eds.), *Cognition and Social Worlds*. Oxford: Clarendon Press.

Trilling, L. (1951). *The Liberal Imagination*. New York: Viking Press.

Tustin, F. (1974). *Autism and Childhood Psychosis*. London: Hogarth Press.

Tustin, F. (1981). *Autistic States in Children*. London: Routledge & Kegan Paul.

Veblen, T. (1936). *What Veblen Taught: Selected Writings* (edited by W. C. Mitchell). New York: Viking Press.

Weber, M. (1936). *The Protestant Ethic and the Spirit of Capitalism* (tr. Talcott Parsons). London: Allen & Unwin.

Welldon, E. (1988). *Mother, Madonna, Whore*. London: Free Association Press.

West, J. (1945). *Plainsville, USA*. New York: Columbia University Press.

Winnicott, D. W. (1951). Transitional objects and transitional phenomena. *International Journal of Psycho-Analysis*, 1953. [Also in: *Through Paediatrics to Psychoanalysis* (chapter 18). London: Hogarth Press, 1958; reprinted London: Karnac Books & The Institute of Psychoanalysis, 1991.]

Winnicott, D. W. (1958). The capacity to be alone. In: *The Maturational Processes and the Facilitating Environment*. London: Hogarth Press, 1965. [Reprinted London: Karnac Books & The Institute of Psychoanalysis, 1990.]

Winnicott, D. W. (1960). Ego distortion in terms of true and false self. In: *The Maturational Processes and the Facilitating Environment*. London: Hogarth Press, 1965. [Reprinted London: Karnac Books & The Institute of Psychoanalysis, 1990.]

Winnicott, D. W. (1962). Ego integration in child development. In: *The Maturational Processes and the Facilitating Environment*. London: Hogarth Press, 1965. [Reprinted London: Karnac Books & The Institute of Psychoanalysis, 1990.]

Winnicott, D. W. (1964). *The Child, the Family, and the Outside World*. London: Pelican.

Winnicott, D. W. (1965). *The Maturational Processes and the Facilitating Environment*. London: Hogarth Press. [Reprinted London: Karnac Books & The Institute of Psychoanalysis, 1990.]

Winnicott, D. W. (1971). *Playing and Reality*. London: Tavistock.

Wittgenstein, L. (1961). *Tractatus Logico-Philosophicus*. London: Routledge & Kegan Paul.

Wright, K. (1991). *Vision and Separation: Between Mother and Baby*. London: Free Association Press.

Young, R. (1994). The vicissitudes of transference and counter-transference. *Free Associations, 31*. [Also in: *Arbours House Journal* (1992): 24–58.]

INDEX

Abraham, K., 202, 238
acceptability, 152
acceptance, 37, 51, 70, 72–93,
    114, 192, 213, 227
  as holding, 74–77
  and integration, 88
accessibility, proper, criterion of,
  48
Adler, A., 256
advantaged people, 38–39
affect-attunement [Stern], 137,
  265
aggression, 259
Aichhorn, A., 236, 241
Ainsworth, M. D. S., 132, 262,
  263–264
alienation, and status differences,
  16–19
alliance, therapeutic, see
  therapeutic alliance
alpha-elements [Bion], 113
ambivalence, 44, 50, 63
American Psychoanalytic
  Association, 237, 257

American Psychoanalytic Society,
  256
anabolizing, 81
analysability, 98, 123, 124–125,
  160, 258
analysis:
  countertransference, 153, 235
  interminable, 90
analyst, blank-screen, 122
analytic space, 110
"Anders", 100, 177–179, 182–187,
  195
anger, 7, 8, 33, 34, 42, 96, 97,
  139, 185, 209, 210
  and deprivation, 34
  as reaction to loss, 33
Anna O, 163
"Annie", 177, 179, 182–187, 195
annihilation, 197
  fear of, 38
anxiety:
  basic [Horney], 246
  extreme, working with, 248–256
  separation, 235, 263

279

vs. integration, 78
therapeutic intervention for,
    59–66
status:
  and imagination, 12–16
  differences in, and alienation,
    12–19
  and language, 19–22
  and repression, 16–19
Steiner, J., 134, 235, 236
Stern, D., 82, 132, 137, 180, 198,
    239, 260, 261, 264–266
Stewart, H., 118
Strachey, J., 121
"Strange Situation" set-up
    [Ainsworth], 263
structure, of personality:
  definition, 172–174
  faulty organization of [clinical
    examples], 176–196
  general concepts of, 169–196
subjective self, infant's [Stern],
    265
Sullivan, H. S., 239, 244, 246,
    248–252, 263
superego, 78, 105, 169, 171, 223,
    256, 257
  control, 50, 156, 159
  holding function of, 79
  -processes, 186
  punitive, 115
supportive psychotherapy, 157
Sutherland, S., 103, 253
symbiosis, therapeutic [Searles],
    83–85, 254
symbiotic relationship, 113, 198
symbol-making, refusal of
    [Wright], 165
Symington, J., 90, 147, 236
Symington, N., 212
sympathy, as holding, 73–74

talking, therapeutic value of, 49
Tawney, R. H., 244
theory of mind [Fonagy], 48
therapeutic alliance, working
    alliance, 63, 103–110,
    125, 169, 182

conditions unpropitious for,
    103
lack of, 105
preconditions for, 193–194
and regression, 186–196
unavailable, 140–143
therapeutic intervention,
    appropriate, 156–168
therapeutic process, importance of
    containment in, 51
therapeutic symbiosis [Searles],
    83–85, 254
therapeutics, 4
  elementary constituents of, 49–
    54
therapist:
  internalized, 66
  ocnophil temptations of, 147–
    148
  as other, role of, 54–66
therapy:
  caring about, 154
  expressive, 151
think, inability to, 104–105
thinking:
  concrete, 140–143
  nature of, 264
Transactional Analysis, 164, 259
transference, 67, 69, 70, 120–140,
    254
  cure, 49
  definition, 65
  disposition [Kernberg], 122
  idealizing, 258
    positive, 211
  interpretation:
    appropriateness of, 118–168
    premature, 141
  manifestations of well-being,
    205–206
  neurosis, 120–140, 149
    encouraging, 127
    inducing, 148
    working through, 128
  phenomena, 159
    therapeutic, 187
    and working alliance, 186–
      196